W9-CNO-097

The Lost Classics Of

ROBERT RUARK

The Lost Classics Of

ROBERT RUARK

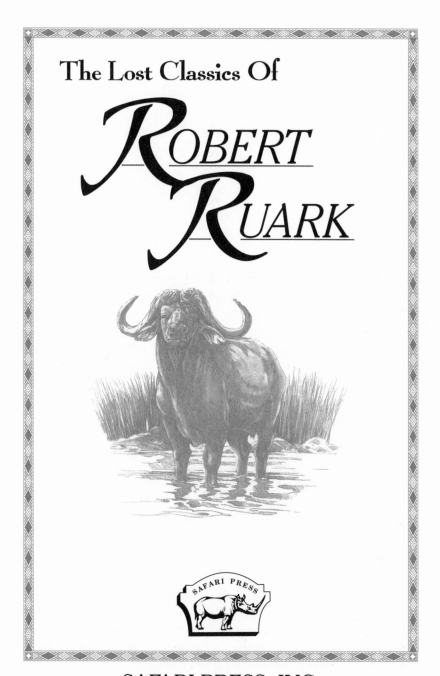

SAFARI PRESS

SAFARI PRESS, INC.
P.O. Box 3095, Long Beach, CA 90803 USA

Ruark, Robert

First Edition

ISBN 1-57157-022-5

1996, Long Beach, California

10 9 8 7 6 5 4 3 2 1

Library of Congress Catalog Card Number: 95-72217

Readers wishing to receive the Safari Press catalog, featuring many fine books on big-game hunting, wingshooting, and firearms, should write the publisher at the address given above.

This is the 63rd title published by Safari Press.

Acknowledgments

As is ever the case in producing a book-length work of this nature, numerous individuals have made a contribution. Lou Razek, who specializes in selling out-of-print sporting magazines through his Highwood Bookshop, generously helped me locate issues of *Field & Stream.* Dale Arenz, an avid collector of old periodicals, provided input and advice from his holdings, and the folks in the Reference Department at Winthrop University (where I hold a "real" job), obtained many items on interlibrary loan.

My wife, Ann, and daughter, Natasha, were as always sources of love and staunch support. Mom and Dad continue to take a keen interest in anything I do connected with the outdoors, and it is to them I owe my introduction to and abiding love for hunting and fishing.

Colleen Storey has brought sundry bits and pieces of material together in a coherent whole, always exhibiting a cheery demeanor as she made sense out of what was sometimes, I fear, my disorganized nonsense. John Cornett, a good friend and long-suffering soul as this project unfolded, has worked closely with me all along. Chuck Wechsler, who has made delightful strides in becoming a true son of the South after moving into the editor's position at *Sporting Classics* a decade ago, has been a bastion of strength. He is a caring, sharing man, a real writer's editor and his persistent prodding kept this book moving toward completion.

Finally, I would be remiss if I did not acknowledge the legions of "Old Men," yesterday and today, who have made it possible for Ruark, for me, and for countless other starry-eyed boys to know and savor the wonders of the wild world. To them, we all owe a debt of gratitude and a duty to try to walk in their footsteps with generations to come.

Jim Casada

Ruark entered World War II as a naval ensign and later served as a gunnery officer in both the Atlantic and Mediterranean. He finished up his military service as a press censor.

Table of Contents

Part One – Old Man And The Boy Stories

Part Two – Down Home

Part Three – The Boy Expands His Horizons

Part Four – Poor Man's Hemingway on Papa

Part Five – Ruark On Ruark

Introduction

*T*o virtually all contemporary lovers of fine sporting literature, not to mention the millions who came to know him through his hard-hitting newspaper columns or best-selling novels, the name of Robert C. Ruark is a household word. Thanks to his timeless and immensely popular series of stories in *Field & Stream* on "The Old Man and the Boy" and a host of other articles and books treating various aspects of life in the outdoors, Ruark earned recognition as one of America's most popular and best-loved sporting writers during the 1950s and early 1960s. These endeavors, however, were but one facet of an extraordinarily productive career that ranked Ruark as a literary figure of considerable magnitude. Yet the winsome child we follow through the joys and tribulations of adolescence and young adulthood in *The Old Man and the Boy* and *The Old Man's Boy Grows Older* (the book-length versions of the collected *Field & Stream* stories) is sadly removed from Ruark the man.

Something of an enigma even in his lifetime, Ruark has, in three decades since his untimely death in 1965, become even further shrouded in mystery. This may seem surprising because many of his books remain popular, and while most originally appeared in large or multiple editions, they are already much in demand by collectors. Since his death, though, little save the standard obituary notices, an indifferent biography, and a succinct sketch in the *Dictionary of American Biography* has appeared on Ruark.

Ruark was born on December 29, 1915, in Southport, North Carolina. He was the son of a bookkeeper, Robert Chester Ruark, Sr., and Charlotte Adkins, a school teacher. Thanks largely to Ruark's reminiscences in the "Old Man and the Boy" stories, we know far more about his childhood than is normally the case. Even though his family moved to the nearby, larger port city of Wilmington quite early in his life, it was in and around his birthplace that Ruark spent the most meaningful and joyous days of his youth.

In the author's note to *The Old Man and the Boy*, Ruark wrote: "Anybody who reads this book is bound to realize that I had a real fine time as a boy." The best and most impressionable of those good times were spent with his maternal grandfather, Captain Edward Hall Adkins, the "Old Man" of Ruark's later writings. Adkins was an endearing figure, full of dry wit, homespun philosophy, and an endless store of outdoor lore, which he patiently shared with his grandson and protégé – the "Boy." The Old Man could be vinegary at times – such as when the Boy departed from good sportsmanship or when the Old Man reluctantly found it necessary to thrash an inebriated, insolent dandy (he called such noxious characters "Willies off the pickle boat") who cursed him and then refused to apologize for their arrogant rudeness. But at heart Adkins was a gentle figure of great humanity. Although the Old Man appeared a bit rough around the edges, underneath his scruffy exterior lay a shrewd mind and a carefully nurtured intellect – "He knows pretty well everything."

Ruark's real home was in Wilmington, North Carolina, but it was this house in Southport, owned by his grandparents Hawley and Lottie Adkins, that figured so prominently in his writings. Nestled under sprawling live oaks on Lord Street, the house is remarkably unchanged from the way it looked in the '20s.

With the guile of years of accumulated experience and a born teacher's abilities, the Old Man imbued Ruark with a genuine love of learning as well as an extensive practical knowledge about the outdoors. Theirs was a timeless partnership, familiar to anyone fortunate enough to have had close contact with one's grandfather in an outdoor setting; what made it unique was Ruark's subsequent ability to capture in prose the nostalgic wonder of those elusive days of youth. In so doing, he gave us, especially in *The Old Man and the Boy*, enchanting pieces of sporting literature.

Ruark's years with the Old Man were all too few. Captain Adkins died when the Boy was only fifteen, but as Ruark gratefully acknowledges in the two poignant tales that conclude the first volume and open the second of the Old Man series, his death was not on opening day and "All He Left Me Was the World." Few individuals are privileged to have such a mentor, and Ruark knew it. In the midst of the sorrow and bitter desolation that followed the Old Man's demise, Ruark found both solace and a strong resolve for the future in the Old Man's legacy:

"It suddenly occurred to me that I was educated before I saw a college. I made up my mind right then that someday I would learn to be a writer and write some of the stuff the Old Man had taught me. There was only one thing I had to do first, and that was to get educated and make enough money to buy back the old yellow-painted square house (lost to creditors as a result of expenses associated with the Old Man's final illness and the concomitant onset of the Depression) with its mockingbird in the magnolia and its pecan trees in the back yard."

A precocious youth already blessed with an ample measure of the spunk and tenacious capacity for hard work that would be among the more redeeming hallmarks of his later years, Ruark entered the University of North Carolina well short of his sixteenth birthday. Suddenly gone were those fleeting halcyon days with the Old Man and "all the honorary uncles, black and white," who had been an integral part of the process of growing up. A much harsher world now faced Ruark, and only with the passage of time and many trials would he learn the truth inherent in Thomas Wolfe's claim that "you can't go home again." Yet in one sense Ruark did go back home. He accorded readers everywhere the rare favor of sharing the Old Man with them, and in so doing he recaptured precious moments of their childhoods as well as his own.

At Chapel Hill, Ruark soon found a niche as a collegian, although there are hints in his later behavior that he somehow felt that both his age and youngish physical features inhibited his undergraduate experience from being all it should have been. A contemporary with whom he worked on the campus humor magazine later gave a fine description of the awkward but ambitious adolescent:

"I think Ruark was the most guileless boy I ever knew. He was as skinny as a boat pole in those days. The biggest thing about him was his grin."

Nonetheless, Ruark garnered experience writing for the *Yackety Yack* and drawing pen-and-ink sketches for both the *Carolina Magazine* and the *Buccaneer* (he was an artist of considerable merit who used his drawings to illustrate some of his books). He even managed to scrape together enough cash, partly through a little judicious bootlegging in the dormitories and by hustling in local boarding-house bordellos, not only to pay his way through college but to join Phi Kappa Sigma fraternity as well.

Years later, when he returned to his old fraternity house, Ruark would reveal a somewhat unsavory side of his character. Apparently attempting to compensate for the fact that an empty purse linked with his age stood in the way of cutting a romantic swath among the ladies, Ruark revelled in bouts of ostentation once he had "made it" as a writer (several photographs survive in carefully preserved albums of a now successful Ruark surrounded by a bevy of local beauties). He took great pride in presenting the fraternity with an ice machine. Ruark justified this unusual gift by saying that ready access to ice for their drinks would free the pledges from needless trips and thereby contribute immeasurably to their academic progress!

For all his infectious love of fun, there was a serious undercurrent deep within Ruark, and whatever his failings, he was never one to shirk hard work. A journalism major, he completed his B.A. in 1935 well toward the top of his class and immediately launched into his career.

Ruark was, in rather rapid-fire succession, a reporter and journalistic jack-of-all trades for the *Hamlet* (North Carolina) *News-Messenger,* a merchant seaman aboard the *Sundance* under a tyrannical captain, an accountant in what he styled a "fraudulent stint" with the Works Progress Administration, and on August 12, 1938, the husband of a young interior decorator, Virginia Webb. During his

The author and unidentified friend after a successful pheasant hunt.

tumultuous and rather tragic marriage, Ruark became an employee of the *Daily News* in Washington, under the incomparable tutelage of its managing editor, Ernie Pyle. There, he rose rapidly through the ranks from copy boy to top feature writer, with an interim as a sportswriter, which exposed him to the "raffish life . . . astounding characters . . . [and] a vocabulary that never failed him when in a few years he was a highly paid columnist." By the time war broke out, he was assistant city editor. Ruark already was, in the grudging estimation of one co-worker, "brash, ambitious, cocky, fast, and good."

World War II interrupted Ruark's meteoric rise in journalistic circles, albeit only temporarily. He entered the war as a naval ensign and later served as a gunnery officer with convoys in both the Atlantic and Mediterranean. Toward the conclusion of the conflict, he saw shore duty in the Pacific, where he was injured in a jeep accident in the Solomon Islands. Following recuperation, Ruark finished up his military service as a press censor, doubtless the capacity his superiors thought best suited to muzzling his uncanny nose for scandalous news. In the middle of the war, Ruark had created a sensation, along with bringing about much-needed reforms, by writing about the shoddy treatment accorded to soldiers serving under "General Lee and a precious group of army colonels in Italy, who thought they would ape the German officer class which they had just beaten." Ruark also wrote several pieces for the *Saturday Evening Post* during this period, and by war's end, there was little doubt about his career path.

Ruark joined the Scripps-Howard Newspaper Alliance and in short order made a major breakthrough by intentionally gaining national notoriety. Calculating how he could best make an impact as a syndicated columnist, Ruark "looked around for the biggest rock I could throw." That rock, a veritable journalistic boulder, was a stridently sexist column on how current women's fashions nauseated servicemen returning home. The piece, which Ruark later described as "naked sex, with a twist," created the splash he desired. Some 2,500 letters, most from irate, style-setting females, inundated the offices of the *Washington Daily News*. Predictably, few found any humor in Ruark's depiction:

"[They sport] nine-inch nails, wear Dolman sleeves, flat-heeled shoes, and have hair hauled up either into an Iroquois Indian topknot with a rubber band around it or else flopping in a net like a sack of mud. [Their] purple lipstick . . . makes them look like the wrath of God."

Roy Howard, Ruark's boss, was suitably impressed, and he gave Ruark the regular column he so desperately craved. Over the ensuing years Ruark produced upward of 4,000 columns – an estimated 2.8 million words – for the Scripps-Howard syndicate. Although he would describe himself as "a pretty ordinary hack," he wrote rapidly and well. Ruark boasted that he could turn out a daily column in a quarter-hour or less, and that he once wrote sixteen pieces in a single sitting in Rome. As if this were not enough, he also produced over one thousand magazine articles during his career.

Ruark's literary star rose rapidly, and in 1947 he produced his first book, *Grenadine Etching: Her Life and Loves.* By this time Ruark was, according to *Life* magazine, the "most talked about reporter" in the country. *Grenadine* enhanced his reputation. Essentially a potboiler, it nonetheless showed the author at his lampooning, iconoclastic best. A biting, rollicking satire that attacked the then commonplace sex and syrup writing of historical novels, it demonstrated Ruark's remarkable ability to lash out effectively at anything that was sacrosanct. He would use the same approach, relying heavily on a facetiously ungrammatical style, in what he described as "a very unfunny sequel," *Grenadine's Spawn* (1953), and in both *I Didn't Know It Was Loaded* (1948) and *One for the Road* (1949).

All of these books sold moderately well, but Ruark was still searching for the literary genre that would prove his true métier. Still, by the early 1950s he was something of a celebrity. He had moved to New York, was a regular at Toot Shor's, drank free champagne at the Stork Club, lived in an expensive penthouse, dressed his wife Ginny (he always called her "Mama") in mink, "knew everybody from Bernie Baruch to Frank Costello," and earned $50,000 a year. All this, yet he was desperately unhappy.

Robert Ruark's sketch of his paternal grandfather. In later years, Ruark illustrated some of his own books.

Ruark and the typewriter that he took with him wherever he traveled.

Ruark was punishing his liver unmercifully through excessive drinking. The malady was a family one. Apparently his paternal grandfather, whom he styled *The Most Unforgettable Sonafabitch I Ever Knew*, drank himself to death. Likewise, he had an uncle who loved his toddy far too much, as Ruark reveals in the hilarious story from *The Old Man's Boy Grows Older*, "Uncle Rob Had Humphrey Bogart Beat a Mile." Ruark, in essence, had overstepped the bounds of fun so loved by the Old Man by searching for it too diligently. He was writing for dollars rather than posterity, and he knew he had better stuff in him. Finally, summoning up enough courage to break away from his lucrative but loathsome world, Ruark fulfilled a long-cherished dream of an African safari. That safari would mark a watershed in his life, and much of his finest work, both fictional and otherwise, would come from his travels in Africa and elsewhere abroad.

Ernest Hemingway had always been his hero, and the two were so similar in their physical features that they easily could have passed for brothers. Ruark liked being called "the poor man's Hemingway," and seemed to pattern Hemingway's style in both the barroom and the boudoir. Indeed, *Time* magazine went so far as to suggest that "if Ernest Hemingway [had not existed] . . . it [would have been] difficult to see how Robert Ruark could ever have been invented." Determined to duplicate some of Hemingway's more laudable experiences, Ruark hired the noted white hunter, Harry Selby, and set out to follow in the footsteps that had produced such masterpieces as *The Snows of Kilimanjaro* and *The Green Hills of Africa*. (Incidentally, Ruark was deeply moved by the death of his idol, and some of the pieces he wrote on learning of Hemingway's death are included in Part Four of this book.)

Revitalized by his African adventures, Ruark turned toward the two types of writing where he would prove truly masterful – sporting literature and epic novels founded on fact. In the former category, Ruark almost immediately produced what would become far and away the best of his early books. In *Horn of the Hunter* (1953), Ruark introduced the Boy, jaded by years of city life, recapturing some of his marvelous childhood in a robust, racy fashion. This was his first important sporting book. While on the safari that produced this book, Ruark also had seen and sensed the seething racial conflicts, compounded by dying colonialism, which would lead to the Mau-Mau rebellion. Drawing on these experiences, he wrote the controversial and immensely successful novel, *Something of Value* (1955).

An instant bestseller, the book made Ruark a fortune in royalties and film rights. *Something of Value* was sharply criticized in many quarters for its garishness and gore. One reviewer charged that "it [was] a trip through an abattoir. The stench overwhelms the mind. Worse, it remains." Another characterized the book as "literally horrible." Yet Ruark was writing uncomfortably close to the facts. As he acknowledges in his foreword:

"There is much blood in this book. There is much killing. But the life of Africa was washed earlier by blood, and its ground was, and still is, fertilized by the blood of its people and its animals. This is not a pretty book, nor was it written for the pre-bedtime amusement of small children."

Not all critics lambasted the book. John Barkham of the *New York Times Book Review* called it "a brand new Ruark" in a "huge and frightening novel." A Book-of-the-Month Club selection, it sold well over a million copies in various formats. The movie rights brought Ruark $300,000 from Metro-Goldwyn-Mayer, a payment which the successful Hollywood version showed was amply justified. There were translations in ten languages, and altogether Ruark made upward of a million dollars from it. More importantly, the book provided him with the affluent leisure to write on subjects that would assure his lasting fame.

Financial freedom brought Ruark his finest years as a writer, but it also exacerbated a variety of personal problems. He had tired of New York's "saloon society:"

"I was getting neurotic about New York. I simply couldn't stand it any longer. [It] was a can of worms. It was lobsters chewing on each other in a pot. It was noise, and dirt, and a dead heat with disaster."

Indeed, his physical breakdown while living in New York had been one of the catalysts that engendered his African trip. He now had the opportunity to get away from the frenetic lifestyle he had never become fully accustomed to and could write more on subjects that were to his personal liking. To this end, and one suspects for tax reasons as well, Ruark purchased a sumptuous villa in Spain. Located in Palamos, near Barcelona, the residence was so grand that its new owner liked to call it a castle. Together with a London pent- house and a new Rolls Royce, it typified the manner in

Ruark's drinking eventually killed him. This photo was taken after an all-night binge in Marseilles.

which Ruark flaunted his success. All was not idyllic, however, for he continued to stow away immense quantities of liquor, and it began to tell on his health. Still, the next few years would be his most productive as a writer.

This was the period of the Old Man stories, and regular safaris in Africa, together with occasional trips even farther afield, produced a steady stream of fine articles in magazines such as *True*, *Field & Stream*, *Playboy*, *Saturday Evening Post*, and *Life*. *The Old Man and the Boy* appeared in book form in 1957 and *The Old Man's Boy Grows Older* in 1961. Ruark's stories delighted *Field & Stream* readers and kept subscribers' appetites whetted for each new episode. As a collection, they are eminently readable and have an enduring appeal. What few people realize is that by no means did all the material that first appeared in the *Field & Stream* columns make it into the two books. The best of those omitted stories are now offered here in book form for the first time.

Spicy, liberally sprinkled with Ruark's pithy language and his vivid recall of both earthy aphorisms and the salty characters who uttered them, the stories range from belly laughing jocularity to tragedy. In all of them, however, the Old Man dispenses his wit and wisdom, tinctured by doses of practical philosophy, on the outdoors and life in general. The stories were and remain a treat – fine and timeless fare to be enjoyed again and again. Ruark once said, "I don't evaluate myself as a heavy thinker," but through the medium of the Old Man he dispensed a great deal of deep thought. Sadly, Ruark himself was ignoring much of the sage advice that the Old Man had proffered.

His own life had become anything but the sublime, slow-moving existence that the Old Man not only advocated but lived. Health problems brought on by alcohol abuse continued, and by 1960 Ruark confided to a friend: "I've been on a strict wagon since the middle of May . . . [but] the outlook is not improved by the dismal news from London that a lifetime of sobriety awaits me." His had become a complicated existence, yet paradoxically, Ruark was happiest with its least complicated elements. As long as he was hunting, had a fly rod in hand, or was sitting before a typewriter, he felt great contentment and joy.

On the surface, the late 1950s and early 1960s were good times for Ruark. He was at the height of his powers as a writer, and those years saw the publication of his finest books. In addition to the *Old Man* volumes, he wrote two major novels, *Poor No More* (1959) and *Uhuru: A Novel of Africa* (1962). The former was a rags-to-riches saga that carried distinct autobiographical tones as well as hints that all was not right with the Boy. As one of Ruark's friends would comment in a posthumous reminiscence, there "were signals to the world that he was no longer worshipping false gods; his trouble was that he did not know where to find any better ones."

Uhuru contains fewer such personal insights, but it is a powerful book. A sequel to *Something of Value*, some index of its impact is provided by the fact that it made Ruark *persona non grata* in Kenya. There were appreciable problems with British authorities as well, largely in connection with the contents of the English edition. The whole subject of "Uhuru" (the Swahili word for freedom or independence) was an extremely sensitive one, and the fact that Ruark managed to raise the hackles of both sides involved in the touchy issue speaks eloquently about his fictional treatment of dying colonialism in Africa.

The author at his typewriter, pounding out one of the more than 1,000 magazine articles he wrote during his career.

In the midst of these years of literary triumph, a variety of developments cumulatively had the effect of creating personal disaster for Ruark. One was the death of his idol and good friend, Ernest Hemingway, in 1961. That Hemingway's career ended in tragic suicide deeply moved Ruark, and he wrote what are undoubtedly some of the finest articles remembering the man whom he called "the master." Much closer to home was Ruark's separation and ultimately messy divorce from his wife of two decades, a relationship that long had been a stabilizing factor in his life.

Following the break with Virginia, Ruark ended another long-term relationship. Commenting that "quite frankly after thirty years in the newspaper business, I suddenly realize that I am nearing fifty and am weary of deadlines," he resigned as a newspaper columnist. Perhaps this was a belated attempt to recapture some of the verve and zest for living that had characterized his earlier years. A

Ruark and his prized Rolls Royce in front of his sprawling Spanish villa at Palamos on the Mediterranean shore.

developing affection for Marilyn Kaytor, the food editor of *Look* magazine, might also be viewed as part of an effort to create a "new Bob Ruark." Whatever the case, Ruark was not to see the fiftieth birthday he was nearing, nor would his engagement to Kaytor culminate in marriage.

In the early summer of 1965, Ruark felt poorly for several weeks, but he continued his frenetic writing pace. In late June, however, he was flown from Spain to be placed in a London hospital. There his liver, ravaged by years of abuse, finally failed. On July 1, Ruark died from massive internal hemorrhaging. On July 10, with virtually every villager of his beloved Palamos in attendance, Ruark was buried in his adopted home. Doubtless he would have agreed with the sentiments expressed by one of his good friends: "Thank God he did not live to be impotent, old and sick like Hemingway." Indeed, Ruark may have subconsciously sensed that his end was near. In "Long View from the Hill," the planned but unwritten volume in a tetralogy with *Something of Value* and *Uhuru*, the book concludes with the central character, an author whose life quite closely resembles Ruark's, dying.

Ruark once confided to a friend: "I started out to be a man . . . glad, sad, occasionally triumphant." In the sense that posterity is the better for the metamorphosis that carried him from being the Boy into a far different world, Bob Ruark was triumphant. He left every lover of nature, every hunter and fisherman, a bountiful legacy. We are infinitely richer for his hundreds of articles and four sporting books (*Use Enough Gun: On Hunting Big Game* was published posthumously). Along with his novels, they constitute a lasting literary monument created at Ruark's typewriter. And now, with the publication of this book, that monument grows even larger. For in the pages which follow, Ruark fans will enjoy dozens of new stories, gleaned from long-forgotten magazines, which heretofore have never appeared in book form.

Jim Casada
Rock Hill, South Carolina
October 1, 1995

A Note On Selection

Years ago I realized that some of the "Old Man and the Boy" stories I had read in *Field & Stream* as a youngster were not in *The Old Man and the Boy* and *The Old Man's Boy Grows Older.* Then, just over a decade ago, while going through Ruark's papers in the Southern Historical Collection at the University of North Carolina at Chapel Hill, it became clear that the same was true of a lot of his other magazine pieces. It was at that point that the seed for this book was planted in my mind.

Originally, it had been my intention to do something strictly with an African focus, but the appearance of Michael McIntosh's *Robert Ruark's Africa* in 1991 changed that. Also, I became involved in a somewhat similar editing project involving Archibald Rutledge's work, and that further delayed bringing this enterprise to fruition. By the same token though, the positive reception accorded my Rutledge trilogy convinced me there was an abiding interest in forgotten works by America's great sporting writers. Thus was born the idea of not merely a Ruark book, but a series, "The Lost Classics," of which this is the first volume.

A lot of digging in old magazine files underlies the production of this book, but I would be willing to bet there are one or two literary gems from Ruark's battered old typewriter that should have been included. With a single exception, "Far Out Safari," all the pieces in this book are, to the best of my knowledge, Ruark writings that have never appeared in book form. That article was included in the deluxe version of McIntosh's book but not in the regular edition, and it is so appealing it seemed appropriate to offer a wider audience access to it.

The first criterion in selection was that the article had not appeared in a book, and only after this had been determined were other factors taken into consideration. I should note, by way of acknowledgment and appreciation, that several colleagues at *Sporting Classics* magazine had a hand in the selection process.

Chuck Wechsler, John Cornett, Duncan Grant and Art Carter all read the pieces I identified and offered their judgments.

What we have here, in other words, are stories we all believe have timeless value and lasting importance. Moreover, we are convinced these stories deserve to be rescued from literary obscurity and shared with today's sporting audience. As you read these selections, we hope you will agree.

Jim Casada

PART ONE

*Old Man
And
The Boy Stories*

Old Man And The Boy Stories

*B*eginning in February, 1953, *Field & Stream* published what arguably is the best-loved and most enduring of all the series and columns this prestigious magazine has ever offered. That issue marked the inception of Robert Ruark's long-running "The Old Man and the Boy" column. Monthly from that point onward, hundreds of thousands of keen fans eagerly awaited each new installment chronicling Ruark's reminiscences of a wonderful boyhood. Although there were some changes in title, the series would enjoy an unbroken run of 106 issues, finally ending in November, 1961.

For the first several years of its existence, the column was entitled, both in the magazine's Table of Contents and with its actual heading, simply "The Old Man and the Boy." Then, beginning with the January, 1958, magazine, the columns carried individual titles rather than simply being headed "The Old Man and the Boy" (although that designation was retained in the Table of Contents). With the January, 1959, issue mention of "The Old Man and the Boy" disappeared entirely, although the timeless partnership between the two protagonists continued to be the central feature of the columns.

Eventually Ruark would collect many of these stories into two anthologies, *The Old Man and the Boy* and *The Old Man's Boy Grows Older*. Indeed, it has been widely (and wrongly) assumed that these two immensely popular books contain all the stories as they originally appeared in *Field & Stream*. Such, however, is not the case. Ruark did use just over eighty of his *Field & Stream* pieces in creating the two books, sometimes combining two or even three columns into a single story. With one or two exceptions, the material in the books shows only minor editorial changes from that which appeared in the magazine.

For present purposes, however, it is the stories which never made it into the two anthologies which concern us here. What follows are the best of the "lost" stories, full of the same wit and wisdom which graced the pieces that have now been cherished by three generations of book lovers. They are vintage Ruark, revealing of the undeniable humanity that was one of his more redeeming characteristics, and replete with the innocence and enthusiasm of youth which so sadly vanished in his adult life. They call back yesteryear, those marvelous days of the youth he knew on the Carolina coast, in a fashion few others have matched.

Here we join Ruark as the Boy, along with the Old Man, for a whole series of trips into the wonderful world he captured so artfully and accurately. For me, it is like I am once more in the barber shop of my childhood, where I always hoped there were a number of customers ahead of me so I would have ample time to read through the latest of Ruark's adventures. Now though, I don't have to worry about hurried reading or interruptions. Instead, I can joy in the revival of a great duo, and to join them in their long forgotten out-door adventures is to sample and savor sporting literature at its finest. Enjoy!

If You Can't Lick The Weather, Join It

*T*ough winter, wasn't it? Seems to me they're all tough nowadays, but of course it may be that I'm getting tender. Anyway, most of the things I like to do just aren't done in winter, not in the so-called Temperate Zone.

The Old Man used to reckon that one man's weather is another man's poison. "The only way to handle weather," he said once, "is to know what you want to do with it and use it accordingly. Quit complaining about it and put up with it for what it's worth. And be prepared for it. The trouble with city people is that they freeze when it's cold and boil when it's hot because they dress the same way for all seasons. An Eskimo knows it's going to be cold, so he stokes himself up on boiled walrus or blubber, builds a house to match his mood and only interrupts the long dark winter to thaw out another chunk of seal. The African savage know it's going to be hot the year 'round, so he wears a strip of banana leaf to hide his nakedness and seeks his coolness under a palm.

"You get a big unseasonable snow, and the man who owns a pair of long-handled red-flannel drawers hollers hooray and goes for a sleigh ride. The fellow that's still stuck into T-shirt and shorts whimpers and wails that the weatherman's betrayed him personally. There ain't no such thing as bad weather, if you come right down to it. Some's just better than others, as there ain't no such thing as a real ugly woman. Some are just prettier than others."

5

This scholarly lecture was delivered, as I recall, on the worst day I can remember. Horrible was a kind word for it. It doesn't snow much where I came from in the Carolinas, but this day it had snowed enough to make a New Hampshire athlete search for his mackinaw and wax his skis. The gray skies were as sad as a Sunday funeral, and the wind howled as the downy snowflakes switched over into scudding sleet. It was the kind of day to toss another pine knot on the fire and hope that no catastrophe short of an earthquake would haul you out of the house.

The Old Man stomped in with his pipe frozen solid, rime on his mustache, and his nose a brilliant cherry red. He seemed as bright as a boxful of birds at a time when the dogs were indistinguishable from the logs on the fire, they were that close to the blaze.

"It's a lovely day today, ain't it?" said he, shaking the snow from his overcoat and warming his chapped hands before the fire. "And by all indications it'll be lovelier tomorrow."

Grandma regarded her mate with disapproval. "Quit dripping all over my rugs," Miss Caroline said. "A lovely day for what: Pneumonia? Hang that wet coat on the back porch."

The Old Man smiled. "It's a lovely day for ducks," he said. "I never saw a nicer day for ducks. The wind will break up the rafts, and the snow and ice will freeze up the big ponds. The ducks'll fly low and come into any little pothole that isn't frozen tight. They'll decoy to anything that looks free of wind. If I was a meat hunter I'd make me a fortune in the morning. Just creeping up on a few unfrozen patches and letting fly with a 10-gauge or some other murderous weapon. Slay 'em by the hundreds."

The Old Man scowled at the idea. "Fortunately," he said, "I ain't a pot-hunter, and I don't own no 10-gauge shotgun. But all the same I intend to take advantage of the weather and shoot rather selectively with that old pump gun that's standing in the corner. Tomorrow I shoot nothing but canvasbacks, bar the occasional pintail and a Canada goose or so. Have I got any takers or are you just going to sit here and shiver and feel sorry because it ain't April?"

I had seen that pointed pipestem before. He strictly wasn't aiming it at Grandma.

"What time do we get up?" I asked. "Before dawn, as usual?"

"Let's don't overdo it," the old buzzard grinned. "It'll be black night until 7 o'clock, and they'll fly all day in this wind anyhow. I should remark that if you had breakfast ready by 6:30 we'd have ample time to cope with all the necessities. But dress warm, boy, dress warm, and don't bother to get me up till the coffee's boiling. I aim to sleep in my long drawers, too. That way you start off warm."

One thing the Old Man taught me – you dress warm from the inside out, not the outside in. You start with a hot breakfast – ham and eggs and toast and a lot of coffee – and then you surround the breakfast with long drawers and a soft sweater and a couple of flannel shirts and two pairs of socks. A pair of woolly britches over that, and hip boots to keep the wind and water off you, and an oilskin jacket and a cap with ear-muffs, and you don't need a bearskin coat. Once that inside furnace starts working, you find you can sweat in a blizzard.

"I know it sounds kind of sissy," the Old Man said as we mopped up the remains of the eggs with the toast, "but certain creature comforts can make a power of difference in how good you shoot. You go get that little kerosene stove we used on the beach this fall while I tend to the coffee thermos."

He tended to another kind of thermos, too, but I suspect it contained no coffee. It didn't *sound* like coffee. It sounded thinner to the naked ear, and possibly contained a vitamin tonic whose sale, at the time, was highly illegal. In any case, it was too special for boys.

We had two or three blinds, to be used according to wind and weather, and this freezing morning we chose a nearby one, with me poling the boat and freezing my fingers through the mittens, my nose running droplets onto the scarf around my neck, the marshes cold and gray and windswept, as only salt marches can be on a day like this. As I shoved the skiff up the little avenues of what was water day before yesterday, the boat's keel made a crackling noise as it forced its way through the thin crusting of last night's ice. The narrow lanes were frozen bank to bank, but when we hove onto a semisweet-water pond, it was only iced around the edges. A mighty flock of mallards took off with irritable quacks when we approached the blind, and the darting *squish-wish* of frustrated teal swept low as we shoved the skiff into the little tunnel behind it. The Old Man more or less slung a dozen decoys into the water helter-skelter, with nothing of his usual attention to meticulous placement.

"Today," he said blandly, "they'll decoy to a couple of old tin cans and some milk bottles. Fire up that stove, sonny, and hand me the jug – the *other* thermos."

I swear, we could have gotten a limit of anything with a couple of old brooms and a slingshot that day. It was almost as if – but not quite – the ducks were trying to come into the blind to get warm. You know Canada geese as wary birds. We collected our limit of the old honkers in two flights, and didn't even bother to change to goose loads, they came in that close.

The roaring wind had filled the skies with disturbed birds, all looking for a place to set. None of the usual artifices which the Old Man employed, and which I know by now, were necessary. It was a mere matter of choice of breed. We got so persnickety at one time that we made a bargain: I would shoot only canvasbacks and the Old Man would specialize in pintails. We sneered at mallards – as it was late in the season, and suspected a tendency to fish eating – and simply stood up and shooed away the teal and the golden-eyes and broadbills and trash ducks that fought their way to the little space.

Time has passed, but I would swear we were out of that blind with the boat loaded to the gunwales and the special jug only a quarter diminished before an hour was up. I have only seen it that way once since, when an old friend Joe Turner, a Washington rasslin'-boxing promoter, and I dared a snowstorm on the Eastern Shore of Maryland. You had to look between the snowflakes to see the ducks, but Lord save us, there were more ducks than snowflakes.

Well, the Old Man and I snuffed out the little kerosene stove, broke the skiff free of the ice that bound her and shoved happily off for home and fire. The snow had started again but the wind had dropped, and the sky was still filled with enough low-flying ducks to have provided a hundred years' imprisonment for a man who wished to over-shoot his quota. When we dragged the boat up on the shingle and shouldered the strings of fowl and the guns, the Old Man smiled sort of sardonically at the putty-gray skies.

"Your grandma ain't going to believe it," he said, "but I think this was one of the prettiest days I ever saw in my life. Any argument?"

"No, sir," I said. "You can have them bluebird days."

I don't ski, as I would rather contract pneumonia without breaking my back in the process, but I can see now where a snowfall that wrecks a city's transportation can be a thing of beauty to a man who straps staves on his feet and goes hurtling down a hill to sudden dissolution.

The average muggy day – semi-hot, with a promise of drizzle – can be heaven to a quail shooter, because the bobwhites seem to come out of their beds on the swampsides and leave a track of scent that makes the dogs' noses more acute. The other extreme is the classic golden day, dry and fit for a calendar illustration, when the birds don't seem to move and the pointer's smeller is hot and he runs through the covey or falls flat on his belly just before the quail erupt.

Of all the quail-shooting days I can remember, the two best were conducted in a driving downpour, when a sane man would have hovered over the fire and waited until tomorrow. Ely Wilson of Kingstree, South Carolina, will recall that on one rainy day, when a semi-mongrel named Joe was making a bum out of his hotly blooded friends, we shot the limit of fifteen bobwhites inside of forty-five minutes, and took only three birds from each covey. Birds were all over the place, leaving a musk as heady as any skunk's. I was back on the same terrain later on that year, on one of those sunny bluebird days, and barely raised a feather.

Apart from accepting the weather, the Old Man early instilled another truism that has kept me nonulcerated for many a year. If you can't work the weather to your will, don't fight it. There is nothing nicer than a roaring blaze inside a snug house when things are really impossible outside. Let it rain, let it pour, let it snow, let it roar; a tidy fire and a noggin of something to half-sole your spirit is not a bad way to spend a day, especially if there is a book handy or a record on the machine.

"The best thing about a real bad day," the Old Man said, "is that you can sit by the fire and tell lies which sound so convincing that they eventually become truth and part of the legend."

"If You Can't Lick the Weather, Join It," *Field & Stream*, May, 1958.

In Your Own Backyard

*I*t was one of those drowsy summer days too hot to move around much and too hot to sit still. The Old Man and I had strolled down to the cedar bench, where he was whittling away at what was left of the bench, and I had run up to Watson's Drugstore to buy us Cokes and me a magazine. I do not mean to make this sound like an institutional ad when I say it was a copy of *Field & Stream*, because aside from the *American Boy* and the *Saturday Evening Post* I didn't read anything else.

I was thumbing through the pages, looking at the pictures because it was too hot to read, when I ran onto a photo of somebody in a pith helmet standing over a dead lion with a gun in his hand. There was another picture on the facing page with the same fellow sitting on top of a rhinoceros.

"Look at this," I said to the Old Man. "Now, *that* is really something. None of this messing around with little stuff. When I get big and make some money, I aim to go shoot me a lion and a rhino and an elephant."

"Admirable, admirable." The Old Man laid down his pocketknife and stuffed his battle-scarred brier. "I like to see ambition in the young. But I saw you miss a running rabbit with a shotgun at about ten yards the other month, and it seems to me I saw you miss thirteen straight quail just last winter. You reckon you're up to lion yet?"

11

"I'd like to try," I replied. "Someday. When you were sailing around in ships, did you ever shoot a lion?"

"No, I never shot none," the Old Man said. "But I saw some. Never occurred to me to shoot one. I wouldn't have known what to do with it after I'd shot it, since there was no way to get it home; and anyhow, your grandma wouldn't have let me keep it in the house. Also, it didn't look like it needed to be shot. There was a whole mess of 'em – male, two or three females, and some cubs – rolling around and playing like puppies. They looked too cute to shoot. Me, I'd rather shoot squirrels. They're harder to hit, and at least you can eat 'em after you've shot 'em."

I riffled through the magazine some more, and came across a picture of the writer Zane Grey with a marlin as big as a battleship. "I'd like to catch one of them, too," I said. "Look at this thing. Says he caught it off New Zealand. It's bigger'n the *Vanessa*." The *Vanessa* was the Old Man's pogy boat.

"All right, if you like work," the Old Man yawned. "I'd just as leave dig a ditch or saw a cord of wood. When I fish, I aim to try for something that don't figure to pull me overboard and drown me. I guess you might say I lack initiative, not to mention courage. How'd you like to go catch a mess of perch? It'll be cool in the branch, apart from the mosquitoes."

"Perch," I said scathing-like. "*Perch*. When you can catch fish like this, you want to go catch *perch!*"

"You can't put a 2,000-pound marlin in a skillet." The Old Man was needling me now, and he knew it; I was just catching on. "There wouldn't be enough grease in town to dampen it."

"Oh, all right," I said. "Let's go catch your old perch. But all the same, one of these days I'm going to shoot me a lion and an elephant and catch me a marlin. And go to New Zealand and all them places."

"I was to Auckland once, when I was in sail," the Old Man told me. "Seems to me it took us about two years to get there, and it was hardly worth the trip. Even when the Maoris were eating the white settlers, it was forbidden to eat them after five p.m. You'd find it mite dull. I suppose we'll find worms under that old rotten log over yonder."

Worms, I thought bitterly. *Perch*. "The next thing you know, he'll be praising up catfish," I muttered.

"I heard you," the Old Man sang out. "They ain't anything wrong with catfish, Dr. Livingstone. In the Nile they got them weighing more than 100 pounds. There's a likely-looking tin can over there to put the worms in, *if* your native bearers can find any."

I went and dug some bloodworms out of the red-soggy, crumbly earth under the rotted log, and we strolled out to where the Tin Liz panted in the heat. The seats were as hot as a smoothing iron, and when you put your bare arm on the edge of the door it was like laying it on a stove. I flinched and hollered.

"It's hotter'n this where you're going when you're grown up," the Old Man chuckled. "I expect it's a heap hotter where *I'm* going some day too." This was one of those days when he wouldn't take anything seriously. Anything you said to him he'd turn and bite you with it. I reckon he'd had a lot of practice defending himself against women in a serious mood, namely Miss Lottie.

We drove a few miles out to the creek, where the little skiff was moored by a landing in the dark, leaf-dyed, fern-fringed water. He was right. It was cooler there on the winding creek, with the cypresses holding their knees high out of the water, and the water oaks dripping Spanish moss, with lumps of mistletoe like squirrels' nests high in the rigging. A swamp can be hotter than a steambath at midday, but it's the first thing to cool off after midafternoon. And it's always pretty chilly in the late evening, when the mists start to swirl off the water, and the first hatch begins to make the trout hungry.

"All right, Dr. Livingstone," the Old Man said, casting off. "Pretend we are Mr. Stanley. Down that away is a very fine hole full of fat bream, as you very well know. Affix one of them bloodworms to your trusty assagai, or what-d'ye-call-it, and catch me some supper. Otherwise your 200-porter safari will starve, and it's too late in the game to yell for Teddy Roosevelt to save us."

"Ain't you going to fish?" I asked.

"I'm too weak from hunger," the Old Man said. "I gave out days ago. I'm being carried along right now on a rough litter by natives nearly as poorly as I am. You better get started to victual this expedition, or we'll all be skeletons by morning. Hear the hyenas?"

I heard a squirrel chittering somewhere off in the swamp and a dove going *hoo-hoo-oo-hoo* mournfully.

"Hyenas," the Old Man said cheerfully. "Come to pick our bones. There goes your cork, Dr. Livingstone. I shouldn't be surprised if you had a 400-pound Nile perch on it."

I jerked the line, and a very handsome bream flopped into the boat. He would weigh a good half-pound, maybe better.

"Suitable for stuffing, I would say," the Old Man remarked. "For stuffing me, I mean. Continue, ere we perish."

He reached under the sternsheets and pulled out a half-gallon jug of a clear liquid. He probed around and found a tin cup, filled it half full, tipped it down, and sucked reflectively on his tobacco-stained mustache. A warm odor of corn mash drifted my way.

"Biltong," the Old Man explained. "It's what the poor folks live on when the hunters don't provide enough game to feed them. Kind of a liquid pemmican, or jerky, and will sustain life indefinitely. There goes your cork, my good Doctor."

It was a monster this time, all of a pound. The Old Man put his bottle of biltong carefully back under the seat.

"We will save some for tomorrow," he said. "A fellow never knows when he will need a noggin – excuse me, strip – of biltong to keep his strength up."

Well, I plain gave up. When the Old Man is in a kittenish mood, you might as well encourage him. I went along with the Dr. Livingstone joke, and called the Old Man Mr. Stanley, and we had a right enjoyable afternoon. The Old Man knew a power about Africa – which is how I first got bitten by the bug – and we kidded back and forth until you'd have thought we were actually in the jungle. A coon came down to drink, and I said, "Look, yonder's a tiger." And the Old Man would say, "Don't be silly. Everybody knows there ain't any tigers in Africa," and all like that. One cat squirrel was chasing another across the high trees, and the Old Man swore they were a couple of gorillas. A deer barked, and the Old Man said it was a lion. When a couple of darkies poled past in a flat-bottom skiff, I shoved our boat behind a bush, because these had to be fierce cannibals of the Lower Brunswick County tribe, and would eat us as soon as say "Evenin', Cap'n," which is what they said.

By the time we had the boat half-full of bream, it was coming on for dark. The night noises began to sound lonesome in the swamp, the birds and bugs were making their usual clatter, and when an old owl tuned up and a fox barked I swear I got the creeps. We'd been playing jungle so much that I might as well have been in one.

As I pushed the skiff back to the landing the Old Man had another slug of biltong, against the evening agues – he said his blackwater fever was plaguing him again. Suddenly he turned serious. "This wasn't *all* damfoolery. I ain't much for damfoolery without a reason for it. There is even kind of a moral in it, if you will hold still for it."

I'd held still for so many of his morals that there wasn't any use saying anything, because it wouldn't have made any difference.

"I hope you grow up and go all around the world," the Old Man went on. "I hope you go to Africa and shoot lions, and to India and shoot tigers, and to New Zealand to catch big fish. I hope you see all there is to see. But the odds ain't very strong that you will, any more than they figure you to be a millionaire or a sword-swallower.

"The trouble with most people is they spend most of their lives wanting something they haven't got a Chinaman's chance to get; and when they get as old as me they've not only not *got* it, but they've missed everything they might have enjoyed if they hadn't been mooning around, waiting for tomorrow, always looking over the hill.

"Right here in your own back yard you can buy a dollar's worth of shotgun shells and shoot a deer, a bear – if you go deep enough in the swamp – a wild hog, a fox, a bobcat, and a few years ago you could of shot a panther. You can shoot turkeys and fox squirrels and rabbits and coons and possum and wild turkeys. You got a back yard full of quail, and the cornfields are full of doves. The cricks are full of black bass and bream, and the river is full of everything from sheepshead to speckled trout. The marshes and the fresh-water ponds are full of ducks. Once in a while you get some good flights of geese. You can surf-cast anywhere around here and catch more bluefish and puppy drum and weakfish than any man needs. You can troll off the shoals, and if you go out a little farther you can catch sails and big mackerel and bonito.

"Now" – the Old Man poked his pipe at me – "that is a passel of action for any man or any boy, and you don't have to travel more'n forty, fifty square miles to do it all. All it costs you is a gun and a fishing pole and a few shells, a dog or so, and the time and effort you put into it. There ain't any sound in the foreign lands that can match a passel of good coon hounds running the woods at night, and for sheer spookiness any woods at night is scary enough to satisfy anybody.

"If you look at it the right way, a rabbit can be as much fun, with a fice dog after him, as any of the great big stuff. It takes more skill to hit a shifty squirrel with a .22 than it does to shoot an elephant with a cannon. A three-pound blue on light tackle, or a four-pound bass, can give you as much work as a marlin. It's just a matter of how you look at it."

I was pretty quiet on the way home as we pumped along in the Liz, with a croaker sack three-quarters full of bream. When we parked under the live oaks in front of the old square yellow house, I got out of the car and hefted the sack of fish. "Some day I'm still going to shoot me a lion," I declared.

The Old Man climbed creakily down and grinned in the light of a rising moon. "I hope you do, Dr. Livingstone," he said. "But in the meantime, if you'll favor me with a few cleaned fish, I will send drum signals to the Great White Queen to start the fire going and slap a little fatback in the skillet. I'm hungry enough to eat a hyena."

I went and cleaned the fish. That's where I always seemed to wind up, cleaning 400-pound Nile perch or skinning greater kudu, otherwise known as cottontails, in our particular jungle.

"In Your Own Back Yard," *Field & Stream*, August, 1956.

Hit 'Em Where They Ain't

*T*he Old Man took to wearing specs a lot in his fading days, but not, I suspect, because he needed them. His eyes were a faded, well-washed denim, but they were sharp as a tack from half a century of looking at blue water and distant trees. I had a suspicion that when he took up spectacles he was indulging himself in another stage property, as his reeking old pipe and his shaggy mustache were props. It is my opinion now that there was nothing but window glass in those gold-rimmed frames, and that he wore them as a badge of dignity and for extra professorial emphasis when he was cowing me into a corner with a fresh batch of knowledge for my unwilling consumption.

The Old Man had his specs tipped down on his nose one day when I barged into the sitting room where he was toasting his shins before the Kalamazoo stove and listening to "The Wreck of the Old

17

Ninety Seven" or some other lugubrious ballad on the handcranked phonograph with the horn-happy dog on it. As usual, I was complaining about something – shortage of birds, lengthening of school days each year, infrequency of fish – something. When you are very young the world is full of injustice, and it's all directed at you.

The Old Man heard me out, then lowered the glasses on his snout another notch and said, "You know anybody named Willie Keeler?"

"Yes, *sir!*" I said. "He was a baseball player. He was with the Baltimore Orioles and the New York Highlanders. He was one of the greatest hitters of all time. He –"

"What did this Mr. Keeler say that fixes him so immovably in your mind?"

"When they asked him to explain how he was such a great hitter he said, 'I always hit 'em where they ain't!'"

"Bravo," the Old Man said. "Maybe you ought to try it – hitting them where they ain't.

"Stay away from the crowds and make your own opportunity. You will be the man who will lug in the only ring-tailed randoolicus when everybody else is complaining about the shortage of ring-tailed randoolicali.

I had a sneaky feeling that this profundity ended my complaint session, because the Old Man put "Birmingham Jail" on the machine and picked up Brother Bulfinch's steady contribution to my culture. Anyway, the thing came to mind the other day when I was reading a *Field & Stream* piece by Ted Trueblood called "Faith, Hope and Success," and it occurred to me that Brother Trueblood was saying about the same thing as the Old Man. Ted's theme was that you should utilize all the practical things you know – and then slosh on a big dipper of confidence and extra hard work. In a word, faith. He points out that this hasn't been written about very much.

I don't rightly know why it hasn't been written up, for this hitting them where they ain't is about as sound a piece of advice as anyone can offer to a sportsman. If you go to some unlikely place firm in the belief that you will be lucky, chances are you will be lucky. And if you go someplace that everybody else regards as useless, there is a good chance that the place has bred up again and you are working a virgin lode of material. And certainly if you can twist the wind and weather to your advantage when the sunny-day sportsman has dropped his tools, you are bound to profit – if only by the absence of a mob.

I have parlayed this axiom into hunting bonuses ever since I was a kid. It not only works for me and Trueblood – it works invariably for the best guides and professional hunters I know. There are half-a-dozen white hunters in Africa who never bring in unsuccessful safaris, because they work twice as hard as the pack, beat the bushes twice as diligently, gamble on the longest shots, and have an ingrained feeling of sincerity and confidence that the long shots will pay if they go where everybody else ain't. These men are booked two or three years in advance with repeat clients, while the others sometimes bring home elaborate excuses instead of trophies.

One of the best deer I ever shot I killed not sixty yards from the smokehouse in the backyard of some country people in North Carolina. I had hunted as hard and as intelligently as I knew how for a week, from predawn to post-dusk. The dogs were smelling well, and deer ran all around me but never over me. All I got a near look at was females and fawns.

On the sixth day of frustration I heard the hounds pick up a trail a couple of miles away and sound off, and for some reason I had one of those goosepimply feelings. I *knew* where that deer was going to run, and I *knew* it was a buck. I got off my stand and ran as fast as I could to a place where I'd have headed if I had been the deer. This was a shabby little run-to-seed truck garden behind a small country farmhouse.

If I am this buck, I thought as I puffed and stumbled along, trying to head him off, *I would figure that if I ran the low woods I would duck the people on the ridges who might be apt to shoot me, and if I could put on a spurt and cross that weed-bearded garden I could sneak across the highway and through a stream and be gone into the bush with the lake not too far on the other side. I would then leap into that lake and flap a saucy wet tail at those hounds and those gunners.* Along the same lines, I thought that if I were a deer I would not be expecting to find anybody sitting in the backyard with a shotgun.

When I got to the little garden I quit thinking like a deer and took up a quiet stand in an overgrown drainage trench at the edge of the garden. There was a pile of junk in the ditch, including an old busted chair, which I sat on. I waited an hour, perhaps, while that deer played tag with the hounds, and then I heard them lose him. They were complaining angrily as they circled to connect with his scent again.

I cannot say why I didn't get up off that chair and start walking back to the car. It was bright midday by now, and nothing much stirs at midday. Anyhow, I was hungry. But the old feeling held. I still knew that deer was going to come tippy-footed past me.

I won't cliff-hang you on this one. Sure enough, I heard a swish and a pitter-patter and in a minute a biggish buck with a whole tree on his head came slipping very quietly and craftily along. I heard him but I couldn't see all of him, just the antler tips as he parted the broomsedge. Then he stopped, testing, and suddenly he took off. As he came to the open space at the edge of the garden he flashed out of the gallberry bush and poured on the coal. I shot him in the neck, quartering, as he cut across the corner, and he took the full, nearly unscattered load of No. 1's in the throat. He turned a flip and sprawled, practically at my feet, dead as old bones. I didn't even have to cut his throat to bleed him before I whistled up a couple of young'uns to help me haul him to the tree where we hung the carcasses for dressing.

That was one small example of hitting 'em where they ain't, using very little but faith to base your batting on. The two best days of shooting quail I can remember were in the rain at the tail end of the season – days so soggy-miserable that nobody but a damn fool would have tried to hunt anything in that weather. But the birds had crept wet-footed out of the swamps and were concentrated on the ridges, and I do mean concentrated.

The ramifications are endless if you combine some basic common sense with faith and a long gamble. Quite often you'll trip, but not so often as you'd think if you try the hard shots and give it the extra effort you'd devote to the mortal cinches. I am certain-sure that the Old Man and I enjoyed what amounted to a private game preserve when I was The Boy. Largely we hunted and fished the places nobody else thought of or didn't bother with because they looked too easy.

I have literally shot pheasant within the city limits of Philadelphia; some of the best quail shooting I had as a youngster was so close to my hometown that the wise guys overran it in their eagerness to head for the wilderness. As a nipper I once shot a limit of squirrels in a grove in which I had seen no squirrel sign in my own hunting lifetime. But I felt squirrelly that day and took the .22 out for a walk with a fat old cocker spaniel, and presto! Where they came from I couldn't say.

The great adventures of my tenderest-footed days, when a rabbit looked bigger than a bear and a robin was huger than a greater bustard in my eyes, were on the offbeat expeditions when boy and dog or boy and boat sort of just sauntered off in unlikely directions and got lost. Mostly I had faith that something would happen, and generally something did. Something always does if you make up your mind in advance that something *will* – and also that you won't be bored if it doesn't. That's half the battle right there.

Not long ago I decided to see if I had lost my touch with this hit 'em-where-they-ain't combination endorsed by the Old Man and a long-dead baseball player. I was in Africa, and I was surrounded by horrible weather and by the impossibility of doing anything about either area or weather; and I got stubborn. Next time up I'd like to tell you about it, for the old formula still works.

"Hit 'Em Where They Ain't," *Field & Stream*, June, 1961.

The Long Walk To School

*I*t's a popular pastime among adults, when the hair begins to gray and the aches of middle age grow stronger, to look back on the prodigious deeds of their youth and proclaim that we've all gone soft and that they don't make boys like that any more. The Old Man had a theory about this. He said that as a man grew older, the miles that he used to walk to the Little Red Schoolhouse grew longer.

"I am convinced," he said, "that what schoolin' I had took place no farther than half a mile from the homestead, but the older I get the longer the trip seems to get. If you asked me right fast how far I walked through snow, I reckon I'd say ten miles without battin' an eye."

I wasn't paying too much attention to what the old gentleman was saying, except I caught the word "snow." It was steamy August and I was torturing the crank handle of an ice-cream freezer. Or, rather, the crank was torturing me. Sweat was gushing down my face, and only the promise of being allowed to lick the dasher kept me grunting at the task as the cream in the cylinder, surrounded by a mixture of cracked ice and rock salt, got stiffer and stiffer.

When it got almost immovably stiff the ice cream was done, and I would be onto that smoothly creamy wooden paddle like a duck on a June bug, and there would be wonderful chunks of frozen peaches making lovely hillocks under the satin surface of the ice cream. This was known as soldier's pay, or extra incentive, and I was allowed an even start on the bulk of the ice cream with family. I usually came out ahead.

It seems to me that this was the best ice cream ever tooled by the

23

hand of man, when you consider the miracles one used to work with Jersey cream, sugar, eggs, and vanilla extract, with a few peach nuggets or cherries stirred into the mixture. They don't make ice cream like that today.

This thought occurred sharply as I was smitten by a violent crick in the back the other day when I was trying to recapture my misty youth by producing some home-churned ice cream instead of sending somebody to the store for a carton, or merely reaching down into the freezer for a rock-hard package that generally tastes of the same sawdust, no matter how brilliant the stripes.

I reckon that in recent years I've ruined an awful lot of good meat cooking out-of-doors in pursuit of youth. I will go fishing or camping just for the fun of being frozen or sunstruck, fly bit or mosquito chewn – anything at all as long as it's uncomfortable. I am a sucker for picnics, and like anything at all to eat if it's either raw or burnt and has sand in it.

In recent years I have eaten elephant heart, raw antelope liver, and half-cooked sand grouse or gazelle chops – meat that had been flying through the air or gamboling on the plains a few short minutes before. Let me catch a fish, and I'm not happy until I've given it a clay pack and shoved it into the coals. If it comes out half raw it doesn't hurt the taste, even on a tongue that may have been jaded by thirty years of nicotine and honed smooth by prohibition gin.

But it is true that the things *were* different when I was a boy, and the Old Man represented the irretrievable mystery of yesteryear. I do not suppose that I would get very far in interesting today's crop of nippers in what to me was high sport and great fun some thirty to thirty-five years a-past. It was altogether too simple then for this age of television and ballet in the circus. Progress, like nearly everything else, is relative, and I often wonder if its benefits are entirely undiluted.

Most of the things we did in the long-buried days happened out-of-doors. The seasons were sharply etched on the calendar as to potential. Winter was the infrequent snow, with icicles to suck and snow ice cream to be made, and traps for rabbits and the little snowbirds and waxwings that miraculously appeared with the first powdering. The traps were simple. A box was tilted and propped with a stick that had a cord attached. A trail of bread crumbs led to the box, and when the prey entered the trap you gave the cord a twitch from your hiding place and the box fell, imprisoning your quarry. Then the only problem was getting the birds out, and they usually flew free.

A thin skin of ice on the sweet-water ponds made duck hunting easier, because the ducks rafted in clumps and bunches in open water and were loath to fly in the flurrying snow. Somehow all animals and birds seemed tamer and easier to hunt in the snow, and it was tremendous fun to track a deer instead of running him with hounds.

Springtime was strawberry time, and green peaches time, and bellyache time, and – blessed of all the blesseds – getting out-of-school time. As May nudged lazily into June and the bobolinks swayed atop the long grasses, and the black cherries oozed sweetness as their trees oozed jewels of gum, the medicine cabinet took quite a thrashing, and the castor oil lowered its level in the penance bottle. And it was time to swim again, strictly against parental orders, so you swam anyhow, and the goose-pimpling waters were rendered doubly pneumonically delicious by their very illegality.

Summer, with the horrors of the schoolhouse all but forgotten, was a steady diet of fishing and swimming. There were some summer camps, even in my time – up in the mountains, mostly. These were basically created for parents who wanted their children out of their hair for six weeks or so, and so remanded them to a kind of benevolent concentration camp with supervised archery, boating, swimming, hiking, campfire-making, basket weaving and suchlike.

The nicest thing about August was that it was a kind of preparatory school for September, when the real adult action started – when you started to train the puppies seriously, when the dove season opened, when the big nor'easters swelled the tides and fetched the marsh hens into sight, when the big bluefish and the channel bass supplanted the inside fish as a point of interest.

October gave you squirrels and chinquapins glossy brown on the bushes, alum-tart persimmons wrinkling, and the quail calling sweetly in the dusk, still innocently secure from the fusillade that would greet them in November. That was when it really got frosty, and the undergrowth withered. The necks of the buck deer swelled, and you could hear the big fellows scraping the last of the velvet off their antlers and snorting in the thickets.

Practically none of this was artificial or contrived. I shot a bow and arrow, but I had made the bow and the arrows according to a recipe in a book by Ernest Thompson Seton. I didn't need a counselor to teach me archery. We could sling a hatchet, tomahawk fashion, and throw a spear, and make a deadfall, and hurl a knife, and row or sail a boat.

The barn walls in winter were generally tacked full of rabbit-skins and the hide of an occasional coon or possum, and I day-dreamed violently of meeting a bear to add to the trophies. I never did, but I saw one's tracks once, and that was almost as good as seeing him and shooting him.

There was also a secret life that adults never shared – a life of interlocking caves, of out-of-the-way islands where pirates surely once had buried their loot, of tree houses and even log cabins, their beams out of plumb, to be sure, but a power of cozy comfort to the weary pioneer.

The train from Southport to Wilmington, North Carolina (called the W.B. & S., which meant "Wilmington, Brunswick, and Southport," but was corrupted to "Willing But Slow"), consumed the best part of half a day to travel thirty miles, but the trip was fraught with high adventure and a sense of vast travel. The trip on the river boat, of which my Uncle Rob was engineer, took longer, but you felt pretty near like Columbus once you passed the stinking fish-meal factory. It took longer to make that thirty miles than it does to fly from New York to London.

It is probably perverse and cranky of me but I can't understand what the modern youngster sees of interest in rockets to the moon and satellites and such when there are still so many things to discover in the tangible sea. Nor how the extravagances of television can claim precedence over camping trips, or even over the limitless, understandable adventure to be found in books that do not deal with space cadets and moon dwellers.

But as a boy grown old, I do not seem to be lonely in this appraisal of things not being like they used to be. The weather's changed, and everybody talks about whether or not it's the atom bomb's fault. The safari business is booming, and is patronized largely by old boys with prominent veins and pot-bellies, men trying to torture themselves into a misty remembrance of things past. You never see any bluebirds any more, and the redheaded woodpeckers have joined the dodo. Things are definitely not the same as when I was a lad, and if you asked me right smart how many miles I walked to school through the snow I would probably top the Old Man and say "Twenty." That would be a lie, because all the time I had a bicycle, and the schoolhouse was just around the corner. It wasn't red either. That was the color of the seventh-grade teacher's hair at just about the time the birds and the bees took on a slightly different significance.

Come to think of it, they ain't making redheaded schoolteachers the way they used to either. Not the last time I looked.

"The Long Walk to School," *Field & Stream*, August, 1960.

A Walk Down The Road

The Tin Liz sighed, sank on her haunches, sighed again and expired. The Old Man got out and looked at her innards suspiciously, crouched down to peer at her lower parts, thumped her a couple of times, like you'd tap a melon to see if it was ripe, and then shrugged his shoulders. He had the yellow, red-headed kitchen match shoved into the pipe before he spoke. He got the pipe going and poked the stem at the rusty old car.

"Clearly a case of death due to old age," he said. "Far as I can figure, she's burnt her bearings, the piston rings are gone, the spring's busted, the gas pump is clogged, the brake linings are burnt out, the axle's sprung, the electric system's finished, and I think somebody forgot to put the crank in. We might as well shoot her like a foundered horse. We are plumb forgot and five miles from home. What do you suggest?"

"I guess we better pick up the guns and leash the dogs and go back," I said. "We can maybe hitch a ride, and then we can go to Gus McNeill's filling station and get him to send somebody out to pick her up and tow her in."

The Old Man snarled slightly, the wind riffling his mustache. He gazed at nothing in particular. "Now, there is my brave pioneer lad, my young Dan'l Boone, the Kit Carson of tomorrow." His voice lifted in a sissified tone. *"We can maybe hitch a ride, and then we can go to Gus McNeill's filling station and get him to send somebody out to pick her up and tow her in."* The Old Man spat. "And *this* is the one that's going to shoot lions and elephants. What do you think the dogs will think of us if we *hitchhike* our way back to a *filling station*" – he sarcastically accented the words – "if we don't give the dogs something to do to earn their keep?"

"Well, sir," I said, "it's a good six or eight miles to where we were headed. You going to walk all that way and then hunt all day, and then walk thirteen miles home?"

"I don't see why not," the Old Man said cheerfully. "Old and ugly and sick as I am, I reckon I can keep pace with any product of the machine age whose legs are so atrophied he needs transportation to go to the store for a box of gingersnaps. And who ever said we had to hunt thataway?"

"Well, there's no birds around here," I said. "Look at it. Broomgrass. Scrubby oak. Cut-down pine. Sparkleberry bushes. Gallberry bushes. Some chinquapin. And right on the highway. Nobody hunts here. It's been shot out."

Himself snorted. "Shot out, is it now? And why would it be shot out, me darlin' lad?" The Irish used to come out of him when he was treading heavy on the sarcasm. "Me gay brothy boy, tell why it'd be shot out, as so ye say."

"Too close to town. To easy to get at. Too many cars stopping along to let the dogs loose and burn down the coveys. Too many turpentine camps and brush fires."

"That's better than I thought you'd do," the Old Man said, leaving the ould sod to people more familiar with it. "You're right in all you say except in just one thing – the land has had a rest, and the birds have had a rest with it. There's no land on the face of the earth that doesn't need a rest, whether you're growing crops or birds or animals. The automobile is the curse of civilization, especially for the wildlife that lives by the side of the road, because any idiot can park his car by a field and, like you say, turn loose the dogs and slaughter a covey and be off with himself before the farmer that owns the fringes finds he's shot a cow and two suckling pigs as well. The hit-and-run hunter doesn't care about conserving the stuff for next year, and for all the next years." The Old Man spat. "If one of these car-without-permission hunters found a covey running down a corn row, he'd shoot it all on the ground and probably sell the birds to boot."

I didn't say anything. I went and let the dogs loose to lift their legs, got the guns in their cases, the thermos bottle, and prepared to march.

The Old Man started off again. "When you had to walk five miles or drive in a buggy for half a day to get where you were going before you could hunt, you appreciated what you were hunting, and took some care of it – *which*," he emphasized, "had something to do with assuring the farmer you wouldn't kill his best brood sow the first time she came at you out of a cornfield. You kind of watched out for your cigarette butts and matches, and tried not to burn his hayfields down, and you might also stop off at the house and give him a couple brace of birds. In return for which he might tell you where he had some turkeys more or less baited, and ask you to spend the night so's you could shoot one the next morning. But the automobile has ruined it. You can go a hundred miles in three hours, and shoot half the way along."

The Old Man glanced at the stricken car. "Look at that hunk of tin tragedy," he said. "We are marooned as much as if we had just been cast ashore on a desert island. Henry Ford made it. All the knowledge of mankind is in it, and look at it. As useless as a busted buggy with a dead mule in the shafts."

We started to walk down the road, heading home. The dogs had been circling, quartering and stopping as dogs will to carve their personal initials on the likelier-looking bushes. All of a sudden I saw a patch of white where the liver-and-white setter, Sandy, had headed into the brush. It refused to move, this white patch. I said to the Old Man, "Either Sandy's froze stiff, or he's found a covey of birds. Look yonder."

The Old Man snorted again. "Couldn't be birds. This place is shot out. I got it on the best authority. Probably nothing but field larks. Sandy had a hot nose when I turned him loose this morning. Better unlimber the guns, though. Probably a rattler or a horse terrapin. Couldn't be any birds along here. Too public. Where's the shell bag?"

I was in a fever when I opened the cowhide cases and started to fit the guns. Maybe you remember, the Old Man had a real peculiarity about guns. He wouldn't use one of those cases that took a whole gun. He said a broken gun never killed anybody, and he wouldn't ride in a car with a gun that was all in one piece. While I was fumbling the guns together – and you can bet the Old Man wasn't helping me any – I kept one eye on the patch of white showing through the dark green of the gallberries, and it never looked like moving.

With shaky fingers I handed the Old Man a fitted-together shot-gun and half a box of shells, and dropped the other half into my canvas hunting coat. We loaded as we walked up to the patch of white, and there was old Sandy, as stark as a statue, and old Frank, looking like a twin to a burnt stump, just behind him.

"I don't think this would be larks," the Old Man murmured. "*Or* a rattlesnake. *Or* a terrapin. Let's us go see."

We walked up to the dogs, walked past, scuffed the twisted low-broom, and what amounted to two million birds got up. I fired into the middle of the two million, and saw nothing fall. The Old Man unleashed his ancient weapon too, although I never heard it. I looked at him and he looked at me. I shrugged my shoulders and he shrugged his.

"Must of been snakes," he said. "But have you got any idea where the single snakes went?"

"They looked like they were going down either into that patch of broom or off into those little scrubby oaks," I said. "How many birds would you say were in the covey?"

"Less than a hundred thousand," the Old Man replied, putting fresh shells in his gun. "Twenty-five at least. Looked like old birds, too. Let's go see if the dogs can smell singles."

We went to where the singles seemed to have lit, and they stuck fast as glue. It was one of the few times we ever overshot a quota, but it seemed in the Old Man's logic that a covey of twenty-five or thirty birds could spare eight, and eight was what we shot.

"Just like," the Old Man said sternly, popping the proceeds of a neat double into his cost, "all the other roadside hunters. Game hogs."

We walked along the road and waved the dogs from one side to the other. In something less than five miles to the city limits, the dogs found five coveys, one of which was bivouacked in the front yard of a suburban friend. We did not shoot that covey, since it involved firing through the windows of the living room.

But we shot sufficient birds to have a heavy-hanging hunting coat by the time we approached the general vicinity of Gus McNeill's filling station. I would like to tamper with the truth a little and say we filled our limit just abaft the gas pumps, but I cannot tell a lie. There were no birds in the vicinity, only Gus and a few shiftless friends.

"Where you-all been?" Gus asked as we trudged down the road, the dogs leashed again, both of us carrying a sheathed gun.

"Huntin'," the Old Man said dryly.

"Huntin' what?" Gus asked.

"Birds."

"Get any?"

"Some."

"Where's your car?"

"Back yonder a piece."

"How far?"

"About five mile."

"How many birds?"

"Twenty, more or less."

"The car broke down?"

"Yep. Can you send somebody to tow her home?"

"Sure. Where'd you get the birds? They been kind of scarce lately."

"Oh, we hunted up 'way ahead of the car. I got a couple of farms the folks let me use from time to time. You know the way it is." The Old Man slipped me a wink. Gus was a shotgun man too.

"You want to use the car tonight, or will tomorrow be okay?" Gus inquired.

"Tomorrow'll do," the Old Man said. "But we would appreciate it if you'd give us a lift home now. My feet are killing me from pounding all this asphalt. Seems to me walking was easier when we had clay roads. At least they fit my feet better."

We drove home, and Gus let us out. I took the dogs to pen and came back to take the guns off the front porch to clean them, and then went back to where the Old Man had a rather massive pile of quail on the back steps.

"*Some farms that folks let me use*. Do not tell a lie," I said reprovingly. "*Never* tell a lie. It says so in Sunday school."

The Old Man was counting the little beautiful bobwhites. "Twenty-two," he announced happily. "All out of a shot-out area. Now, what did I tell you about the curse of the machine age? If that Liz had held together, we would of run right past the birds, and probably come home with nothing. The auto is the curse of the hunting man. And just think, all we had to do was walk down a road."

"Do *not* tell a lie, like Miss Lottie says," I said sternly, for me.

"Miss Lottie be blowed," the Old Man said, still happy. "She never knew anything about quail hunting or game conservation. We are game conservationists, protecting the national resources from tourists. We are protecting them for ourselves, which is conservation of a sort, even if it's selfish."

"I suppose I'd better start cleaning them, like always," I said.

"Tonight I'll help you," the Old Man said, and I like to have dropped dead from shock.

"A Walk Down the Road," *Field & Stream*, September, 1956.

Rainy Day Reminiscences

*I*n the South there isn't a whole lot to do in the month of August, because this is dog-days month and it's hotter than those hinges you hear about, and muggy to boot, with a lot of thunderstorms. Everything is burned up. It's too early for the bluefish to run and too late for some of the other fish, and you've played enough baseball. It's getting awful close to school time again, which is a depressing thought, and what makes school time worthwhile, the hunting season, is almost as far away as Christmas.

I remember I was complaining about this one day to the Old Man – a sticky, miserable day with the sky sort of yellow-gray, the kind of day when your clothes seize onto you and you itch all over and wish it would rain and be done with it.

"I never see such a natural-born complainer in all my days," the Old Man said. "I swear I believe you take after your other grandpa. Nothin' suits you. If it's football season, you're yellin' about baseball. You seem to be trying to keep living about a year ahead of yourself. One day you'll be old as I am and wonder what the Sam Hill you did with all those days you wasted wishing it was some other time of the year."

The Old Man lit his crook-stem pipe and spit. A butterfly shuddered under the shock and sort of crippled off with one wing low.

"You bring out the worst in me, boy. You're turning me into one of them evangelists. I am a one-horse Billy Sunday. Here you are, just about halfway out of the shell, and already you're telling me you're bored. Ain't no unlicked whelp got any right to be bored, any time, any place. Just being your age is enough to keep you charged with sparks."

I kept quiet. The signs were that the Old Man was cranking up for a lecture. I never minded these lectures when some sort of concrete illustration went with 'em – such as a hunting or fishing trip – but it looked to me like we had nothing better to look forward to than a rain-squall.

I was right, too. A clap of thunder fit to wake the dead split the sky apart, and just ahead of it was a zigzag streak of lightning so close that you could hear it crackle. We went in the house. The black clouds crowded low on top of the yellow clouds, and the skies just opened up and cried. It was raining so hard that it sounded like a team of horses on the shingles, and when the rain hit the dust it made little dimples and puffs. Everything outside the house was a dirty-dog-gray.

The Old Man smiled. "Nothing in God's world I love so much as a real rip-snortin' thunderstorm," he said. "Makes a man stop and think. Never knew a woman yet who wasn't more afraid of the noise than of the lightning. Just like the Injuns always thought the noise from a gun was the killer – not the quiet little bullet.

"I love a squall because it washes the world clean. It's a purge, like calomel in the spring. There's a lot of blim-blam and boom-boom and slashin' rain, and then it turns off cool and everything's quiet and sweet and clean and well-washed again. You sit quiet in a snug house and you hear old Jupiter up there heavin' them thunder-bolts around, and you forget it's just hot air meeting cold air. Nothing I know of is as sweet and soft as the skies after a squall – and nothing is as really comfortable as the pounding of rain on a roof when you ain't wet. 'Specially if you know how to use this wonderful vacation from the outside world."

Well, I thought, here she comes. I was right again.

"You take the Injuns," the Old Man said. "They were grateful for a rainy day. They set snug in the tepee or the long house with the chimney flaps trimmed right, and gave thanks to the Manitou for a day off. They did a passel of things they hadn't got round to, due to being too busy making the squaws work.

"They mended their fish-nets. They repaired their snowshoes. They looked to their traps. They shook down their hunting gear. They greased their spare moccasins, and counted their wampum. They slept some and ate some and smoked and told each other a lot of lies about how many grizzly bears they'd shot and how many palefaces they'd scalped. They scratched their lice and thanked the Manitou for the deer and the turkeys and the corn crop and the pinto ponies and anything they could lay a thank-you to. We been trying to civilize Injuns for years, when all the time they're a heap smarter than we are. They prepare today for what might come up tomorrow, instead of waiting for tomorrow to come and find them unprepared. Also, I never heard of no Injun with an ulcer."

The Old Man tapped his teeth with the pipestem. "You looked at your gun lately?" He shot the question at me.

"No sir," I said, before I thought.

"You'd make a hell of an Injun," the Old Man said. "All your papooses would starve to death. Maybe you and me better stir our stumps and overhaul a little gear."

We went up to the attic where we kept such unwomanly truck as hip boots and guns and fish rods and knives and hatchets and bait cans and tackle boxes – and, I suspect, where the Old Man cached his spare supply of nerve medicine. There is something right wonderful about an attic in the rain. You are closer to the rain, for one thing. Also, there is a smell about an attic – raw, resin-oozy pine boards and musty papers and a sort of happy unfinished atmosphere, as if this would be a mighty fine hide-away if you ever got out the hammer and saw and put the finishing touches on her.

Also, the women leave you alone when you go up to the attic. Maybe they just don't want to climb the stairs bad enough to have their delicate nervous systems disturbed by all the mess that a couple of men can make in a room that doesn't come under female supervision every day. I reckon it's a concession they make for being such fuss-budgets about keeping the parlors clean and not spilling ashes on the rug.

Another thing about attics is the piles of old magazines, like the *Country Gentleman* and the *National Geographic*, and ratty old books, and even old newspapers telling about Archduke Ferdinand getting himself assassinated, and old trunks tied up with sash-cord, and old clothes that somebody a long time dead used to wear. It is a pleasant reservoir of things to do for the future, because if you ever got hard put to it you could always come up and plunder the trunks and read all the stuff you never had time to read before somebody took the books and magazines out from under the window-seat and hustled them upstairs.

"Suppose you clean the guns," the Old Man said quietly. "I'll have a look at the fishing tackle. Won't be very long before the blues and the puppy drum are running again in the sloughs over to Corncake."

I knew very well I had cleaned and oiled those guns – my sixteen and the Old Man's guns as well – when we put them away in March. But the best-kept gun will collect a fine film of light-pink rust from the condensation over a period of damp months, and my shotgun and the Old Man's pump and the little .22 and the old .30-30 all needed a little tending to. I got out the gun oil and the greasy rags and the ramrods and started to work. The Old Man started to strip a couple of surf reels and take down the mechanism.

We took our time. We weren't going anywhere. The rain drummed down steady and strong. While I was wiping off the shotgun I suddenly wasn't in an attic. I forgot the rain. I was out in the woods. I was shooting my first bobwhite. I was sitting half frozen in a duck blind, and I could hear the *whissshh* of the teal sliding in and the creaking flap of a goose coming close and the slip-stream of a high pintail flock. I was waiting in the cool, scary quiet of a cypress swamp, waiting for the belling of the dogs to come closer and listening acutely for the scraping of a buck deer's rack on the gallberry bushes.

When I held the shining barrels to my eyes, looking for the

remnants of lint from the wiping rag, I was standing in the far corner of a cornfield, watching the doves being driven from stand to stand, hearing the guns go off, seeing the late-afternoon sun flash on the rosy gray of their breasts, and hearing the sharp whistle of their long, back-raked wings. I went back to the angry gobble of an old tom turkey squalling off in the swamp, and I heard the chuckle of the hens. I could smell the sweet crushed fern in the bays, and taste the sharp tang of the clear brown swamp water in a tin coffee pot. There came clearly the sharp sizzle of bacon frying on a frosty morning and the clean crunch of a brown-burnt corn dodger in my mouth.

I noticed that both the Old Man and I were hunting as we fiddled with the gear. He had a big old surf reel stripped down to practically nothing and was doing something with a very small screwdriver. I looked at the split-bamboo rods that Linden Knox had made for me, and at the reel, and at the loose-looped pile of salty gray cuttyhunk, and I reckoned I knew what was making the Old Man hum.

He had to be standing, wet to the waist, in a slough, with the moon just jumping up and the salty night air gone chill, and the sea birds crying and a great big channel bass hung fair and fine on the mullet-baited hook. The rod would be bent into a semicircle and the Old Man would be backing up, very carefully, until he was all the way in the sea-oats and the big silver log of fish came out of the sea like Venus and flopped in the silver sand. There would be a drift-wood fire, burning blue from the salt, and a thermos of hot coffee and some ham sandwiches waiting for him when he slid the hook out of the puppy drum's mouth.

I finished with the guns and walked over to the ratty old pile of books, and riffled through the pages. There was a bound volume of an old English magazine called *Blackwood's*, the pages yellow and spotted from age and damp, but right in the middle there was a story about witchcraft in the Burma jungles, and I got so fascinated that I couldn't put it down until the Old Man hollered to come help him rewind the line on the reel.

We got out some neat's-foot oil and greased up the hunting boots, and the Old Man checked all his bass plugs, and I read some more about the retreat from Mons in the yellowed newspapers, and then came across some cartoons that my Pa had done for the newspaper when he was a part-time artist and not an accountant – in spirit, anyhow. One was a picture of the Kaiser, John Bull and a Frenchman, all singing "Peace, Sweet Peace" after the war was over. The title was "Golly, What A Discord." My Pa was a pretty good artist, considering that in those days you had to draw for reproduction by scratching the lines in chalk plate with a stylus that had a sharp hook on the end.

As I remember, there was even a copy of *Godey's Lady's Book*, but that wasn't near so interesting as the old Sears Roebuck catalog, which had more saddles, guns and other exciting things in it than any single volume of anything ever published.

The rain finally slacked off a little bit, but it was getting dark. We had just turned on the single naked bulb that hung, flyspecked, from the ceiling when there was an unmistakable female screech from the bottom of the stairs that could only have been Miss Lottie, my grandma. She was inviting us to dinner – before it got any colder and she threw it to the dogs. The Old Man looked at me and shrugged. He tapped the dottle out of his pipe and stuck it in his pocket.

"You still bored with a rainy day in August?" he asked, with that I-told-you-so flicker behind his glasses.

"No sir," I said. "I expect this is one of the most exciting days I ever spent in my whole life."

The Old Man grinned. "You might make a pretty good Injun after all," he said. "But we better get down to the boiled dog in a hurry or the squaws are apt to scalp us."

"Rainy Day Reminiscences," *Field & Stream*, August, 1954.

The Smell Of Christmas

*T*o me it scarcely seems possible, but this issue you're reading marks the sixth anniversary of "The Old Man and the Boy" – seventy-two pieces without a missed deadline, although there have been some frighteningly near squeaks. Perhaps now my friends might like to join me in a sort of author's-eye view of what has been the pleasantest writing chore I ever took on.

About 180,000 printed words have been dredged out of a boyhood trove of memories, the basic idea being that in an era of atomic power, zip guns and juvenile gang warfare something of excitement might be recalled from an ice age in which kids were *given* knives and guns as a reward for behaving themselves.

In talking over the project originally with *Field & Stream's* editors, it seemed to be possible to create something of a Tom Sawyerish, Huck Finnish nature without boring either the Old Man or the Boy in the process. The column at first was aimed at kids but speedily betrayed its author and accumulated a preponderantly adult audience.

The speed with which the rough format took shape was almost frightening, certainly uncanny. It was as though the stuff had been locked up, waiting for someone to shove a key in the door and let it come tumbling out. In six years I haven't once been really hard pressed for an idea.

As you are well aware, "The Old Man and the Boy" has dealt with a small local segment of the American scene; so it is rather strange that its installments should have been produced in practically every corner of the world. The first two were written on a steamer bound for Genoa; subsequent ones were recorded on an African safari. In the years that followed, "The Old Man and the Boy" was written in such disparate places as the Hotel Savoy in London, the Hadden Rig sheep station in New South Wales, and in a camp in Goroka, high in the mountains of New Guinea, as well as in Rome, Paris, Madrid, the Philippines, Tokyo, Hong Kong and a number of other places I won't take the time to list. Altogether, it has been one of the best-traveled columns in history, and it is odd that the only place in which it has not been written is the locale where the incidents happened – Southport and Wilmington, North Carolina.

Not once has my other work competed with "The Old Man and the Boy." I wrote two novels and three nonfiction books, plus magazine articles, and of course there has been my thrice-weekly newspaper stint. But always, somehow, the Old Man took firm precedence over the others.

Often the material almost wrote itself. I suspect that in reporting the fevered present I had somehow forgotten the old things: the smell of Christmas in a country house; the bugling of hounds hot after a coon; the sight of the wizened old Chinaman's face of a possum curled in a tight ball in a persimmon tree; a colored boy singing to keep off the hants as he drove the cow home through the lowering evening woods; the spumy smash of norther-driven waves on a lonely beach; the rich swelling of song at a colored camp meeting; the convivial gayety at an oyster roast, when the fruit jar passed freely in the shadows and the square dancers struck up a slightly unsteady reel.

"The Old Man and the Boy" made me think – made me fine-tooth-comb my memory. The smell of Christmas is a case in point. The old-fashioned Christmas smell was predominantly that of crushed evergreens against the constant resiny aroma of a snapping fire. One was a cool smell, the other hot, but both joined forces. This backdrop was overlaid by the heady odors that drifted from the kitchen – the sage which went into the turkey stuffing predominating.

The whole was tinctured with spices and by alcohol, because brandies and wines were lavishly used in the preparation of sauces and in building the fruitcakes. There was, as well, an infusion of tropical scent as the infrequent Christmas citrus fruits – the opulent golden oranges – added an oily sharpness to the mixture. This was counter-balanced by the clean, cidery bite of the hard, white-fleshed, scarlet apples. Bright Christmas candies – the clover-shaped and heart-shaped sugary ones you never saw at any other time of the year, and the striped hard ones with the soft centers – helped the greasy Brazil nuts along, as did the winy aroma of the great clusters of raisins, sugary-sticky to the touch. The spices that went into the eggnog or the hot Tom and Jerrys stood off the warm friendship of the rum that gave character to the cream.

Now, I had to turn back the clock a far piece to sort out all those various effluvia in my mental nostrils, and in the process I ran onto other stimuli. I could suddenly remember what it was like going to bed between icy sheets in an unsteamheated house, and the torture of leaving a warm bed to crawl into your clothes in the black predawn of a duck-hunting day – of the tiny furnace that a hunter's big breakfast built in your stomach when your ears were dropping off from the cold and your legs were numb from the knees down.

It was easy, then, to reconstruct the bright droplet that always stood at the cherry end of a boy's frozen nose as he shivered in a duck blind and prayed for the mallards to come in. And such things as the dewdrops of spray standing distinctly on the Old Man's mustache, and the smell of an old man – "old men and old dogs both smell bad" – which seemed compounded of tobacco juice, corn whisky, open fire and just plain old man.

I was moved to think again, for the first time in many a year, of just how hell-conscious a small boy can be, and of that frightening span of two or three years when I was sure I was going to hell for telling a lie or for cutting Sunday school or for saying damn, and of how I was sore stricken with the enormity of eternity. These severe strokes of conscience generally took hold during a late afternoon in a swamp, when the doves mourned and the early evening snaps and pops and hoots began. Even today, as an adult, during a late fishing afternoon in a darkly mysterious swamp, surrounded by cypress knees and Spanish moss, I feel something of that old fear of the wrath of God, and a chilly finger runs up and down my spine.

It was not until I undertook this series that I realized just how much a boy dwells in his stomach. It seems to me in retrospect that very few chapters lack an almost lyrical appreciation of food and its preparation. The other night I was rereading some of the stuff, about terrapin stew and oyster roasts and such truck, and I got so hungry I crawled out of bed and padded into the kitchen to lay waste the icebox.

I had never written much about food until I took on "The Old Man and the Boy," but I noticed that this new novel of mine, just finished, is so full of food that the people who have seen the script are calling me the poor man's Edna Ferber. I have also noticed that directly because of "The Old Man and the Boy" my descriptive powers have sharpened perceptibly when used in other work.

The depth of my appreciation of the boons granted me by the series is immeasurable. Among other things, it provided a stout staff to lean on when I cut loose from a life I didn't like and took up a life I *did* like. So long as I had "The Old Man and the Boy" I had steady work, plus time to gamble on other things. In terms of physical health, peace of mind and opportunity to experiment with other forms of writing, you could not compute what the series has been worth.

Basically, though, my gratitude extends to the hundreds of thousands of people who have read the stuff since its inception, and who got the idea right away and spoke out loud and clear to say so. In the sputnik age, I was immensely cheered to learn that there were so many people still around who attached value to certain things that were not necessarily made of plastic or exceeded the speed of sound.

Possibly you will think it curious that I write this sort of inside piece on "The Old Man and the Boy," but once in a while I have an idea that readers might like to know something of what goes on inside an author's head. Also, you might say that at the end of this sixth year I am slightly carried away by sentiment, and wish to express deepest thanks to the Old Man, the Boy and all their friends.

"The Smell of Christmas," *Field & Stream*, December, 1958.

Bobwhites & Buffalo

I mind it very clear, that day when I came in as proud as a peacock with a bushel of birds, arrogant as only the very young can be. I spread the quail out on the front stoop for the Old Man to admire.

"You must of been shooting pretty sharp," he said. "I'm sorry I wasn't there to see you. Find a whole lot of coveys?"

"No, sir," I said. "Found just one, a great big one. Got 'em scattered out in that broom grass around Willett's farm, and old Frank was really going good. I murdered 'em."

"Your choice of verb is excellent," the Old Man said. *"Murdered* is the precise word. What do you figger to shoot there next year – *air? Larks?"*

My face must have drooped. "There was an awful lot of birds," I said. The Old Man had a way of blowing the wind out of your sails, just as he could fill 'em and send you spanking along at the rate of knots. The Old Man spat disgustedly. He tugged on his mustache for a minute and then spoke awful sarcastic.

"Remind me to write a letter to your English teacher," he said. "Your vocabulary is getting what I would call *super*-precise. *Was* a lot of birds is dead right. *Is* a lot of birds is dead wrong. You just killed a covey, give or take a few, and by the time the foxes and wild tame-cats and spring freshets and disease get through with what's left, there won't be nothing at all left for you or me or anybody else to shoot next year. It makes you a kind of criminal. You have invaded the public domain, like a robber holding up a bank. You are stealing from your own country."

Well, I never thought of me as a crook. The covey had flushed

47

perfectly and fanned out into the broom sedge, and old Frank's nose was keen as mustard, and the birds held good, and I was shooting awful good for me. Before I knew it I had a coatful of birds. I felt fine when I was shooting. I didn't feel like I was robbing a bank."

"From time to time," the Old Man said, "I have mentioned the buffalo, one of the greatest assets America ever had for a variety of reasons. There ain't any now, bar a few private herds of the privileged survivors. You will now absorb a lecture on the buffalo, and I trust it will lead to the perpetuation of the bobwhite quail in Brunswick County, North Carolina. You didn't see no buffalo today, did you?"

"No," I said.

"Well, we had 'em here once," he went on grimly. "Before my time, but we had 'em. We had more next door in Virginia, but one time they were all over the United States, in swarms. And people like you killed 'em off. Just like you assassinated that covey of birds. Prepare yourself for a little education, but first go clean the birds. Even the Injuns made use of what they slaughtered."

The Old Man was pacing and fuming and chomping on his pipe when I came back from picking and drawing the birds. "Set," he said. "I aim to declaim."

I sat. He declaimed.

"The American bison, or *Bison bison*, was first dug up by a Spaniard named Cortez in 1521, or thereabouts. He saw him in Montezuma's home town, which is now Mexico City, in a private zoo. Another Spaniard named Alvaro Nuñez Cabeza de Vaca (Cabeza de Vaca means "Cow's Head") got himself shipwrecked off the Gulf Coast of southwest Texas and ran into the first wild buffaloes. He thought they were a curious kind of humpbacked cattle. We had a lot of Spaniards running around the country at that time. The next one to come onto the buffalo was a fellow named Coronado, who I'll tell you about later, because he left a mess of Inca treasure scattered around that people have been looking for ever since. Coronado, he wrote that New Spain (Texas, Colorado, New Mexico and Oklahoma) had more 'crooked-backed cattle than Old Spain has sheep.'

"The English were a little slow on the encounter, but somebody named Sir Samuel Argyll run across a bunch close aboard Washington, D.C., in 1612, where they were chewing down the forest, and from then on everybody saw 'em. We had a power of these beasts in those days. They ranged from Canada to Carolina, and all the way across the Mississippi to Mexico. They migrated all over everywhere. They went a little travel-crazy and just busted out."

The Old Man paused to light his pipe.

"You know how much is a million of anything?" he asked.

"Mosquitoes, maybe," I said. "Gnats."

"Well," he said, "figure seventy-five million gnats weighing up to two thousand pounds apiece, and you got some idea of the number of buffalo that were running around loose when the country was new. You know how many one-ton wild gnats we got now?"

"No," I said – "sir."

"None," he said, "I will continue to declaim. The Plains Indian economy was based on the buffalo. Any fool who can read knows that. He lived off the buffalo. He made his robes and his clothing and his tents of buffalo hide. He fed his family buffalo meat. If he needed a fancy hat, he stuck buffalo horns onto his headdress. He even made his fires of buffalo chips, which dried better than cow dung and burned with a pretty, clear and quiet flame, kind of like drift-wood. He followed the buffalo migration and feedings. This meant a mess of movement, because a buffalo's feeding habits would take him from one hundred to four hundred miles away from base. But the Injun economy was so firmly stuck to the buffalo that whole tribes starved when the expected migrations didn't arrive, or weather or disease cut down the size of the herds.

"The buffalo was Big Medicine, even after the white man came, or especially after the white man came. Once in a while an albino buffalo, with pink eyes and near-white skin, would appear on the scene, and the man that killed him was king of his community, because they believed all the other buffalo would come back to pay homage to their albino chief. On all the human migrations west, the pioneers followed buffalo trails, which had got to be Injun trails, which got to be oxcart trails, and that is why we have cities like Portland, Oregon, or San Francisco, California. More or less, anyways.

"Before the white man come in force and brought horses and rifles, the Indian didn't make an appreciable dent in the buffalo population. West of the Mississipp', that is. They dwindled down to a precious few by about 1800 on the eastern side on the big river, but that was disease and blizzards and a lot other things, like encroaching civilization and lack of pasturage.

"But it was when the Indian got ahold of the horse and learned about guns that the poor old buffalo really took a plastering. Some reckon that around 1830 the Injuns were killing about two million buffalo a year, and some reckon five million. That's a big piece of meat. When you figure that the white man wasn't hunting in much force, and add wolves and floods and disease and blizzards and drought, how many buffalo died is impossible to estimate.

"By the early 1830s, they were selling 200,000 buffalo robes a year, taken from the Western Plains buffalo alone, and that would have meant a slaughter of at least three million a year, since the Injuns were using what they couldn't sell – or rather, selling what they didn't need to use. Old Frémont, the trader, says he found a great 'distress' among the Indians along the Platte because of the 'failure' of the buffalo. *Failure* was a mild word for it. What with the wolves and plague, and straight-out murder, there wasn't no heavy amount of buffalo apt to show up.

"Now," the Old Man said, "we get into my generation. You're too young to remember when Buffalo Bill Cody had his show here, but I did manage to take your Cousin Ted. I won't go into old Pahaska's morals regarding women and whisky, but I will kill him dead on the buffalo business. Pahaska means long hair, a name the Indians gave him. I think he was mostly fraud, but no matter. He could hold a lot of likker.

"The Union Pacific Railway split the main Plains herd into two sections when they were moving the iron tracks west. How many hired killers they had, shooting those big new Sharps cartridge rifles, I couldn't estimate, but they were feeding the Irish immigrant help as they went, and selling the hides for bonus. From that point on it was called 'South Herd' and 'North Herd.' That's when we come to mister Colonel Buffalo Bill Cody, or Pahaska.

"He signed on with Kansas Pacific Railroad, and earned himself a reputation like *you* earned today. They called him Buffalo Bill, because he is supposed to have killed about 4,000 buffalo in 18 months, apart from innocent Indians, and on one day he killed 69 buffalo, betting money against Billy Comstock, another hunter."

The Old Man paused for breath and snorted. "He run a lousy circus, too," he said. "They should of put him on exhibit with the other animals. I think he grew that beard because he lacked a chin.

"Well, what Col. Buffalo Bill Cody left on the South Herd, the Santa Fé Railroad accounted for. The white hunters were killing about a quarter-million every year, and the Indians were getting in their licks, and by 1889 there just weren't any herds apart from a few scattering groups. On the North Herd, some figures I saw started out with fifteen million in 1865, with a million killed the year before. There were two years when a half-million were slaughtered – out of one herd, mind you, and when it come down to 1889, there were 150 buffalo left. The previous year they'd killed the same figure, 150. That's making it come out nice and even.

"The buffalo had a lot of enemies apart from man, but he was uncommonly well-equipped to deal with them. His hide, with all that wool, kept the flies off him, kept the snow off him, and he could turn on a dime when he had to fight wolves away from the calves and the calving cows. He was fierce enough to handle what he had to handle. He was a pretty good family man, and he could be counted on to breed for the three or five years he bossed the herd. The cows were long-lived, and they had a calf a year, sometimes twins, for twenty years, even more.

"They were immune to most of the diseases that attack cattle. They were good foragers, and could live off less acreage than modern cattle. They were resistant to weather, and the main weather that killed them was rotting ice, when they migrated – stampeded, really – across the mushy ice and got drowned. They could hold out against a blizzard that would kill a cow, and they could find food in deep snow when the elk and the other wild game were starved dead. Fire cut them down, mostly when some drunk Injun set fire to the plain and destroyed their food. They got caught in bogs, because of their stampeding habits.

"But mostly what killed them off was man. Not the horseless Injun with the bow, but the Injun on a horse with a gun, who killed them to sell to the white man, who then found out it was easier to kill the Injun and the buffalo himself and avoid the middleman. And then he run out of space, of course, as the continent filled and towns grew up. One way or the other, the buffalo would have come down to very little, giving way to cattle and people and gardens."

The Old Man quit talking, took a long breath and stabbed his pipestem at me.

"But it wasn't *all* necessary," he said. "We didn't have to wipe out the lot to make room for progress. And there ain't any railroads coming through here feeding its working force on quail, or dressing them in quail feathers, or making fires with quail chips. There is no economy wrapped up in the quail except that he is a pleasant friend to have around to eat the bugs that eat the crops, whistle pretty, provide sport for people and dogs and generally behave himself as a good neighbor. He adapts to civilization, unlike the buffalo, and if I ever hear of you shooting up a covey again I will skin you alive. You ain't Buffalo Bill Cody, and I'll have your scalp."

"Yes," I said. There didn't seem to be any more I could say.

"Bobwhites and Buffalo," *Field & Stream*, February, 1957.

The First One Was In A Stable

"As you likely know," the Old Man once said, "I ain't a feller to hand out too much free advice, because I don't reckon a man can digest but so many eggs at one sittin'. But I aim to leave you with one high-minded thought. When you got yourself a tragedy, don't cry. Make like you're in an adventure that is happening to somebody else."

This was a day we'd planned on for a whole year, the opening of the quail season. It started to rain on Thursday and it was still coming down in sheets on Saturday. There wasn't any question of hunting. You could have been drier in a river, and the dogs would have smelled the birds better if they had one of these fancy modern aqua-lung arrangements. It was even too wet to fish, and I was fit to blow a gasket. You go to school all week, looking forward to Saturday as your play-pretty, and then they turn the world upside down to let it drain on you.

"It ain't fair," I said, still hopping mad. "Why don't it rain on Monday? Why has it always got to rain on Saturday? Why. . .?"

"Relax," the Old Man said. "Mark Twain used to say that everybody talked about the weather but nobody did nothin' about it. Think of Noah. Pretend you got an Ark all full of every kind of bird and beast there is, and you're steamin' straight for Ararat with no compass. There ain't nobody there but you and that one silly dove with its olive branch to help with the navigation."

I begun to snicker. "I'd of shot the dove." I said.

The Old Man begun to snicker too. "I doubt it," he said. "I've seen you shootin' doves. This dove would of had a hell of a good chance to get missed."

Somehow this one piece of advice stuck with me, like so many of the Old Man's casuals that seemed just lazy talk then and flew back to roost years later, when I needed a little momentary help. Like anybody else, I've had considerable tragedy, or what seemed like tragedy. And if you take a look at it, as if it is happening to somebody else, suddenly it isn't tragedy any more. It's high adventure, like in a war when the ship gets hit. You think: "So that's what it's like to get blown up in the bloom of youth" – as if somebody else was getting blown up. And then when she don't blow, you've got yourself a bonus.

Maybe it's Pollyanna but it works. Christmas was always wonderful in the Old Man's day and age. The house was full of wonderful smells and wonderful food. School was out for a couple of weeks and Santa Claus was duty bound to bring you something wonderful, like a shotgun or a bicycle or a pair of hunting boots and a mackinaw – all the fascinating stuff that you saw in the Sears Roebuck catalogue. Then there was the free week until after New Year's to try out all the stuff in the woods, with your pockets full of nuts and raisins and store candy and your new boots blistering your heels and the gun looking oily slick and smelling like only a new gun can smell.

Then one day the Old Man is gone, and now *you're* the Old Man, although you've just touched 21, and you're busted in a strange town, with no prospects ahead, living in a ratty rooming house, and it is Christmas Eve and there is literally not one friend to pass it with. You can smell, in the back of your mind, the roasting turkey with sage dressing and the wondrous warmth of the brandy-soaked fruit cake and the aroma of crushed evergreens and people laughing over the hot toddies.

And there you are, a tragic figure.

I moped around the office a mite and then I thought about the old gent's approach to a rainy day when the bird season opens and you can't shoot. I was $12-a-weeking as a copy boy for a paper in those days, which is not opulence in Washington, D.C.

"Well, God bless us all, cried Tiny Tim," sez I. "After all, I am only Oliver Twist, asking for more gruel. Mr. Dickens and I are in this thing together. I am lone and lorn and far from home and everybody's busted and it's raining and it's Christmas Eve and the villain is going to foreclose the mortgage and somebody shot Santa Claus and I only got one suit and one dollar and in a way it's very funny. I ought to pay money to see how funny it can be. If it happened to somebody else, that is."

So I walked a few dozen blocks back to the rooming house and there was a Christmas package from home which had been delayed in the mail. It contained a check for $5, a bottle of bourbon, some homemade cookies and a half-gallon jar of pickled artichoke roots. Santa Claus had arrived.

The arrival of Santa Claus touched off a chain reaction. There was a pretty little Jewish girl, also busted, living in the rooming house, and a rather shoddy lady who, I am afraid, made her living as best she could. There was a busted-down trap drummer and some other seedy souls, including the landlady. Everybody was broke and everybody was lonesome, because this was depression time. But we made it to the kitchen and everybody produced something, whether it was a bottle of olives or a bottle of blend or kosher pickles. I am afraid we all woke up with hangovers, but it was a powerful, cheerful Christmas.

The memory of that particular Christmas came back strong and clear a year ago, this time in Tanganyika, where I was hunting sable and kudu with my friend Harry Selby, the professional hunter. Down in Tabora, I had come down sick with something or other, and by the time we got up to Singida, Mr. Selby also looked very odd. His face was as big as a basketball, his eyes slitted, and his temperature rode high. It turned out that his youngster, my godson, had given Father

Selby the mumps for a Christmas present, and the mumps presently became complicated by pneumonia and malaria.

Selby was damned near dead by the time we got an airplane in to fly him out. Frank Bowman came down on it to keep the critters from stomping me in Harry's absence. Frank and I shot a good big kudu and took off just ahead of the rains – we thought – and then it got to be something out of a soap opera as it might have been written by Ernest Hemingway.

We were headed for the Serengeti and a favored spot of mine called Ikoma, a matter of considerably less than 300 miles. The truck kept catching fire. The jeep developed the croup, the glanders and pernicious anemia. We were running just ahead of the rains. The rains caught us as we achieved Ngoro-Ngoro, which is rather a large hill, such as about seven thousand feet worth of hill, and whose track is composed equally of gloriously greasy red clay and soft cotton soil that seizes like concrete.

The truck's engine caught fire again at the top of the mountain, and the black clouds moved up and passed us. We had nearly made it to the plain of Serengeti when the rains roared ahead of us and we had to offload the truck and shove it downhill. We got stuck only a few times on the Serengeti, but when we arrived at Ikoma, the Grumetti River was up over the banks and we couldn't ford the vehicles across. In all, it took us a week to do two days' easy journey, and we never knew whether we'd spend the winter in any spot we hit.

It was not very long before Frank had to go back to Nairobi for some family business or other, so we made a makeshift airstrip and in swooped the iron bird again, this time bearing Don Bousfield. We hunted a little bit, and then Don's wife, expecting a baby, was having some serious trouble, and again came the iron bird for Don, this time bearing John Sutton and Mrs. Virginia Ruark. This pair managed to last out the preholiday season, but we almost overturned in the ferry at Musoma.

Long since, I had harked back to the Old Man, and was more or less enjoying the vicissitudes. The hell, I said, I don't care if I'm stuck here the rest of my life, and you can't fight City Hall On High, and so you may as well relax and enjoy the rain. It *rained*, too, and kept on raining. At a rough cost of a thousand bucks a week.

But somewhere in the process I managed to collect what I was aiming for: a really good sable and a really good kudu, plus a bonus leopard that some of the experts had been trying to get for a couple of years. And I was able to arrange a post-Christmas shooting trip for some friends, Bob and Jane Low of Madrid, a party which came off so smoothly that Bob got the lot in less than a month and we were able to fish in Mombasa as extra bonus. And Bob's trip included a very good elephant and a leopard, always tricky to come by.

Bob's elephant, an 86-pounder, tusk-wise, was nearly a tragedy, too, because all had seemed bleak. The plains were swimming in water, the grass was collar-button high to a tall giraffe, and the game was scattered all over miles and miles of bloody Africa. On a reccy-run – an inspection tour with a fly-camp operation out of a Land Rover – John Sutton nearly killed himself and Low with exhaustion. But they reccy'd right, despite the weather, and when Bob went out the next time he came back the same day with this good bull. At the time most hunters were starving for the sight of an elephant who'd weigh 60 pounds per tusk.

Well, it worked out fine except that after everybody else had gone away, I was hunting elephant and being the old, old Bwana 'Mkubwa, I had neglected to take the antimalaria pills and came down hard with a case of malaria that just about did me in before they found out what was pulling the meat off me at the rate of about four pounds a day. And even that seemed a little funny, because I kept feeling that it wasn't happening to me, it was happening to somebody else. This got to be particularly amusing in Khartoum, when I was speaking Spanish gibberish, completely out of my head, while waiting for one of England's fabled Britannias to get off the ground in Johannesburg or Nairobi or Rome, where they were squatting like broody hens because of engine trouble.

"Well," I muttered, "Old Man, laugh this one away. Figure that you've got something that'll kill you, and in Khartoum at that, and give me that old cheerio approach. Khartoum, yet."

And, even in the delirium, the Old Man came back with an answer. It's what he told me when he was about to die, and knew it.

"You got to do it one way or the other sometime," he said. "And if there was a way to beat it, I would have heard about it."

And that was pretty comforting too. It wasn't me stretched out on two chairs in Khartoum, waiting for an aircraft that was possibly as sick as I. It was somebody else, a stupid stranger and not me.

"The First One Was in a Stable," *Field & Stream*, December, 1957.

Grab Your Hat And Go

I was slopping around in Texas recently, doing little if any damage to the dove crop, and reminding myself that the dove is the only bird I know that is immune to static ballistics. I mean to say, once you've got your swing grooved on duck or quail or grouse or chukars, the killing gets to be pretty automatic. Maybe the African sand grouse shares some of the dove's ability to loop and dart and swoop, to fly fast or lazy, and to change his pace like a good pitcher, but I doubt if it compares with the dove in versatility of erratic action.

But this is not a piece about doves. It is primarily a piece about snakes, but it will wind up dealing with people. As I say, I was doing a little bird-dogging on a wounded dove in Friou County when I heard a nerve-shattering sound that I can best describe as that of a Cuban band composed entirely of maracas. A lady companion had nearly stepped on a rattlesnake about five feet long and as big around (it seemed) as an inflated inner tube. She thoughtfully shot its head off, and I retreated to the road to quiver.

And that brought back the saying the Old Man once dropped on me when I was stepping gingerly through some broomgrass. "A rattlesnake," the Old Man said, "doesn't really like to bite people. He just resents intrusion into what he considers to be a snake's domain, and the striking is a reflex."

I soaked up a lot of the old gentleman's philosophy and some of it stuck, but I never forgot one solid axiom. "Most people," the Old Man said, "don't know when to leave. That's when they get bit – even by rattlesnakes that don't like to bite people."

If his reasoning was a little obscure to me then, it no longer is. I have been reviewing my life lately, with some disfavor, and it suddenly occurred to me that most of the troubles man encounters come of poor timing. Leave early, and you don't get slugged on the chin. Leave early, and you don't get named as correspondent. Leave early, and you're a hero. Stick around, and you can make out to be a bum.

It's the same way with hunting and fishing. The same five men who can remain fast friends on a backwoods deer trip for a week can turn into enemies on the eighth day. Moral: When you've had it, go home. It is kind of like the tail end of a party. If you don't take that last snort, you don't start inspecting your best friends for faults. But hanging on to the bitter end is always the snake in the grass – or in the mind.

"A man," the Old Man said, "can make an awful lot of easy enemies, but he isn't really in the enemy business until he makes one out of a friend."

And by that he meant a hunting or fishing friend. I know about that one. I hunted and fished with one man most my life, and at the end of this partnership I am certain that we shared a healthy hatred.

I was always the easy rider, and this gentleman was a pusher. He hogged the shots and claimed the biggest fish and hollered at other people's bird dogs. At the finish we just pretended nobody was there when we met on the street. And come to think of it, nobody was.

I hearkened back to this recently when, as I've said, I was picking over the fleas on my conscience. And it occurred to me: Was I always the easy rider, he the pusher? Was he full of the defects I see so clearly now, or did he have some little ones I magnified through boredom with his company? Maybe the answer is that the partnership lasted just a little too long – that one of us failed to go home at the right time.

As I said a month or so ago in these columns, there's nothing like a long boat trip or an African safari to separate friends and infuriate people. The little imperfections that you never noticed before, or smiled at, now swell painfully, like a sty on the eye or a boil on the nose. You go along twenty years not noticing certain mannerisms – a habit of clearing the throat, a small defect of speech, a tendency to repeat, and all of a sudden you lose the friend and find the faults.

The Old Man made a host of friends, and lost very few of them. Though he used the word "sportsman" very seldom, if at all, he knew what he wanted in the way of a hunting or fishing partner. And he used his friends sparingly, so to speak. "A friend," he'd say, "is like a bottle of prime whisky – the older the better. Trouble is, too many men never let their friends or their whisky age. They use 'em up fast. Now, I like to know that there's a jug in the back of my closet under a pile of decoys, and I find solace in paying it an occasional visit. But I know when to come away. Same way with friends."

Sometimes, of course, it's not easy – even impossible – to come away. I had a guy on safari a lot of years ago whom I'd come to know as a pretty fair fellow indeed. I'd been with him on an occasional woods shoot, and he measured up pretty well. So I figured he'd fit into the African bush. But I hadn't reckoned on his appetite or his sulks or his sighs. It's no sin to be hungry, and certainly no crime to sigh. But when you make a god of your belly, when you are always sulking and sighing because dinner is late, or pleading for a candy bar, the combination of sighs and sulks gets to be unendurable over a long haul.

But even on safari there are opportunities for departure, and when one came my hungry friend knew enough to take advantage of it. Which was lucky for both of us, because I had about reached the point where one more sigh would have sent me reaching for a panga to skull him.

A couple of months back I told you about my hunt with Ricardo Sicré, a Spanish gentleman of Madrid. Temperamentally I am about as un-Spanish as you can get, and Ricardo is not exactly a relaxed southern colonel. But we got along fine. I lay a big part of our success to a place called Pamplona, in Spain. Pamplona is noted for its frenetic atmosphere during its big festival, when they turn the bulls and the people loose in the streets, all at the same time. I made it for a week with several people, and we were still on speaking terms at the end of the trip.

So on the basis of this trial marriage I asked the same people to go hunting with me in Africa. We managed to beat up three months in different sections and I must say there are no complaints on my side. Of course, they may be knocking me.

I claim that Pamplona made the difference. You get a bunch of strange people sitting up all night and chasing bulls through the streets, and maybe drinking too much and being exposed to too many naked faults, and if they come off solid you can risk your time with them in Africa.

The Old Man used to say that if he shot pool with a man, he could tell how he'd act in the woods or on the water. Pool, he said, brought out all the hidden thievery in a man's soul. I think he had a pretty good point there, but he had better ones in not over-staying your time and in snakes not really wanting to bite people.

"Only people want to bite people," the Old Man said. "And only because of the flaws they find in their friends."

When you start looking for them, go home.

"Grab Your Hat and Go," *Field & Stream*, December, 1959.

PART TWO

Down Home

Down Home

*E*ven after his writings had earned him fortune and fame, not to mention the opportunity to travel to every corner of the globe, Ruark still held a special place in his heart for the South. Until his dying day the Southern heartland held fast to a corner of his soul, and anyone who takes time to analyze his writings soon realizes as much. All of the "Old Man and the Boy" tales are redolent of hearth and home in a special and moving way, and scattered elsewhere throughout Ruark's writings are revelations of how he would yearn for a return to the simpler days and simpler ways he knew as a youth growing up along the Tar Heel coast.

He eventually came to realize, as did fellow North Carolina writer Thomas Wolfe, that you really "can't go home again." Yet that realization in no sense lessened the pull of the homeland, nor did it in any way detract from his ability to capture the mood and milieu, which have always given Southern sport a special aura and the region's writers a special appeal.

Here we have three fine examples of just how talented Ruark was in this regard. In "Dixie Deer Hunt" he captures the essence of a sport that may well be relegated, within a generation or two, to the world we have lost. In "The Brave Quail" he crosses the border to neighboring South Carolina to share with us the glories of bobwhites when bevies of the saucy little bird were abundant. I've been privileged to hunt some of the same ground he describes around Kingstree and have even met descendants of some of the local folks he describes. Sadly though, the descendants of the birds they hunted are much harder to meet up with than those of their human counterparts. Victims of countless adversaries, numbers of the noble quail are but a shadow of what men like Ruark, Bernard Baruch, and Havilah Babcock knew in yesteryear.

In "Nimrods Anonymous" Ruark ventures a bit farther afield, and one senses that he found something especially appealing about the laid-back lifestyle he could enjoy in Cajun country. Maybe that was a subconscious reaction to his own fast-paced existence, one characterized by a hectic work schedule and incessant travel, which allowed precious few changes for simple pleasures and real relaxation. Yet it was during such all-too-rare moments, whether on safari in Africa or "down home" in Dixie, that Ruark was happiest. It was also these experiences, as both this section and the one following suggest, that gave him the raw material for some of his finest writing.

Dixie Deer Hunt

*F*or one hundred years the men took down their guns from the rack and went into the woods when the supply of venison ran low in the smokehouse. They would range themselves at short intervals in the scrub pine and gallberry bushes that dotted the savannas, or grassy plateaus, of eastern North Carolina. A couple of men with half a dozen nondescript dogs would go into the branch – an overgrown thicket with a small stream – and with a great hallooing they would turn loose the dogs. Before long, the dogs would "jump." Deer, started out of their nests, would crackle through the swamp, while the hounds split their throats and the drivers shouted.

These men know the terrain as a New Yorker knows the subway system. A male deer, started at such and such a place, would take one of several trails, and a man with a gun would be at the end of each trail. A doe, less wary than the buck, might go another way, and she would run much closer to the bugling of the dogs. A man with a gun would wait for her too.

During the morning there would be half a dozen gunshots, and at noon the men would start home with gutted deer strapped to the rumps of their horses. It was simpler than slaughtering cattle, more fun, and just as certain.

Or a man would take a torch and go into the forest at night. Coming suddenly upon a field where deer fed by moonlight, he would throw the rays from his light into the eyes of the grazing animals. They stood still and stared at the torch, while a companion walked almost to touching range and fired between the green, dazed eyes that blinked back at him. A man with a gun and ammunition faced no meat shortage.

So it happened in 1890 that the men who lived near Lake Waccamaw, a day's long horseback journey from Wilmington, North Carolina, saw less and less deer sign in the swamps and the savannas. Blacktongue had killed some and fire more, and indiscriminate shooting, in all seasons, had reduced the does to a flighty band, incapable of dropping sufficient fawns to keep the quota at the norm.

A dozen landowners, with names like Council, Holmes, McFadyen and Flowers – men who controlled hundreds of thousands of acres – signed a pact not to shoot or allow the shooting of a single deer or turkey on their ground for a period of five years. When a man violated the agreement, his neighbors tried him, convicted him and ostracized him so coldly and completely that he must move away from the area or walk among scornful glances and hostile silence.

"As a boy, I remember hiding in a cotton gin to hear one of those trials," K. Clyde Council, now an elderly resident of Lake Waccamaw, said not long ago. "I was scared stiff. I knew, sure, that they were going to hang him. They didn't, of course, but they were so mad I figured they were bound to string him up."

Out of that gentlemen's agreement, in 1890, grew the North State Hunt Club. Its first president was J. K. Council, of Lake Waccamaw, a wealthy landowner whose son, K. Clyde, was president last year. It is a most unusual organization in many respects, if only because it is a shooting club whose chief purpose is to avoid killing many deer. Its rules are more stringent than military regulations. It is exclusive to the point of impregnability – membership generally passes to sons from fathers, and its limit to twenty-five members forbids long waiting lists.

The club is fascinating because the formal rules of fox hunting have been incorporated into its function; yet these sportsmen chase deer with dogs and shoot them with 12-gauge shotguns loaded with Double-0 and No. 1 buckshot, at first glance a complete reversal of sportsmanship. The North State members and their guests have a curious idea that it is more fun to run a deer and listen to the hounds than it is to reduce the animal to a bloody carcass, and so they kill only enough to keep venison on the table. As a matter of fact, in a country which is capable of yielding a dozen deer a day to twice that many men, North State hunters often have dined on beef in the mistaken idea that they were eating venison.

The North State Club holds three week-long shoots every year – the October hunt, when the season opens and the bucks are still wild and flighty; the Thanksgiving shoot, when they are rutting and have grown, in a measure, incautious; and the Christmas hunt, which as a general rule is closed to adult guests. It is then that the members take their youngsters and teach them how to drive a buck, how to sit quietly in a clump of palmetto while the mosquitoes bite them bloodless – and impress on the future members the unforgivable sin of shooting a doe, even by accident.

On 15,000 acres of privately owned and leased land, the club maintains a permanent reservoir of from 500 to 1,000 deer, from whose number a maximum of forty to fifty is taken annually. A sanctuary, relatively, its creatures have overflowed and populated other areas, in which similar clubs – a half dozen of them – have grown up and patterned their rules on the North State formula.

In and around Lake Waccamaw today, despite heavy commercial hunting and all-season killing of the deer by the less sporty residents, deer are numerous to the point of nuisance. They run through the lawns and eat the flowers out of housewives' flowerbeds. They tear out green crops by the roots on moonlit nights, and dash stupidly into the paths of autos on one of the most-traveled highways in the South. I once shot an eight-point buck 100 yards from the highway, in a friend's backyard through which the buck was cantering with the aimless assurance of a drunken yokel.

The almost fanatic influence of the members of the North State Club has penetrated the county, with the result that deer have thrived even though some residents are not averse to a jack-lighting expedition to fatten their larders, and occasionally cut down on a deer without investigating its sex before firing. While the non-*aficionados* will shoot a doe in the dark of the woods, they no longer do it with bravado, because the perennial wardens, nudged to alertness by the North Staters, are apt to invoke the limit in punishment.

In more than a half-century of shooting in a dish-flat land where fifty men armed with shotguns stand at 200-yard intervals on the average hunt, the North State club has never had an accident, either fatal or trivial. And yet this is a neighborhood where men are killed almost every year by trigger-happy hunters who shoot at every quaking bush. The club's most rigid rule, the no-doe regulation, is chiefly responsible for the absence of accidents.

Shooting a female, accidentally or otherwise, is regarded as a more heinous crime than wife beating, arson, premeditated murder, narcotic trafficking or adultery. Even when doe killing was legal, the men of the North State Club fined their members for knocking off a lady deer.

No man who waits until he sees horns ever fires blindly into a bush, to discover later that his best friend's wife must go shopping for something suitable in black. And such is the weight of scorn that a member or guest of the North State Club would prefer a public whipping to acknowledging that in a moment of excitement he had done in a mother of potential bucks.

Does are killed on an average of one a year. Once, a state game commissioner, who would rather have been shoved in the stocks for a week, accounted for a doe when he fired at an animal which jumped out from behind a bush. A buck had walked into the same bush, it seems, and had discovered it to be already tenanted by a female. When the doe came out, the hunter, his eyes full of horns, cracked down. The fine was fifty dollars and the loss of his license immediately.

Another gent shot at a buck, and as he pulled the trigger, a doe leaped out of the grass between them. She died swiftly, and the buck fell over, too, a little later. Same fine, same suspension of license. The only nonfinable, nonsuspensionable slaying of a doe in the history of the club came about recently. The dogs were running a doe, and when she leaped, her foreleg pierced a stumphole and broke. As a humanitarian measure, three men – including the game warden – shot her. The meat was more tender that week at the club barbecue.

The country around Lake Waccamaw is as flat as a flounder, and a rifle bullet travels until it spends itself, and may be lethal for miles. As opposed to a state like Pennsylvania, where the rifle-toting deer-stalkers generally manage to knock off a good percentage of hunters as well as animals, the North State Club section of Carolina has no accidents, because a shotgun is harmless at more than ninety yards. If a rifle turns up in camp, it is locked away. The lockup measure is taken against the occasional guest who gets likkered up in the day-time. No drinking is tolerated until the finish of the afternoon hunt.

Gluttonous killing by the North State members is discouraged by several methods. For one thing, no meat may be taken from the camp until the end of the season. A deerslayer may take away the head and hide, but not so much as one chop. Only enough animals are shot to feed the hunters – roughly, a deer a day feeds the camp. If, on some lucky day, the men knock down three or four bucks, this constitutes the quota for the week. The hunt goes on as usual, but the hunt master places the men on the least likely stands and encourages the hounds to drive the deer the wrong way.

It is axiomatic that there is no way to make a deer run the way you want him to, but the drivers who flush game for the North State Club can come close to disproving that statement. If it is impossible to put a man on a certain stand and guarantee that a deer will pass him, it is very possible to guarantee that the deer won't skip by within gunshot.

Mr. John Council, who generally serves as boss of the hunt and the old-timers who surround him in the club, have deep feeling about deer. Mr. John and his brother, Mr. Clyde, were telling me about it.

"When you run a certain deer season after season," Mr. Clyde said, "you get kind of fond of him. You know him by sight, and maybe you can tell his track from another deer's, and you know what time he's apt to be found, and where you're apt to jump him. You even get to know which way he'll run. He gets away from you year after year. The dogs bay louder when they're after that particular one, seems as if. You play with him for a long time, and then somebody shoots him. Makes you feel terrible, like you'd lost an old friend. The game's over with that one, and it seems kind of like a sin to eat him."

Although there are only twenty-five members of the club, each man is allowed one guest, which generally assures half a hundred people for each hunt.

A typical gathering will include several millionaires, some poor folk in jeans, a baby doctor, a judge, a banker, a tool manufacturer, a sheriff, a lawyer or so, a life-insurance executive, a contractor, a cotton-mill owner, a truck-line operator, a butcher, some farmers, and generally a few service guests, such as a Netherlands East Indies marine, an Air Force lad or two, or a submariner lieutenant off a pigboat which has paused at the deep-water port of Wilmington.

The occasional Yankee visitor, accustomed to arduous deer stalking in the North, invariably is surprised at the lazy ease with which the hunt is organized and operated. Nobody is anxious to suffer for sport. Dawn arising is considered silly, and if the men have finished breakfast and are on their stands by 8:30 A.M., it's time enough.

Non-local visitors always make a great point of showing up the night before the hunt, to sleep in the white-washed lodge and sit around the fireplace telling lies to each other. For some reason they delude themselves that they are going out tomorrow and rough it, for they invariably dress in canvas pants, high boots, plaid shirts and the usual accessories of a man who intends to fare forth and beard Nature in her own territory. This is obvious nonsense, because the hunters are delivered to their stands by automobile, walk distances from 200 to 1,000 yards over logging roads, plop their rears onto camp stools or a convenient log, haul out a book and wait for the hounds to chase a buck past them. Only the few men who go with the dogs into the swamp to roust the deer out of their beds have much of a brush with briers and bogs and creepers, because the best stand of the day often is a seat to one side to a well-swept, string-straight railroad bed or the junction of a grassy country road.

Around the fire of an evening there is no gambling, because a club rule prohibits it, on grounds of breeding ill-will, but there are usually a couple of bottles passing back and forth. As is usual with men unleashed from wives and business, the humor is rough. There is forever a furious argument over college football, since several of the hunters interest themselves actively in their various alumni associations. Mr. John Umstead, an executive of the Jefferson Standard Life Insurance company, can, if given time, prove that the past, present or upcoming football team of the University of North Carolina is the superior of the Washington Redskins, Ghengis Khan's Mongol hordes, or the late great 3rd Army. Bedtime, even among men who spend their time brooding over the OPA, jurisprudence and the state of the nation, usually comes early.

The hunt itself is a simple thing. Mr. John Council lines everybody up in the yard and hollers, "Count off!" in a fashion to arouse envy in the Army for having missed a fine hunk of potential sergeant. He checks off the hunters as to auto loads, and places a sort of corporal at the head of each squad. The corporal is a savvy guy who knows the country, and when Mr. John says, "Take your people to Joe Henderson's south forty by the black-gum with the burnt stump, about so far from Burning Witch branch," the corporal does not say, "Huh?" He piles his people into the car and off they go.

The squad leader unloads his men and stations them a couple hundred yards apart. The hunter immediately sits down, lights his cigarette, reaches for a detective story, watches the yellowhammers fly back and forth, and hopes that the deer will not stomp him to death when it passes.

The only folks who do any work are the drivers, who plunge into the branches with three or four hounds apiece – and when I say hounds, I might mean pure-bred Walkers or a disreputable combination of hound and bull and fice – and proceed to stir up the potential steaks. This is labor that involves falling into sink pits and stump holes, slicing up the face with briers, tumbling into streams and walking miles through jungle thickness. It is for the driver's benefit that nobody is allowed to fire at anything but deer and predatory animals. When a gun goes off, the harassed driver walks a couple of miles to see what has happened. If the hunter has spent his powder on a squirrel, the driver is apt to up and brain him with his gun butt.

This is the place for definition of a good deer hound. Regardless of blood lines, he should be a dog who sneers at bears and foxes and even does. He should keep his big mouth shut until he roots a buck out of his bed, and then he should cut loose with a deep-chested "ahoo-o-ahoo-o" fit to shake the woodpeckers off the trees. Yap-yap dogs are sneered at, as are hounds which make a great fuss over backtracks and ancient spoors. A good deer hound should be a cold-headed businessman who keeps his lip buttoned until he is actively in business, and then he should run his quarry until somebody drops, either from gunshot or fatigue.

The entrancing thing about this kind of hunting, apart from the fact that you can sit down to do it, is that everybody generally sees something, and listening to twenty hounds working on ten deer is an experience guaranteed to shake any man out of his calm. As you ride to your stand, it is nothing unusual to see half a dozen deer mince leisurely across the road or arise, as stiff-leggedly as a rheumatic old man, from under a tree by the railroad, and insultingly bounce into the swamp. And never was there a man with enough ice in his blood to sit on a stand and hear the belling of the dogs come closer and closer without pricking his back hairs and accelerating his heartbeat. If the animal is a doe, vaulting saucily along in an immunity she knows very well, the shock effect is the same. The only difference is that nobody shoots. Although the bucks are as wise and as wary as Russian diplomats, the females revel in their safety. They will lope along a scant fifty feet in front of the dog, come to a spraddle-legged halt and look you in the eye with the amused tolerance   of a cocksure woman. The bucks, inwardly aware of the liabilities connected with horns, travel as much as two miles ahead of the hounds, and can sneak across a knee-high patch of sedge with   the silence and skill of a combat-trained soldier.

Every so often a buck makes a mistake and crosses within range of a standee, who will lift his shotgun and burn him down or miss him clean. As opposed to a rifle bullet, which makes a small clean hole and wounds without crippling, the shotgun is a very humane weapon. A handful of pea-sized buckshot, hurled at close range, is an effective killer, whereas a deer which has been gut-shot by a rifle may live for days. With dogs to trace a wounded deer, the North State people rarely lose one.

They cut the hunt into two parts, starting out freshly after lunch with a new band of hounds. The afternoon area depends on whether the morning shoot has been effective. Two or three deer downed in the morning means a dull afternoon hunt, but if the hunters have flunked the A.M. effort, then the hunt master will string them out around a particularly desirable stretch of land which several bucks are known to use. Then nearly always you hear the sound of guns and the pickup truck rolls into camp with meat.

As the night drops swiftly, again a roundup of deer, dogs and men is made, and the cars head back for camp. Dinner is something to make you cry. There are a dozen or so side courses, but the main thing is venison – loin chops and succulent bits done over a slow charcoal grill, moist and brown and tasty. Anyone who eats less than six helpings is a sissy.

After dinner comes the kangaroo court, which may sound childish, but powered by bourbon and delivered dead-pan, often is uproarious. A man who has missed a deer that day attempts to convince a 100-percent-prejudiced jury that he was justifiably in error. The court –

like the smearing of a youngster's face in the bloody paunch of a buck to celebrate his first kill – dates back to the earliest days of organized hunting.

Long ago the penalty for missing a shot was the forfeit of a keg of liquor, to be contributed at the next hunt by the convict. So many people missed so many deer that the lodge assumed the appearance of a bootlegger's cache. The penalty was made milder, and chopping off the offender's shirttail replaced the whisky forfeit.

Clothing shortages recently have further remodeled the penalty. The negro cooks and attendants agitated for reform. In a time of shirt shortages, they said, it was a sin and a shame to ruin a good shirt. Better the shirt should be stripped from the sinner's back and donated, whole, to the steward's department. As of now, the best dressed men in the county are the cooks.

The cost of maintaining the North State Club is very low, computed in terms of what the Northern sportsman is apt to pay for a few day's fun in the woods. The members are assessed $100 a year, and pay seventy-five cents each for themselves and guests at every meal. The dues provide money for upkeep of the lodge, the salary for a ranger who keeps his eye on the land, and the cost of an occasional lease of extra, desirable territory. The hounds are furnished by individual members, and sometimes by guests.

"Dixie Deer Hunt," *Saturday Evening Post*, April 27, 1963.

The Brave Quail

*C*et's say it's a nice crisp autumn day, with the sun warm and the breeze winy, and you are approaching a copse of brier and leveled timber on a high hill with pine trees growing on it. One of your dogs is cantering easily, nose proudly in air, with a cock to his ears that convinces you he knows where he is heading. The other dog is circling rapidly, nose to ground, and all of a sudden both hit happily on a strange sort of radar beam. The nose-in-the-air dog wriggles down close to the earth and performs a hula with his hips. The circling dog crowds into the act, and the contest is suddenly clear. One of those dogs will freeze, and may even lift his right, left, front or hind foot. His tail will either stick straight up or straight behind him like a baton. And it will not quiver. Whichever dog loses the contest will honor the winner by dropping and freezing.

The man walks up behind the dog. His face is white. He sweats. His hands are shaking. His heart is pounding a rumba-beat. He is carrying a shotgun, generally with a 26- to 28-inch barrel. The gauge of the gun is an index to the ability of the man to prove his manhood at that moment. If it is a 12-gauge, he is so-so at his business. If it is a 16, he is pretty good. If it's a 20-gauge he is excellent, and if it's a .410 he is bragging.

This man's mouth is cottony. At the very moment he feels like a bullfighter awaiting a *toro bravo*, a big-game hunter preparing to meet an African buffalo's charge, a soldier verging on a desperate destruction of a machine-gun emplacement. His reflexes are cocked, and his reputation is at stake. Also, his stomach is full of squirrels.

He prods the hummocks with a foot, and possibly the dogs sneak ahead to freeze again. The man draws his breath sharply inward. He kicks again. Nothing happens. Again. Nothing. The dogs inch forward.

The man scuffs his boot. The lead dog switches his snout and points it downward. The man says the old cliché: *This is it.* He kicks, and the world erupts around him. The noise has something of the sound of an exploding land-mine, something of the rapid belch of an Oerlikon 20-millimeter. It is otherwise indescribable.

Small birds burst from the ground. They take off in all directions. They are traveling at more than forty miles an hour, and they present a target as large as a big orange. If they are to be killed they must be killed before they have traveled sixty yards, and if the cover is heavy they may need to be shot within twenty yards. They may have to be shot from the hip, or off the biceps, or even off the nose.

First, though, the gunner must select a bird from the thundering mass of rocketing fowl, because the man who shoots into the brown takes home no meat. A split-second selection must be made. The quail comes into the eye, the gun goes under the eye, the trigger is pressed, and if the man is good the bird drops in a shower of feathers. If the man is very good, he then switches to another bird, which he selects from the speeding gang, and fires again. If he is very good, *very* good, another bird drops.

Then the man turns around with his face split by a grin. He pats the dogs as they fetch the dead game. He lights a cigarette, and for a moment he is Belmonte, the bull-fighter. He is Dwight Eisenhower. He is Clark Gable. He is the late Frank Buck. He is David, standing over the prostrate form of Goliath. He is one hell of a big guy – to himself, if he is alone – to the others, if he is accompanied.

This is because, using the ancient Chinese invention of gunpowder, a great deal of luck and the skill of his dogs, he has just killed a couple of creatures that, while delicious to chew on, can be consumed in a couple of munches. He has just slain a little bird called a quail, bobwhite, or partridge, according to where he lives.

The American bobwhite quail has never been known to attack a man, even in defense of its young. Yet the dictionary lists a verb, "to quail," which means to curdle or coagulate. This curdling and coagulation occurs each fall, according to local game laws, when big brave men, armed with shotguns, step past a pointing dog and await the roaring rush of wings that signal the take-off of a little speckled brown bird that is prey to hawks, eagles, cats, foxes, rain, drought, high grass, low grass and man himself. Man – armed man – is scared stiff of the quail. He is easily as frightened as the *matador de toros* who faces the bull in the *corrida* on a sunny afternoon. After all, the *torero* will only be scared by a maximum of three bulls. Quail, on the other hand, get up in flocks.

Some twenty-five million quail die annually in this nation in order to prove that a man is superior to a bird. The quail breeds well; a couple of clutches will build a covey up to twenty-five. He sticks to his own ground. The "same" covey will inhabit the same acreage for years if sufficient seed birds are left to rear a family. As a child I shot the great-great-great-great-grand-children of my first feathered friends in the four acres that comprised my own backyard. But he is not too long for this world unless he is rigidly protected. Weather, varmints, mankind and the auto have conspired to make him a potential candidate for extinction, except in areas where he is conserved by law and human consideration.

The quail has never been satisfactorily explained in terms of his relationship to man, his peculiar fascination for man, or the occasional nobility or fraud he inspired in man. He seems to have been created especially for his catalytic approach to the genus *Homo*, and comes off heavily best by comparison.

You may say, for a start, that as a result of association with quail, all quail shooters are liars. They are also braggarts, when the opportunity allows, but they are self-apologists and ingrown liars first. Quail shooters do not merely lie to other people. They lie first to themselves.

I know this because I am a quail shooter, raised in the company of quail shooters.

By the same standard you will rarely find a dedicated quail shot who is not a pretty nice guy. He has to be a nice guy, because he is performing for the benefit of the dogs, himself and his companions, and all are expert in the detection of fraudulent behavior in the field. Lying afterward is permissible; ducking the basic conflict between bird and man is not. A man who comports himself shoddily in the presence of quail is stoned in the trade marts and derided in the taverns. Friendships have been broken when one friend detected an unpleasantness in his buddy's approach to quail.

Mr. Bernard M. Baruch, the millionaire elder statesman, is fond of saying that there are two things a man cannot abide being kidded about: his prowess with the ladies and his ability to shoot quail. Mr. Baruch is a fair expert on both matters, especially on the latter. He has been a passionate quail shooter for something like 65 years, and is, at 81, possibly the best senior quail assassin in the land.

Mr. Baruch shoots quail three months a year. For the past fifty-odd he has shot them in the vicinity of Kingstree, South Carolina, where he has leased and maintained thousands of acres nearby his plantation, Hobcaw Barony. Shooting quail, to Mr. Baruch, is a grave ritual, and he claims that his longevity is largely due to the sport. It has kept him active long after his contemporaries have retired to the bath-chair.

The old gentleman takes his quail a touch more seriously than he used to regard the stock market, and his millions attest that he never approached the market on a frivolous basis. There is no levity about B. M. B. when the subject of quail comes up, although he can kid about the other shooting sports, and long ago gave up duck and turkey shooting.

Quail killing at Mr. Baruch's is regarded as the top shooting privilege in the nation today. General Omar Bradley shoots birds with Baruch, as do a gross of other citizens with recognizable handles. Mr. Baruch coddles his birds as other rich folk look after their jewels.

The preservation of his quail is a local industry. His acres are constantly patrolled by a fleet of overseers, under the strong hand of a Mr. David McGill, who does not shoot quail himself. Cats, run wild, are exterminated. Bounties are paid on varmints. At the end of the season the woods are burnt free of underbrush, so the little birds will not be trapped in the matted grasses. Poaching is more of a sin in that neighborhood than voting Republican. Clutches of eggs are lifted from the wet spots to higher ground.

I do believe Mr. Baruch would shoot a man who would shoot a sitting quail, and I am certain he would fire any friend who ever exceeded the South Carolina limit of fifteen birds per day. He limits the number of birds to be killed in any one covey to three, on a given day. Although he shoots six days a week for three months every year, his birds are rarely shot over more than twice, or three times at the most. In this way Mr. Baruch maintains a backlog of birds that is almost unknown in a country in which indiscriminate shooting is ruining the bobwhite as a game bird.

Mr. Baruch does not approve of more than one gun per party, so that each hunter starts out with his own entourage. At the moment the old boy runs three rigs. They consist of Mr. McGill, who generally takes over B. M. B.'s personal safari, and two Negro boys, and two other sets of three men each.

Dave McGill rides a horse and handles the dogs. The two colored lads have separate functions – one marks down the dead birds and the other watches where the singles fly. They are usually mounted on mules.

Mr. Baruch rides a horse, as does his nurse, Elizabeth Navarro, who sometimes goes along with him. Miss Navarro is not a quail shot, yet. She shoots squirrels with a .22 rifle, but since she has acquired a little mansion of her own, close to the quail grounds, she is beginning to make noises like a quail *aficionada*.

It is a remarkable sight to see an 81-year-old man fork a horse, ride him three hours in an afternoon and alight as much as fifty times in that day, and still best most of his guests with the gun.

Mr. Baruch is 81, after all, and he is deaf as a post, and when he shoots he does not wear a hearing aid. Most quail shooting is based on the association of sound and movement. A bird roars up to your right, your left, or behind you, and you whirl and gun him down – or miss him, as the case may be. Anything that does not rise in front of Mr. Baruch he does not shoot at, because he must depend entirely on sight. This cuts off a good sixty percent of his possible shots.

Yet the old gent consistently comes home with the best part of his limit, and will often bring in the full fifteen – more than the combined score of his best-shooting guests. His record of fifteen birds in seventeen shots he recently bettered by fifteen birds in thirteen shots, an amazing score for anybody, and utterly incredible for a four-score-year-old man with no hearing to help him.

Fifty percent is considered excellent in quail shooting. A man who can average thirty percent, for shells expended, is good. Sixty percent is fantastic, except among pot-hunters, and seventy-five percent is nearly unheard of. Getting a limit at all, even with the profusion of game that Baruch's grounds boast, is a signal for champagne at the big house.

Yet the senior statesman frequently kills *three* birds on a covey rise. He shoots a double-barreled 16-gauge. He likes to take a pot at the outriding cock bird as it roars aloft to signal the rest of the flock. Then he swiftly breaks the gun, ejects the spent cartridge, and blasts twice at the main herd as they jet themselves away. Often as not he is successful.

On the long ride back home Mr. Baruch does not talk atom bomb, world affairs, or finance. He talks quail. It is a peculiar fascination of bird-for-man that even rubs off on the help, who are not allowed to shoot. When a guest comes in after a good day, all hands beam. When a guest comes in after a sour day, all hands are silent and respectful, as at a wake. This is a time-hallowed treatment of the wing-shot. *Never cross a hunter when his timing is off* is ingrained in the tradition.

My friend Ely Wilson, a pleasant Negro gentleman who runs my hunt when I am lucky enough to go down to South Carolina, falls into a fit of desperation for hours if the dogs are not working well, or if I am in my usual state of firing much and dropping little. Ely would stay up all night to look for a bird that is known to be shot down but is difficult to find. On at least one occasion I have watched him search for an hour in a swamp looking for a crippled bird that the best retriever in the world, a nondescript and now deceased critter named Joe, had given up on. Ely finally found the cripple in a creek, and caught him with his hands. There is a lack of nobility in the man if he goes away and leaves a wounded quail. Ely is so good that on one occasion he finally found a highly rumpled corpse of a quail that General Bradley had shot two weeks before. The bird had lodged in a tree.

"I lost him once," Ely said, "but I just *knew* that bird was around here somewhere."

Not many hunters are lucky enough to indulge themselves under such luxe circumstances as the men who have made a hobby of creating their own game preserves, but the thrill of chasing the bob-white is as great for the poor man as for the tasseled tycoon. Hundreds of thousands of quail shooters achieve the same sensation when the little brown bazooka takes off under their feet – a sort of delicious momentary terror followed by triumph or despair. The satisfaction of the autumn day, the working dog, the dramatic moment of point is as great for a small boy with a mongrel and a ten-dollar smokepole as for the well-heeled big-shot with the hand-carved Purdey or Greener or Sauer shotgun.

Some people step into their backyards to shoot quail; others spend thousands of dollars annually for the same privilege. But they all share one defect of character: all quail shooters are abject liars. I know, for I have been lying steadily about quail and bird dogs since I was eight, and got physically sick from excitement when I killed my first one.

The quail shooter's mind works roughly like this:

They aren't making the same kind of cartridges any more, because when you point them at the bird the bird don't drop. Obviously something wrong with the powder. . . . The sun was in my eyes. . . . The damn bird flew around a branch just as I shot.

The dogs have lost their sense of smell. . . . The rabbit hounds ran up all the quail. . . . One of the other hunters was in the way, or I would have killed two. . . . It was getting too dark to shoot with safety.

All the birds got up wild, away ahead of the dogs. . . . I slipped and fell. . . . I had a headache and my timing was off. . . . When I was going good after the first two coveys, we couldn't find any more for an hour and I cooled off.

The safety on my gun jammed. . . . The little single dog wouldn't hold to a point.

These are the things you tell yourself. You tell other people that you only used half as many shells as you really used, and then you say that you had to run down a couple of wounded birds and shoot some more.

You impugn the honor of the retrievers. You mention that you shot at least half a dozen you didn't bring home, but the dog's nose was off, or the bird fell in the swamp, or they are making the birds tougher now than they used to. Then you find that you are counting in the birds that you didn't collect with your full total. I have known men who could go to any bank and walk out with a colossal loan, on their face alone, to callously raise the total of their quail bag by fifty percent a couple of days later, and for no reason except the salving of their ego. And remember, a quail is not a rhinoceros. It is less than a half-pound of flesh and feathers.

The quail shot also lies about the dogs he has known. Such as my old Llewellin setter Frank, long gone to his fathers, result of hanging himself as he tried to hurdle a fence to get at something comely in the way of a gal-dog. Frank was an expert in the quail profession. Today I wouldn't believe myself under oath when I talk about old Frank of Tennessee.

Frank was a connoisseur of shooters. If you were going good, Frank would cooperate. That's to say, Frank would work. If you were shooting badly, Frank would go home. I missed thirteen straight shots one day, and finally, in desperation, took a crack at a bird that had roosted in a tree. This is unusual behavior for quail, and for me, too. I missed the bird in the tree.

Frank took one look at me, and sneered. He went home, and refused to hunt for a week. I could take him out into the fields, but he would just sit and sneer.

Frank was what is known as a force-broken retriever. That means he didn't like to fetch things for the sheer love of it, but had been induced to retrieve by rigid training. Frank never so much as wet a bird, let alone crush one. He would come with the quail hanging limply from his lower lip, and he would rear up, put his paws on my chest, and nudge the bird inside my hunting jacket.

One day I was training a pointer puppy named Tom, who was fast as Jackie Robinson, and this adolescent upstart beat Frank to a point. Birds roared up. I shot and killed one, then held onto the old dog to give the youngster a sense of gratification in his work. Puppy found the dead bird and retrieved him faultlessly. I patted the puppy. Told him he was a fine, noble puppy. Old dog looked at me and glared.

Then the puppy found a couple of single birds. Shot again – I was going good that day – and another bird dropped. Again held the old dog to let the puppy strut his stuff, which he did. Old dog glared some more.

Then Frank, the old codger, found another single. Bird got up and I killed him. Frank went and got his own bird. He brought the bird to me and looked up. He said a variety of things, all profane, with his eyes.

Then he bit the bird in two pieces. He spat the bird out on the ground. Then he turned on his heel and stalked off. He didn't speak to me for a week afterward. This was a dog I have seen point a covey with a dead bird in his mouth. This was a dog that I have seen hold one bird in his mouth and press another, wounded bird onto the ground with his foot.

At least I believe I have. Us liars are never quite sure later.

This Frank, a setter, was the all-round best gun dog I ever saw, in general savvy, but he was not much better than Sam, a big young pointer operated by Mr. Henry Nelson of Kingstree, South Carolina, or the late Joe, owned by my friend Ely of the same community. It does not make too much difference about the breed. Joe was a hodge-podge of nothing much, but on his good days he could make a bum out of anything with Ch. in front of his handle. On one exceptional day when Joe found everything except Adolf Hitler, his boss got off the horse and briefly placed Joe in the saddle.

"This dog too good to have to walk between coveys," Ely said.

A couple of liars I know in Fort Lauderdale, Florida, claim to have hunted over a dog which would find a covey of birds, wait a reasonable time for the hunters to appear, and then back off to find the hunters and beckon them up to the birds. There was a story, too, about a dog so stanch that he was lost for years. They finally found his skeleton frozen into a point over a bevy of skeletonized quail, but that is a little rich for even a practicing quail-liar to believe. We all know bones fall apart.

Each man builds his bird dog in his own image, but the definition of a good dog, like the definition of a good man, is one who knows and *respects* the bobwhite. No sincere hunter will over-shoot a covey, out of concern for next year's sport. No good dog will flush a covey of birds until the hunter is at his side. No good dog will encroach on the point of another. A smart dog knows more than any man about the likeliest spot to find his quarry. No good man or good dog is happy to leave a wounded bird unfound. No good man hogs the best shot, as no good man is disrespectful of the rights of his hunting companion. Altogether the quail manages to bring out a great deal of fineness in both dogs and men.

Unfortunately the available quail are becoming less available for the average man with a gun. There were practically no posted lands when I was a nipper. Now nearly all populous game land is posted and protected, leased or owned by serious hunters. A hunter may no longer park his buggy by a strange peafield and expect to find a covey of birds unless he is friendly with the farmer or leases the land. The automobile, in the last twenty-odd years, has contributed greatly to the come-down of the quail, because it has made him available to a vastly increased number of occasional hunters, many of whom are careless of conservation. There are people who will shoot a bevy down to its last survivor. Added to the other vermin, plus the occasional awful inroads of weather, the indiscriminate hunter has come close to ruining the free domain of the friendly bobwhite. The brave quail is also the frail quail, who loves to live near man and has suffered some pretty awful consequences thereby. Just like man himself.

Protected, however, and shot with reverence and moderation, the quail still comprises the noblest American sport in the eyes of many men who have gone against grizzlies and rassled single-handed with mountain lions.

If there is a broad explanation for the fascination of quail shooting, it must be that no man can bet on just how good he'll be on any given day. The challenge of bird to man is permanent. You will catch a full night's sleep, find perfect shooting the next day, and miss everything that flies. You can get drunk as an owl, sit up all night, fly a plane from dawn until noon, and with a bellyful of butterflies kill all that rustles. My personal record of fifteen out of eighteen shots was set on a basis of no sleep at all for two nights, due to work and travel, with a splitting headache and hands that shook like maraca gourds. Recently I had eleven in the bag with thirteen shots. We couldn't find bird No. 12, and this so upset my timing that it took me twenty-two shots to get the other four quail. And we literally chased the last one to death.

Apart from his courage and trickiness in the field, the bobwhite has the power of inspiring magnificent nostalgia in the evening, when the fire snaps and hisses and the bourbon melds gently with the branch-water. He tastes as good on the plate as he looks in the field, and no bird of paradise was ever handsomer to the hunter than this little brown gentleman's gentleman. He often ennobles the man who shoots him, a trick that has not yet been perfected by humans in relationship to each other.

"The Brave Quail," *Field & Stream*, December, 1951.

Nimrods Anonymous

*Y*our correspondent is what is known as a compulsive hunter, an affliction that is, I believe, rated next to whisky drinking and horse playing as a threat to the American home. It is more expensive than maintaining a stable of chorus girls. It leads you from the hearthside and strews your path with temptations.

Also it perverts the soul. I have never known a hunter – especially a quail shot – who wasn't an outrageous liar, a braggart, a pitiful alibier and a neglecter of his job. Yet every year comes the urge to shake the moths out of the trusty fowling piece and fare forth to slay the unwary titmouse, at God knows what cost to domestic and economic stability. You know the old stuff. Snuggle next to nature. Stride around in the forest primeval. Color in the cheeks. Hearty dinner in front of the blazing fire. Autumn leaves. Dogs. Health. Thundering quail erupting from the brush. Beard the bear in his lair. Untamed turkey for Thanksgiving.

Nuts! What you catch is pneumonia.

A wild duck, for instance, is a disagreeable fowl that keeps lousy hours and never is happy without frosted feathers. He lives in dismal swamps, miles from civilization, and, unless he is specially cooked, tastes like a slab of fishmonger's boots.

Yet ordinarily sane men fly hundreds of miles on the slim chance of getting close enough to one of the critters to slay him, at the approximate cost of seventy-five dollars per duck. They tumble out of boats, drown, freeze to death, become mired in bogs, suffer mosquitoes, slave like chain-gang laborers, and all for two pounds of feathers encrusted with No. 6 shot.

89

These mordant reflections occurred as our hero recently sat on a tussock of Louisiana marsh, gay and debonair, with a crown of mosquitoes wreathlike around his head. The seat of his pants was wet, and cold ooze had seeped inside his hip boots. He had been up since 3:30 A.M., a horrid section of the day devoted chiefly to death and duck hunting.

He had pushed a dugout through a few thousand yards of ooze, sinking up to his hips in a gumbo that smelled like a paper mill. The biceps of his stout right arm was a futuristic painting in purple, yellow, and angry red, induced by the mulish kick of a 12-gauge shotgun with delusions of heavy artillery.

Our hero was hungry – sleepy. His bites itched. His nose was sunburned. But our hero is happy.

Why he is happy no sane man would be able to explain. But no duck hunter is sane. He smokes an opium all his own. He is happy because in the muck at the bottom of the pirogue sprawl four defunct ducks. The nearest glares malevolently with a dead eye, and indignation is in his ruffled feathers. He has croaked with a crawful of shot to please a silly fellow called man, who would rather eat a steak, and who lacks the intelligence to come in out of the rain.

I have been a sucker for this kind of thing ever since I assassinated my first English sparrow with a slingshot. Let the phone buzz with some project to fly to Kamchatka, over the weekend, to shoot ptufted ptarmigan, and I am your boy. Job goes out the window. Wife goes home to mother. Normal routine goes haywire. Likewise bank account. But Daddy goes a-hunting to bag baby Bunting's lousy little rabbit skin. Better he should buy baby a sable stole, retail, and save money.

You fly all the way from New York to New Orleans to shoot four lousy little ducks today and four lousy little ducks tomorrow, and then you fly back again. Even the ducks are smarter. They only fly one way at this time of year.

I worry about ducks. I worry about the fact that the oil companies, in the marshes, are spoiling duck food and fresh-water ponds. I sit in a blind and curse the law that allows hunters to shoot in the evening, scaring the curl off the drake's tail and driving the geese out of the country. I agitate for legislation allowing the destruction of the blue-winged teal, in a split season, for as the situation stands they come in, eat up all the legitimate duck food, and then fly gaily off to Mexico before the season opens. The Mexicans catch them in nets, after they have fattened off our grub. With the world going to hell, I sit and ulcerate over ducks.

And then I fret about my health, too.

According to the statistics, the men who piloted the Japanese kamikaze planes – the suicide Joes – were safer than the man who loads his 20-gauge gun with No. 8 shot and goes out with the idea of herding a snipe into a narrow corner.

There was a piece in *Hygeia* magazine, the house organ for the American Medical Association, that says it isn't the vagrant bullet that lays the deerslayer low, it's the heart misery. You put on your red hat and load up Old Betsy, and before you can spit a curve into the wind you've keeled over with a thrombosis.

They say that out of eighteen hunting casualties in Michigan last year, ten were due to coronary conditions. That's fifty-five percent, and what it means is that some fat banker overstepped himself. A man whose daily exercise is confined to chasing the stenographer around the office is in no shape to go out in the bush and attempt to type-cast himself as Dan'l Boone. The old arteries just up and holler, "Hold, enough!"

This would be a recreational hazard I'd gamble on, ordinarily speaking, since we have a slow track and short-winded secretaries in our office, and as a result I am in fair shape. But up comes this gloomy state of Michigan with a mess of extra injunctions, all designed to keep you out of the swamps. It's the Department of Health, now, with more taboos than you'd find among the head-hunters in the Pacific.

Don't use anything except pasteurized milk, cream and cheese, it says. If you can't find pasteurized milk, carry canned milk. Be sure to wash the fruit you steal from the farmer's orchard, but be sure and don't wash it in a stream you haven't tested.

Die of thirst if you must, it says, but don't drink a gill of water from a hostile creek without dumping in a can of common laundry bleach. Lug along a first-aid kit to protect you from blisters, bruises, scratches, punctures, burns and the off chance that your hunting partner's wife confuses you with an elk. Above all things, take a course in how to stop bleeding by using pressure on the arterial supply above a serious wound. Avoid poison ivy as the very Black Death.

I should like to inject the suggestion here that it would be more than wise to learn how to perform an appendectomy with an old tomato can, and to deliver sextuplets. You might also buy a box of penicillin and a small ambulance.

As a man who still gets a small bounce out of rereading James Fenimore Cooper, I cringe for my contemporaries. Leatherstocking must be writhing in his crypt, in concert with Capt. John Smith, Pocahontas and the aforementioned Master D. Boon, which is how he once spelled it on a tree.

I can remember the days when, if you wanted to go hunting, all you did was kick the houn' dog out of the fireplace, pick up the gun, and start walking. If you got thirsty, you elbowed a couple of hogs out of the crick and shoved your face down in the water until you weren't thirsty any more. You ate anything that struck your fancy, and it was considered bad form to shoot yourself or your best friend in a moment of gay stupidity. I don't recall ever needing a trained nurse to accompany the dogs, who were generally smarter than I.

Nothing bad ever came of this, but I suppose you must put it down as a youthful antipathy to germs and strenuous exercise. I find that today Old Deerslayer ain't as full of zing as he used to be. He wheezes easy and is regarded as a moron by the local yeomen.

They say it's a healthy thing for the soul of a city dweller occasionally to return to the deep sticks, if only to rediscover his own practical stupidity.

Me, I am an honorary Cajun, sure, maybe. But I would starve to death, me, if I had to be a self-sufficient dweller among the bayous and marshlands of Louisiana. I don't know how to do any of the things, any more, that the hunters and trappers consider necessary to existence. I can shoot all right, but shooting and walking are skills acquired simultaneously down here. No significance attaches to either. I can wash a hell of a lot of dishes. I can pluck a duck and am really superbly deft at eviscerating a duck with one wrench on the innards. That's all I can do.

"You gut the duck *bien,* you," says Monsieur Purvis Théal, my shooting partner in the bayous. "You gut a duck good as anybody I know. But, Robair, not enough. Need more things to do."

I cannot, for instance, manage a pirogue without drowning myself. A pirogue is a soapdish of a boat which is chopped from a single section of log, pointed at both ends, and can be poled in an inch of water. It is balanced like the mechanism of a watch, and will capsize if you shave too closely on one side of your face.

I do not know how to trap a muskrat. I cannot talk to the ducks or call a goose down out of the high sky. Yet I have seen Ted O'Neil, a biologist who lives in the woods, stretch his neck and give a yowp that fetched a goose practically into the blind from a thousand feet. All I could see was a speck up there in the blue, but Ted identified it as a young goose who was lost from his mama.

"I will make a noise like his mama," says Ted, emitting a dulcet yodel.

The lonesome goose dropped his flaps and came down in a power dive. You could have killed him with a broom.

In the past few years I have girdled the globe a few times, and I have more friends in Africa than in New York. But I cannot walk the "prairie" in Louisiana, even in hip boots. The prairie is a vast oozy marshland where the rats and the ducks dwell. I sink to my neck and struggle helplessly while Monsieur Bibi Humble, aged eighteen, strides along as if on a sidewalk. When I get hopelessly mired, I bleat pathetically, like the lost goose looking for its mama, and Bibi or Théal comes and derricks me out.

I can eat an oyster, and I can even open one without cutting off my hand, but I cannot look at a stretch of water and say positively that there is a bed of oysters in it. I can't squint at a section of marsh and announce authoritatively that it is eaten out by the rats, hence worthless. I cannot make orange wine or whittle a decent pushpole for the pirogue. I can't even cook. I am a bum in their book.

When my friend Théal goes back home to Abbeville, it is necessary to place him aboard the bus and pin his ticket to his coat. But out in boundless wasteland he never saw before, he moves as confidently as a New Yorker walking from Forty-second to Forty-third street.

I don't know a *poule d'eau* from a *roseau*, a *dos gris* from a *bateau*, and it is all highly embarrassing. A *poule d'eau* is a coot. A *dos gris* is a bluebill duck. A *roseau* is a reed, and a *bateau* is a flat-bottomed boat. I am worth less than sixty dollars a month on talent, and all I can do real good is gut a duck.

But I have invited my Cajun friends to visit me in *my* marshes, the limitless prairies of New York. Before I pass final judgment on my stupidity I am anxious to see how they make out in the subway. I may not be able to call a goose, but I am death on highflying head-waiters, and once I even intimidated a cab driver. These are skills too. Me, on my own bayous, maybe I am a pretty good Cajun, after all. Sure, me.

"Nimrods Anonymous," *Field & Stream*, September, 1951.

PART THREE

The Boy Expands His Horizons

The Boy Expands His Horizons

*F*rom boyhood, Ruark dreamed of pursuing sport in distant, exotic locales. He got just enough of a first-hand taste of this as a youngster, when he accompanied the Old Man on a waterfowling and fishing expedition to Louisiana's Cajun country and a memorable pheasant hunt on an exclusive estate in Maryland, to whet his appetite for even bigger and better things. The Old man planted the seeds for future shikari and safaris with plenty of vicarious exposure to distant climes and their potential for exciting times. This came through the Old Man's knack for storytelling (which Ruark obviously inherited) and an early exposure to adventure literature. As a youngster, Ruark would later write, "my imagination – having fed on Dickens, Melville, Edgar Rice Burroughs, Robert Louis Stevenson and Ernest Thompson Seton – often left me feeling like a hero of high adventure stories." What he didn't say, although it was undoubtedly true, was that the craving to achieve that hero status intensified with adulthood.

Then too, long-term exposure to the wolf of poverty howling just outside the back door during his late adolescence and early adulthood heightened Ruark's determination to enjoy, someday, some way, the sporting opportunities open only to the affluent or well-connected. His college years in the depths of the Depression were difficult ones, partly because he was only fifteen when he enrolled at the University of North Carolina but also because he was miserably, constantly poor. By his own admission Ruark indulged in some pretty questionable money-making schemes while in college, with bootlegging being a pretty regular source of income, and according to one close acquaintance and fraternity brother he was always borrowing money.

Accordingly, when Ruark finally had made a name for himself and had reached a reasonably comfortable financial plateau, it should come as no surprise that he turned lovingly to Africa as a way of simultaneously realizing a boyhood dream and flaunting his new-found wealth. His intentions to go on a safari were announced by the editors of *Field & Stream,* playing up the "dream come true" theme, and Ruark's exposure to the Dark Continent would prove to be a major watershed in his career.

It launched an unending and to some extent unrequited love affair, for Ruark was every bit as smitten by the wild wonders and vast horizons of Africa as had been great nineteenth-century hunters like Sam Baker and Fred Selous. As he put it: "Africa was the land I loved most." It was also the land which gave him the inspiration and material that produced a transition from first-rate journalist to best-selling novelist. There would have been no *Something of Value* or *Uhuru* without Africa, nor would what is probably Ruark's crowning literary achievement, *Horn of the Hunter,* have been written. Quite simply, exposure to Africa made him rich, and the continent stole his soul in the process.

Along with a dozen or so safaris in Africa, Ruark was also able to pursue sport in India, the Far East, Australia, New Zealand and indeed pretty much anywhere his fancy dictated he might wish to go. These excursions were by no means inexpensive, and as always Ruark worked, and worked hard, to pay for his play. Some of the magazine articles that resulted from his sporting travels eventually were collected (posthumously) into *Use Enough Gun,* and more recently Michael McIntosh focused specifically on his African experiences for the anthology, *Robert Ruark's Africa.*

Still, several examples of his finest writing on sport in farflung corners of the globe have heretofore eluded modern readers, and what you will find here reveals, in striking fashion, Ruark's abilities to present a tale well told. He did indeed get mauled by a big cat, and while one has to wonder if he had indulged in a bit too much sauce in advance, there is no denying the power of his recounting of this brush with danger. Even where there is no degree of danger though, be it on a traditional deer hunt with dogs down Dixie way or trout fishing in the Land of the Long White Cloud (New Zealand), it is a joy to join Ruark as he makes virtual reality of youthful visions. Here we offer several stories which resulted from him widening his horizons.

Ruark Realizes Boyhood Ambitions

*I*t is seldom that a man has a chance to realize *one* dream. Two dreams are considerably more than par for the distance. When the same man can combine two dreams in a single stroke, he is a very lucky fellow, as so, indeed, am I.

When I was a very small boy, my folks gave me a gun and a dog. I broke in on sparrows with an air-gun when I was six, and was shooting quail with a 20-gauge shotgun when I was eight. Santa Claus, as I recall, also gave me a subscription to *Field & Stream* before I turned ten.

You might say that *Field & Stream* was my early bible. I worshipped the likes of Archibald Rutledge, David Newell and Ray Holland a far piece ahead of Ernest Hemingway or Thomas Wolfe. I had good dogs as a kid, and a great many marvelous things happened to me in the woods. For a long time I had a small boy's dream of writing a story about my dogs and my quail – and, of course me – and having it printed in a magazine with a cover by Lynn Bogue Hunt. That was the going-to-sleep dream. I never expected to achieve it, but dreams are not taxed for small boys, not even the wildest ones.

Somewhere along the way, when I was out after squirrels or creeping after ducks or following my old setter Frank after bob-white, I got involved in an even more ambitious dream. I had early fallen under the spell of Edgar Rice Burroughs and his *Tarzan of the*

Apes. Somewhat later came more realistic approaches to Africa – the Martin Johnsons, *"Trader Horn," "Sanders of the River."* I got involved with the travel tales of Somerset Maugham, and it seemed I would bust a gusset if I didn't get to see jungles and lions and cannibals someday.

I believe I planned to follow the Alger technique. I would return a lost wallet to a banker, and get a job in his bank. Then I would marry his daughter, inherit his riches, and one day I would pack up and take a safari into Africa. I would see, and maybe shoot, old Numa the lion, and Sabor the lioness, and Tantor the elephant. (Mr. Burroughs' nomenclature for Tarzan's playmates was even more colorful than Swahili.) And then maybe, when I was rich and famous, I would write about Africa.

The implementation of dreams rarely follows the script, but the endings sometimes turn out surprisingly well. Well, I married no banker's daughter. I got into the seafaring business, and later into the writing trade, and then into the war business, and then again into the writing trade. I never got rich or famous, but I got action.

I saw Mr. Maugham's South Seas, and I have made five round trips to Africa. I wrote a lot of stuff for a lot of people – syndicated newspaper columns, and a raft of stories for a great many magazines, and several books. Then one day I remembered something from away back.

I sat down and knocked out a piece on what I know about quail and dogs and men that hunt quail, and sent it to *Field & Stream*. Hugh Grey bought it and put a plug for it on the cover. In North Carolina, of twenty years ago, a small boy suddenly had become a big man in his neighborhood, even if the process was considerably delayed.

Having hurdled one, I took on the other. For no real reason at all, except that I had a 20-year itch, I rigged my own safari to Kenya and Tanganyika. It was *mine*. Nobody sent me. I paid for it myself. Nobody went along but Mama, and the white hunter, and a company of African boys. I refused to share the trip with anybody else, even though I had offers of plenty of company.

I spent the two happiest months of my life in the bush of British East Africa. The time was so spent that it was impossible not to write about it. There is not much real personal adventure left in this world – not many boyhood dreams that lose nothing, but gain, by fulfillment. So I have combined two dreams in one: I have been on a safari, and I have written about it for my first hero-fixation in the magazine field. Some of it has been done for other magazines as well, but not with the same sense of long-term, boyish gratification.

If there is any moral to this preamble to a series of African pieces, it is that dreaming costs nothing, and might even come true. In my case it did.

"Ruark Realizes Boyhood Ambitions," *Field & Stream*, March, 1952.

Leopards Are Different

*I*t was a cold, clear night in the little camp at the Grumeti in Tanganyika. A sharp, winy night, like New England in the fall, with the stars distinct against the sky. The boys had built a roaring blaze out of dead thornbush logs. The dinner was responding kindly to a third cup of coffee. Everybody was tired. It had been a big day. There had been the immense waterbuck in the morning and the red-headed lion in the afternoon, and the business with the lioness and the cubs.

Suddenly the wind veered. A smell swept down on the breeze, a dreadful smell.

"O–ho," Harry Selby said. "Chanel No. 5, if you are a leopard. That delicious aroma could be your pig and your Grant gazelle. It may smell awful to you, but the bait has hit just about the right stage of decay to be better than Camembert to our noisy friend of the fig tree. I was never able to figure why the cleanest, neatest animal in the bush waits until his dinner is maggoty before he really works up an appetite. Let's see. We've had the bait up five days now. The boys say your pussycat's been feeding since yesterday. He ought to be through the pig now, and working on the Grant. He ought to be feeling pretty cheeky about his vested interest in that tree.

"I don't know what there is about that tree," the professional hunter went on. "I think maybe it's either bewitched or made out of pure catnip. You can't keep the leopards out of it. It's only about five hundred yards from camp. I come here year after year, and we always get a leopard. I got one three months ago. I got one six months before that. There's an old tabby lives in it, and she changes boy friends every time. We'll go to the blind tomorrow and we'll

103

pull her newest fiancé out for you – that is, if he's eaten deep enough into that Grant. That is, if you can hit him."

At this stage I was beginning to get something past arrogant. Insufferable might be the right word.

"What is all this mystery about leopards?" I asked. "Everybody gives you the old mysterious act. Don Ker tells me about the safari that's been out fourteen years and hasn't got a leopard yet. Everybody says you'll probably get a lion and most of the other stuff, but don't count on leopards. Leopards are where you find them. We got two eating out of one tree and another feeding on that other tree up the river, and we saw one coming back from the buffalo business yesterday. They run up and down the swamp all night, cursing at the baboons.

"You sit over there looking wise, and mutter about if we see him and if I hit him when we see him. You've been polishing up the shotgun and counting buckshot ever since we hung the kill in the trees. What do you mean, if I hit him? You throw a lion at me the first day out, and I hit him in the back of the neck. I bust the buffalo, all right, and I hit that waterbuck with one in the pump, and I break the back on a running eland. What have I got to do to shoot a sitting leopard at thirty-five feet with a scope on the gun? Use a silver bullet?

"Leopards ain't like other things," Harry said. "Leopards do strange things to people's personality. Leopards and kudu affect people oddly. I saw a bloke fire into the air three times once, and then throw his gun at a standing kudu. I had a chap here one time who fired at the leopard first night, and missed. We came back the second night. Same leopard in the tree. Fired again. Missed. This was a chap with all manner of medals for sharpshooting. A firecracker. Splits lemons at 350 yards, shooting offhand. Pure hell on running Tommies at 600 yards, or some such. Knew everything about bullet weights and velocities and things. Claims a .220 Swift's plenty big enough for the average elephant. Already had the boys calling him One-Bullet Joe."

"So?" I inquired.

"Came back the third night. Leopard up the tree. Fired again. Broad daylight, too, not even six o'clock yet. Missed him clean. Missed him the next night. Missed him for the fifth time on the following night. Leopard very plucky. Seemed to be growing fond of the sportsman. Came back again on the sixth night, and this time my bloke creases him on the back of the neck. Leopard takes off into the bush. I grab the shotgun and take off after him. *Hapana* – nothing. No blood and no tracks. Worked him most of the night with a flashlight, expecting him on the back of my neck any minute. *Hapana chui* – no leopard. My sport quit leopards in disgust, and went back to shooting lemons at 350 yards."

"How do you know the marksman touched him on the neck?" I asked sarcastically. "Did he write you a letter of complaint from Nairobi?"

"No," Harry said gently. "I came back with another party after the rains, and here was this same *chui* up the same tree. This client couldn't hit a running Tommy at 600 yards, and he couldn't see any future to lemon-splitting at 350. But his gun went off, possibly by accident, and the old boy tumbled out of the tree, and when we turned him over there was the scar across the back of his neck, and still reasonably fresh. Nice tom, too. About eight foot, I surmise. Not as big as Harriet Maytag's though. He was just on eight-four."

"If I hear any more about Harriet Maytag's lion or Harriet Maytag's rhino, Mr. Shelby," I declared with considerable dignity, "it will not be leopards we shoot tomorrow. It will be white hunters, and the wound will be in the back. Not the first time it's happened out here, either. I'm going to bed, possibly to pray that I will not embarrass you tomorrow. Even if I am not Harriet Maytag, I still shoot a pretty good lion."

There was an awful row down by the river. The baboons set up a fearful cursing, the monkeys screamed, and the birds awoke. There was a regular panting, wheezing grunt in the background, like the sound made by a two-handed saw on green wood.

"That's your boy, chum," Selby said brightly. "Come to test your courage. If you find him in the tent with you later on, wake me."

We went to bed. I dreamed all night of a faceless girl named Harriet Maytag, whom I had not met and who kept changing into a leopard. I also kept shooting at lemons at three and a half feet, and I missed them every time. Then the lemons would turn into leopards, and the gun would jam.

Everybody I had met in the past six months had a leopard story for me. How you were extremely fortunate even to get a glimpse of one, let alone a shot. How they moved so fast that you couldn't see them go from one place to another. How you only got one shot, and whoosh, the leopard was gone. How it was always night, or nearly night, when they came to the kill, and you were shooting in the bad light against a dark background on which the cat was barely perceptible. How if you wounded him you had to go after him in the black, thick thorn. How he never growled, like a lion, betraying his presence, but came like a streak from six feet or dropped quietly on your neck from a tree. How, if four guys went in, three always got scratched. And how the leopard's fangs and claws were always septic because of his habit of feeding on carrion. How a great many professionals rate him over the elephant and buffalo as murderous game, largely because he kills for fun, and without purpose. And how unfortunately most of what you heard was true.

I had recently talked with a doctor who had sewed up three hunters who had been clawed by the same cat within the last six months. A big leopard runs only 150 pounds or so, but I had seen a zebra foal, weighing at least two hundred pounds, thirty feet above the ground and wedged into a crotch by a leopard, giving you some idea about the fantastic strength that is hidden by that lovely spotted golden hide. I reflected that there are any amount of documented stories about leopards coming into tents and even houses after dogs and sometimes people and breaking into fowl-pens and leaping out of trees at people on horseback.

"A really peculiar beast," Harry had said when we jumped the big one coming back from the buffalo. "Here we find one in broad daylight right smack out in the open plain, when there are people who've lived here all their lives and have never seen one. Here is a purely nocturnal animal who rarely ever leaves the rocks or the river-edge, standing out in the middle of a short-grass plain like a bloody topi. They are supposed to be one of the shyest, spookiest animals alive, yet they'll come into your camp and pinch a dog right out of the mess tent. They'll walk through your dining room on some occasions, and spit in your eye. They're supposed to have a great deal of cunning, yet I knew one that came back to the same kill six nights in a row, being shot over and missed every time. But they've a great fascination for me, and for most people.

"The loveliest sight I've ever seen since I started hunting was a leopard sleeping in a thorn tree in the late afternoon. The tree was black and yellow, the same color as the cat, and the late sun was coming in through the leaves, dappling the cat and the tree with a little extra gold. We weren't after leopard at the time, already had one; so we just woke him up and watched him scamper. He went up that tree like a big lizard."

I was getting to know quite a bit about my young friend Selby by this time. He was a professional hunter and lived by killing, or by procuring things for other people to shoot, but he hated to use a gun worse than any man I ever met. He has the fresh face and candid eyes of a man who has lived all his life in the woods, and when he talks of animals his face lights up like a kid's in a toy store. He had nearly killed us all, a day earlier, coming back from a big *ngoma* – lion dance party – in the WaIkoma village. There were some baby francolin in the trail, and he almost capsized the Land Rover trying to miss them. What he liked was to watch animals and learn more about animals. He refused to allow anyone to shoot baboons. He hated even to shoot a hyena. The only things he loved to shoot were wild dogs, merely because he disapproved of the way they killed, by running their prey in shifts, pulling it down finally, and eating it alive.

"You're a poet, man," I told him. "The next thing, you'll be using the sonnet form to describe how old Katunga howls when his madness comes on in the moonlight nights."

"It would make a nice poem at that," Harry said. "But don't

spoof me about leopards in trees. Wait until you have seen a leopard in a tree before you rag me. It's a sight unlike any other in the world."

When we got up that next morning, the scent of the rotting pig and the rotting Grant was stronger than ever. Harry sniffed and ordered up Jessica, the Land Rover. We climbed in and drove down the river bank, with the dew fresh on the grass and a brisk morning breeze rustling the scrub acacias. As we passed the leopard tree there was a scrunching sound and a rustle in the bush that was not made by the breeze. A brown eagle was sitting in the top of the tree.

We made a daily ritual of this trip, after we had hung the bait the first day, in order to get the cat accustomed to the evening visit. Always we passed close aboard the blind, a semicircle of thorn and leaves with a peep-hole and a crotched stick for a gun rest. Its rear was open to the plain, and its camouflaged front faced the tree. By now it would seem that the leopard had been feeding on the two carcasses we had derricked up to an L-shaped fork about thirty feet above ground and tied fast with rope.

You could just define the shape of the pig, strung a little higher than the Grant, as they hung conveniently from another limb, in easy reach of the feeding fork. The pig was nearly consumed now, his body and neck all but gone and his legs gnawed clean to the hairy fetlocks. The guts and about twenty pounds of hindquarter were gone from the Grant. The steady wind was blowing from the tree and toward the blind, and they smelled just lovely.

Harry didn't say anything until he had swung Jessica around and we were driving back to the camp and breakfast. "You heard the old boy leave his tree, I suppose. I got a glimpse of him as we drove by. And did you notice the eagle?"

"I noticed the eagle," I said. "How come eagles and leopards are so chummy?"

"Funny thing about a lot of animals," Harry observed. "You know how the tick-birds work with the rhino. Rhino can't see very much, and the tick-birds serve as his eyes, in return for which they get to eat his ticks. I always watch the birds when I'm stalking a rhino. When the birds jump, you know the old boy is about to come bearing down on you. Similarly, you'll always find a flock of egrets perched on the backs of a buffalo herd. You can trace the progress of a buff through high grass just by watching the egrets.

"I don't know how they work out their agreements," Harry went on. "Often you'll see a lion feeding on one end of a kill and a couple of jackals chewing away on the other. Yet the lion won't tolerate a hyena or a vulture near his kill.

"Now, our friend, this leopard which you may or may not shoot tonight, or tomorrow night, or ever, has this transaction with the eagle. The eagle mounts guard all day over the leopard's larder. If vultures or even another leopard comes by and take a fancy to old Chui's free lunch, the eagle sets up a hell of a clamor and old Chui comes bounding out of the swamp to protect his victuals. In return for this service the eagle is allowed to assess the carcass a pound or so per diem. It's a very neat arrangement for both."

We went back to camp and had the usual tea, canned fruit and crumbly toast. It was still cold enough for the remnants of last night's fire to feel good.

"We won't hunt today," Selby said. "We'll just go sight in the .30-06 again and you can get some writing done. I want you rested for our date with Chui at four o'clock. You'll be shaking enough from excitement, and I don't want it complicated with fatigue."

"I will *not* be shaking from excitement or fatigue or anything else," I declared. "I am well known around this camp as a man who is as icy calm as Dick Tracy when danger threatens. In near-by downtown Ikoma I'm a household word amongst the rate-payers. I am Old Bwana Risase Moja, slayer of Simba, Protector of the Poor, Scourge of the Buffalo, and the best damn bird shooter since Papa Hemingway was here last. I promise you, you will not have to go into any bush after any wounded leopard this night. I'm even going to pick the rosette I want to shoot him through. I intend to pick one of the less regular patterns, because I do not want to mar the hide."

"Words," Selby said. "Childish chatter from an ignorant man. Let's go and sight in the .30-06. We'll sight her pointblank for fifty yards. They make a tough target, these leopards. Lots of times you don't have but a couple of inches of fur to shoot at. And that scope has got to be right."

"How come scope? I thought you were the original scope-hater. At thirty-five yards I figure I can hit even one of those lemons you're always talking about with open sights, shooting from a forked stick."

Harry was patient, as if talking to a child. "This is the only time I reckon a scope to be actually necessary out here. The chances are that when that cat comes it will be nearly dark, well past shooting light. You won't even be able to see the kill with your naked eye, let alone the cat. The scope's magnification will pick him out against the background, and you can see the post in the scope a lot easier than you could see a front sight a foot high through ordinary open sights. And if I were you, I'd wear those polaroid glasses you're so proud of, too. Any visual help you can get you will need, chum."

We sighted in the .30-06, aiming at the old blaze on the sighting-in tree. Then we trundled Jessica back to camp, pausing on the way long enough to shoot a Thomson gazelle for the pot. It was a fairly long shot, and I broke his neck.

"I think I can hit a leopard," I said.

"A lousy little Tommie is a different thing from a leopard," Harry replied. "Tommies have no claws, no fangs, and do not roost in trees."

We slopped around the camp for the rest of the morning, reading detective stories and watching the vultures fight the marabou storks for what was left of the waterbuck carcass. Lunch time came, and I made a motion toward the canvas water bag where the gin and vermouth lived.

"*Hapana*," Harry said. "No booze for you, my lad. For me, yes. For Mama, yes. For you, no. The steady hand, the clear eye. You may tend bar if you like, but no cocktails for the Bwana until after the Bwana has performed this evening."

"This could go on for days," I grumbled. "Bloody leopard may never come to the tree."

"Quite likely," Harry remarked, admiring a small glass of luke-warm gin with some green lime nonsense in it. "The more for me and Mama. A lesson in sobriety for you."

A bee, from the hive in the tree behind the mess tent, dive-bombed Harry's glass and swam happily around in the gin-and-lime. Harry fished him out with a spoon and set him on the mess table. The bee staggered happily and buzzed blowsily.

"Regard the bee," said Selby. "Drunk as a lord. Imagine what gin does to leopard shooters, whose glands are already activated by fear and uncertainty."

"Go to hell, the both of you. I'll eat while these barflies con-sume my gin."

The lunch was fine – yesterday's cold boiled guineafowl flanked by some fresh tomatoes we had swindled out of the Indian storekeeper in Ikoma, with hot macaroni and cheese that Ali the cook produced from his biscuit-tin oven and some pork and beans in case we lacked starch after the spaghetti, bread and potatoes. Harry allowed me a bottle of beer.

"Beer is a food," he told me. "It is not a tipple. Now go take a nap. I want you fresh. I hate crawling after wounded leopards who have been annoyed by amateurs. It's so lonesome in those bushes after dark, the leopard waiting ahead of you and the client apt to shoot you in the trousers the first time a monkey screams."

I dozed a bit, and at four o'clock Harry came into the tent and roused me. "Leopard time," he said. "Let's hope he comes early. It'll give the bugs less chance to devour us. Best smear some of that bug dope on your neck and wrists and face. And if I were you, I'd borrow one of the Mem-sahib's scarves and tie it around most of my face and neck. If you have to cough, cough now. If you have to sneeze, sneeze now. If you have to clear your throat or scratch or anything else, do it now, because for the next three hours you will sit motionless in that blind, moving no muscle, making no sound, and thinking as quietly as possible. Leopards are allergic to noise."

I looked quite beautiful with one of mama's fancy Paris scarves, green to match the blind, tied around my head like an old peasant woman. We climbed into Jessica. Harry was sitting on her rail from the front-seat position. The sharp edge of her after-rail was cutting a chunk out of my rear. We went past the blind at about twenty miles an hour, and we both fell out, commando-style, directly into the blind. The jeep took off, to return at the sound of a shot or at black dark if no shot.

I wriggled into the blind and immediately sat on a flock of safari ants that managed to wound me severely before we scuffed them out. I poked the .30-06 through the peep-hole in the front of the blind and found that it centered nicely on the kill in the tree. Even at four-thirty the bait was indistinct to the naked eye. The scope brought it out clearly. I looked over my shoulder at Selby, his shock of black hair uncluttered by shawl or insecticide. A tsetse was biting him on the forehead. He let it bite. My old 12-gauge double, loaded with buckshot, was resting over his crossed knees. He looked at me, shrugged, winked and pointed with his chin at the leopard tree.

We sat. Bugs came. Small animals came. No snakes came. No leopards came. I began to think how much of my life I had spent waiting for something to happen – of how long you waited for an event to occur, and what a short time was consumed when the event you had been waiting for actually did come to pass. The worst thing about the war at sea was waiting. You waited all through the long black watches of the North Atlantic night, waiting for a submarine to show its periscope. You could not smoke. You did not even like to step inside the blacked-out wheel-house for a smoke because the light spoiled your eyes for half an hour. You waited on islands in the Pacific. You waited for air raids to start in London, and then you waited some more for the all-clear. You waited in line at the training school for chow, and for pay, and for everything. You waited in train stations, and you sat around airports waiting for your feeble priority to activate – you waited everywhere. From the day you got into it until the day you got out of it you were waiting for the war itself to end, so that it was all one big wait.

Sitting in the blind, staring at the eaten pig and the partially eaten Grant and waiting for the leopard to come and hearing the sounds – the *oohoo-oohoo-hoo* of the doves and the squalls and squawks and growls and mutters in the dark bush ahead by the Grumeti River – I thought profoundly that there was an awfully good analogy in waiting for a leopard by a strange river in a strange dark country. I began to get Selby's point about the importance of a leopard in a tree – waited for, planned for, suffered for – to be seen for one swift moment or maybe not to be seen at all.

These are the thoughts you have in a leopard blind in Tanganyika when the ants bite you and you want to cough and your nose itches and nothing whatsoever can be done about it. Five o'clock came. No leopard. *Hapana chui*, my head said in Swahili. I looked at Selby. He was scowling ferociously at a flock of guineafowl that seemed to be feeding right into the blind. With his hand he made a swift, attention-getting gesture. The guineas got the idea, and marched off. Selby pointed his chin at the leopard tree and shrugged. Now it was six o'clock. I thought about the three weeks I sweated out in Guam, waiting for orders to leave that accursed paradise, orders I was almost sure of but not quite. When they came, they came in a hurry. They came in the morning and I left in the afternoon. Six-thirty. *Hapana chui*.

It was getting very dark now, so dark that you couldn't see the kill in the tree at all without training the rifle on it and looking through the scope. Even then it was indistinct, a blur of bodies against a green-black background of foliage. I looked at Selby. He rapidly undoubled both fists twice, which I took to mean twenty more minutes of shooting time.

My watch said twelve minutes to seven, and it was dead black in the background and the pig was non-visible and the Grant only a blob and even where it was lightest it was dark gray. I thought, *Damn it, this is the way it always is with everything. You wait and suffer and strive, and when it ends it's all wasted, and the hell with all leopards*. Then I felt Harry's hand on my arm. Down the river to the left the baboons had gone mad. The uproar lasted only a split second, and then a cold and absolute calm settled on the Grummetti. No bird. No monkey. No nothing. About a thousand yards away there was a surly, irritable cough. Harry's hand closed on my arm, and then relaxed. My eyes were on the first fork of the big tree.

There was only tree to watch, a first fork full of nothing. Then there was a scrunching noise like the scrape of stiff khaki on brush, and where there had been nothing but tree there was now nothing but leopard. He stretched his lovely spotted neck and turned his big head arrogantly and slowly, and he seemed to be staring into my soul with the coldest eyes I have ever seen. The devil would have leopard's eyes, yellow-green and hard and depthless as beryls. He stopped turning his head and looked at me. I had the post of the scope centered between those eyes. His head came out clearly against the black background of forest. It looked bigger than a lion's head.

You are not supposed to shoot a leopard when he comes to the first fork. The target is bad in that light and small, and you either spoil his face if you hit him well, or you would wound him and there is the nasty business of going after him. You are supposed to wait for his second move, which will take him either to the kill or to a second branch, high up, as he makes a decision on eating or going up in the rigging. If he is not shot on that second branch or shot as he poises over the kill, he is not shot. Not at all. You can't see him up high in the thick foliage. And Harry had said, "On a given night there has never been more than one shot at a leopard."

I held the aiming post of my telescopic sight on that leopard's face for a million years. While I was holding it the Pharaohs built the pyramids. Rome fell. The Pilgrims landed on Plymouth Rock. The Japs attacked Pearl Harbor.

And then the leopard moved. Only you could not see him move. Where there had been leopard there was only fork. There was not even a flash or a blur when he moved. He disappeared.

Then he appeared on a branch to the left of the kill, a branch that slanted upward into the foliage at a 45-degree angle. He stood at full pride on that branch, not crouching, but standing erect and profiling like a battle-horse on an ancient tapestry, gold and black against the black. There was slightly ragged rosette on his left shoulder as he stood with his head high.

The black asparagus tip of the aiming post went to the ragged rosette, and a little inside voice said, *Squeeze, don't jerk, because Selby is looking at you and you only get one shot at a—*

I never heard the rifle fire. All I heard was the bullet *whunk*. It was the prettiest sound I ever heard. No, not quite the prettiest. The prettiest was the second sound, which said *blonk*. That was the sound the leopard made when he hit the ground. It sounded like a bag of soft cement dropping off a roof. *Blonk*. No other sounds. No moans. No growls. No whish of swift, bounding feet on bush.

A hand hit me on the shoulder, bringing me back into the world of living people. "*Piga*," Harry said. "*Kufa*. As bloody *kufa* as a bloody doornail. Right on the button. He's dead as a bloody beef in there. We were as near to losing him as damn to swearing, though. I thought he'd never leave that bloody fork, and when he went I knew he was heading up to the crow's nest. You shot him one-sixtieth of a second before he leaped, because I could just make out his start to crouch. You got both shoulders and the heart, I'd say, from the way he came down. Aren't they something to see when they first hit that fork, with those bloody great eyes looking right down your throat and that dirty big head turning from side to side! You shot him very well, Bwana Two Lions. Did you aim for any particular rosette, like you said?

"Go to hell twice," I said. "Give me a cigarette."

"I think you've earned one," Harry said. "Then let's go retrieve your boy. I'll go in ahead with the shotty-gun. You cover me from the left. If he's playing possum in there, shoot him, not me. If he comes, he'll come quick, except I would stake my next month's pay that this *chui* isn't going anywhere. He's had it."

Harry picked up the old 12-gauge and I slipped the scope off the .30-06 and slid another bullet into the magazine. We walked slowly into the high bush, Harry six steps ahead and I just off to the left. I knew the leopard was dead, but I knew also that dead leopards have carved chunks out of lots of faces. Selby was bobbling the shotgun up and down under his left shoulder, a mannerism he has when he wants to be very sure there is nothing on his jacket to clutter a fast raise and shoot. We needn't have worried.

Chui – *my chui* now – was sleeping quietly underneath the branch from which he had fallen. He had never moved. He was never going to move. This great, wonderful golden cat, eight foot something of leopard, looking more beautiful in death than he had looked in the tree, this wonderful wide-eyed, green-yellow-eyed cat was mine. And I had shot him very well.

"You picked the right rosette," Harry said. "Grab a hind leg and we'll lug him out. He's a real beauty. Isn't it funny how most of the antelopes and the lions lose all their dignity in death, while this blighter is more beautiful when he's in the bag than he is in the tree? Look at those eyes. No glaze at all. He's clean as a whistle all over, and yet he lives on filth. He eats carrion and smells like a bloody primrose. Yet a lion is nearly always scabby and fly-ridden and full of old sores and cuts. He rumples when he dies, and seems to grow smaller. Not *chui*, though. He's the most beautiful trophy in Africa."

"How does he compare with Harriet Maytag's leopard?" I asked, rather caustically, I thought.

"Forget Harriet Maytag, chum," Harry said. "I was only kidding. As far as I'm concerned, you are not only Bwana Simba, Protector of the Poor, but a right fine leopard man, too. Here come the boys. Prepare to have your hand shaken.

The boys *ohed* and *ahed* and gave me the old double-thumb grip, which means that Bwana is going to distribute largesse later when he has quit bragging and the liquor has taken hold. We piled the big fellow into Jessica's back seat and took off for camp. Mama nearly fainted when we took the leopard out of the back and draped him in front of the campfire. The wind had changed again and she had heard no shot. When the boys left in the dark with the Rover, she had assumed they were going to pick us up.

The leopard looked lovelier than ever in front of the campfire. His eyes were still clear. His hide was only gorgeous. Even the bullet hole was neat. He was eight feet and a bit, and he was a big tom. About one fifty on an empty stomach.

"Tail's a bit too short for my taste, though," Harry said. "Harriet's had a longer tail."

"Harriet be damned. After you're through with the pictures, mix me a martini."

Harry took the pictures. He mixed me a martini. I drank it and passed out – from sheer excitement, I suppose, because I hadn't had a drink all day.

The next evening when Harry and Mama went down to see about the female, with cameras, she had already acquired another tom. This leads me to believe that women are fickle.

The tom came in across the plain, which leopards never do, and passed within a few feet of the blind. He growled mightily as he bounded past. The Mem-sahib gave up leopard photography. She said that Selby was obviously deaf, or he would have heard the leopard coming through the grass.

"Leopards Are Different," *Field & Stream*, April, 1953.

Game Animals That Fight Back

*P*erhaps you first go to the deep bush of India or Africa with the idea you might get hurt. Maybe it proves something to the inner man – that you've got guts enough to spit in a lion's eye and walk off winning. And mostly you can . . . until God and circumstance and some critter foul up your luck. Big-game hunting is dangerous, and it is well not to forget it. But there are certain calculated risks one takes, of course, and you win them, and you feel pretty smug. Once in a while an uncalculated risk fixes your clock for fair, however.

Because some game such as the elephant, buffalo and gaur is huge, it may seem to the uninitiated to be slow and clottish. And lions? A joke – just like big dogs you shoot once in a while for a friend who wants a rug. Other people get chewed, never you.

Yet regardless of size, they all can be appallingly quick, strong and tough. I would like to mention a leopard I was wearing instead of a wrist watch last year, and check back on some of the incidents that tell me nobody in the hunting trade can keep winning so long as the animals fight back. I don't care how big they build the bores of the double rifles; I don't care how flat the trajectory on the marvelous new magnum, or how miraculous is the television picture of a variable-power scope. You play around with these wild critters long enough and one of them will carve a chop off you. A dying lady pig made a pass at me just the other day, and I lost my pants in the process.

The leopard that bit its initials on me was dead when I walked up. It was a little female which I shot out of cold spite because she was in heat and a tom leopard I wanted wouldn't come to the water-buffalo bait. He was arching his neck and caterwauling up and down the riverbed but his mind was *not* on food. We waited him out until black dark and then headed back to the *dak* bungalow, in a most unprepossessing area of India's Madhya Pradesh, to which I was not a newcomer, having shot three tigers and some other stuff there about ten years before.

So we head home to our dismal *dak* by the railroad station, and there in the road sits the leopard bitch which caused me the frustration. I broke an old rule about never shooting at night, flashed a torch on her, and walloped her straight down the front with a soft-point .30-06. It was a Remington rifle which had slain a hundred leopards, in my hands and out. She went over backward and almost became a rug.

There is some point to note here that I *should* know as much about leopard shooting as anybody, because Harry Selby, one of the best in the business taught me. Harry has been working at the trade for thirty years, and I have indulged in it for a mere fifteen.

One thing I do know about leopards is that none is dead until you have it skinned out and salted down. So you always carry a shotgun for the final approach, even if you know it's dead, and you always come up *behind* the leopard, and if it even wrinkles its hide you give it two blasts of buckshot in the back of the neck. This is with a *dead* leopard. A wounded leopard in thick brush – when it is stalking *you* – is quite another story, and certainly another technique.

In this case, by the light of a wan moon and a feeble lantern, I approached this leopard and saw a hole as big as a dinner plate blown out of her back where the softnose had emerged from the chest shot. But I had the shotgun in hand, with the Indian bearers waved back, when suddenly I saw her flinch. She was no trophy, so I gave her two wallops in the back of the head at about ten feet. Two buck-shot blasts at ten feet will take the head off anything, including Charles de Gaulle.

The cat lurched into a small patch of bush and was again dead – triple dead. I went carefully around . . . and found I only had one other shotgun shell in my pocket. Hugh Allen, an English friend with me, came up carrying the rifle which had suffered a split cartridge case from the first shot. He handed me the rifle so I could jimmy out the cartridge, and took custody of the shotgun.

At about that time the boys came up to the dead cat and one heaved a stone at the carcass. This revived the leopard.

She roared out of her deathbed, looking like all the gaudy magazine covers ever painted and making more noise than was possibly heard at the retreat from Dunkirk. The black lips writhed back over the red gums with the white tombstone teeth, and her filthy talons spread in an all-seeking embrace. Hugh Allen fired the other shell from the shotgun, but all of a sudden I had a lapful of live leopard.

I might as well tell you now that none of the locally bought ammunition was any good, Indian hunting skills being what they are. Later we plucked the buckshot out of the skin like flies off a piece of pie. The rifle shot had been all right (except for the split case) and the leopard actually *was* dead – or at least would have been if one of the Indians hadn't flung the rock.

But she was not dead when I performed a Spanish bullfight maneuver and gave her my wrist to chew on instead of my neck, and the clawing hind feet ripped air instead of my soft underbelly. While she was chomping on the arm, she knocked me off balance and bore me down to the stony ground. The Indian "gunbearers" took off and liberated the lamp with them just as the moon disappeared behind a cloud.

The rest is reasonably fuzzy, except for fright. Hugh Allen beat her off me with the shotgun, and then jammed the barrels down her throat, but not before he had taken a wicked gash in his arm. I was bleeding like a stuck human, from three separate bites where her teeth had closed on my left arm, and from several more upper-arm gashes where the claws had ripped.

It was like a scene straight out of a Doré Hell – Hugh spouting blood, trying to keep the thrashing cat on the ground with the barrels in her mouth, and me trying to pry a stuck cartridge case out of the barrel and jack another one into firing position. I don't know exactly how I did it – maybe with my teeth! – but I finally got the rifle in working shape and blew the snarling thing's head off at a distance of six inches, taking care not to shoot Hugh, and then Hugh and I started tying tourniquets on each other.

I didn't know if I was bleeding to death or not, because the pain doesn't come immediately. All I know is that it took six dirty handkerchiefs – all of mine and all of Hugh's – to stanch the flow for the bumpy two-hour midnight drive back to camp and some neat Dettol to clean the holes and some neat gin to revive the flagging spirit.

I don't want to draw this out any longer; I was unconscious for nearly a week from infective fever despite the good work of a medical missionary who gave me some antitetanus and some penicillin and stitched up the gaping holes.

We consider now that I have shot possibly twenty leopards, and have had only one foolishly wounded – gut-shot from a friend's hair-triggered rifle that went off where I was not aiming. This one tracked me through enough bad bush to give me a fairish third of a novel. Another, wounded because I either flinched in a tough shot in high grass with only the throat to aim at (or else the scope was out, which is what I prefer to think), we finally had to chivvy out of the greenery with some firecrackers.

Call it bad luck, accident or what will you, I nevertheless have had three hairy times with some twenty leopards I've shot . . . and I'm only a guy who hunts perhaps once or twice a year. How does it go for the white hunter who takes out safaris back to back with all manner of client shooters?

The catalogue within the last few years of dangerous going-ons is endless and as varied as a bouncing roulette ball. White hunter Harry Selby has dignified the wake of much more than 100 leopards, and very nearly had his throat torn out by a "dead" one that came at him in classic fashion with a toehold on the running board of a power wagon. Harry has attended the death of possibly a thousand buffalo . . . and got painfully tromped on in a rich suburb of Nairobi when his doctor rang him up to come shoot a couple of buff out of his flower garden. The unseasonable rains had driven a buffalo bull and a cow literally into the city from the nearby Ngong hills, and Selby almost met his finish in a bed, for God's sake, of petunias.

The other closest call that Selby had was from a buff that roared out of a bush with no warning – and no buffalo charges unless he's cornered or wounded. Selby shot it from the hip, in the neck, and discovered on the corpse an ulcer as big as an omelet from an old native arrow wound. The poison hadn't been fresh enough to kill and the buff had been brooding over his maltreatment for weeks, perhaps months, merely waiting for somebody to murder.

Maybe I'm wrong about the closest call on Selby. On my first safari with the talented young man, he damned near got killed by a zebra which had been heart-shot (by me) and throat-cut (by Metheke, the gunbearer).

It was the last day of safari, and I needed some more zebra skins. With an hour to go I walloped a big stallion up the backside and he ran 200 yards before he dropped from the raking shot. We got back in the car, drove up to the dead animal, and the gunbearer cut its throat to sanctify the corpse slightly officially for our Mohammedan members.

Selby had got out of the car and was standing against the Land Rover's open door. Suddenly the heart-shot, throat-cut stallion reared up, loosed a fearful roar, and charged Selby with mouth agape sufficiently to accommodate a train, forefeet flailing. He knocked Selby backward into the front seat of the Rover. I leaped into the back seat, grabbed a gun and shot the zebra down its gaping mouth, blowing out its brains. The beast fell permanently dead now on Selby, jamming him behind the wheel, with Selby cradling the bloody head and oozing brains in his arms.

"Get this goddamned thing off me!" Selby roared, seeing no humor in the fact that the boys and I were rolling on the ground, screaming with laughter.

I told this one around Nairobi, with some embellishment, and especially to Tommy Shevlin, an old friend from Palm Beach who has been on many a safari.

"Tell this to Fred," Tommy said, gesturing at his white hunter, Freddie Poolman, who was wearing a bandage on his right hand. I told the story, and then looked at the bandaged hand.

"Now don't tell me you got charged by an enraged dik-dik," I said (A dik-dik is the smallest African antelope, about the size of a large jackrabbit.)

Poolman looked at me without amusement.

"And what," he asked, "is so frilling funny about being charged by a wounded dik-dik?"

Turned out he had been, and the little beast had spiked him neatly through the hand with its tiny horns.

Buffalo, I would hazard, probably kill more natives and beat up more hunters than any other beast. The buff is difficult to finish unless you get him mortally with the first shot: he develops an added adrenaline blastoff that makes him almost unkillable. He is also usually hunted in thick bush and is inordinately crafty in doubling back and lying in wait for the man who is tracking him. He is also easy for native poachers to shoot – and wound – but unless the poison is very fresh he becomes a menace to the community until some game warden kills him.

He is also a fighter in his own backyard. I have seen numerous contests for preeminence in the breeding herd, with father and son slugging it out for the favor of the cows. The loser in one of these intramurals nearly collected Reggie Destro, a cautious and clever white hunter from Kenya.

Reggie was stalking up to a herd, not yet taking his rifle from a gunbearer who was at his elbow, when a youngish bull tore bellowing from the bush a few feet away. Reggie's gunbearer was brave enough, but the native instinct in emergency is to run first and think later. The automatic native ran three yards before he remembered that he was a gunbearer and that he had Reggie's rifle. In the time it took him to come back those three yards and give the rifle to Destro, the bull was on Reggie, ruining his left arm and twisting the heavy double rifle into a pretzel. Reggie's arm was useless for months, and the weapon never recovered. One of the clients shot the bull – a disenchanted younger male kicked out of the herd by a pa or uncle and lingering behind, brooding.

Nearly every white hunter I know has been tossed by a buff at some time or other, but generally not so seriously as Destro or as Mike Rowbothom, who was in the deep late-afternoon bush after a client-wounded animal who got ambushed by the bull. Mike gave the charging animal two in the face at a range of about two feet with his .470, which fires a whopping bullet about the size of a dill pickle. Yet there was still enough gas left in the critter to bust a couple of Mike's vertebrae.

I give the buff credit for being the chanciest of all the dangerous stuff. He hears magnificently. He has eyesight like a vulture. He can smell the tiniest taint drifting in for miles. He can turn on a dime, and bull his tonnage through any bush. He is singleminded in his hatred, and he will lick the flesh off your feet with a tongue like a woodrasp if you don't climb high enough in a tree. He can kill you either with a swipe of horns, a butt of his massive boss, or casque, or with a stab of horns. He will kneel on you, dance up and down on you, and what is more he will track you and ambush you from behind. I will take him over rhino any day – most hunters get trodden by rhino if they hunt them long enough – but not so fatally as someone who really tangles with an elephant.

Rhino stories, unless fatal, are generally funny. One of the funnier had to do with old Tom Murray-Smith, a pro of ancient vintage and a man whose bravery in his fading years reached foolish proportions. Tom plunged into the bush after a client-wounded rhino and the thing charged from some thick bush. Murray-Smith backed up and stepped into a pig hole, with the rhino on top of him. Losing his rifle, Murray-Smith took firm hold on the rhino's front horn and clung for dear life, with the rhino bumping him violently up and down. The gunbearer came up, recovered the rifle, and shot the rhino off his master.

"Well," said Murray-Smith, "all I could think of at the time was that the horn seemed to be quite a bit *longer* than when I told the client to shoot it."

Lions have been crowding into the news lately. An American named Joe Shaw, client of an Angola safari firm, was killed when he went against advice into thick bush after a lion of proved nasty disposition just last year. John Kingsley-Heath, a broadly experienced professional was fetched in, mauled and tattered, to Nairobi recently. There was some doubt that Kingsley-Heath would live, and then more doubt that he would walk. The details of this accident are vague and varied, but the likeliest version is that a lion approached the rear of the leopard blind, the client took a shot at it with a light rifle, wounded it, and Kingsley-Heath gave the lion himself to chew on until somebody showed up with heavy reinforcements. It should be pointed out here that when you go into a leopard blind, you usually take just a light rifle and a shotgun with buckshot for insurance.

Not so long ago on the Serengeti Plain in Tanganyika, a strolling lion went into a non-hunter's tent, stepped over a couple of tourists, dragged out one of the sightseers and killed him, eating a good portion of the body. I used to love to sleep out in the open with lions roaring all around me, but since that Serengeti incident I feel a little safer under canvas with the fly-front firmly drawn.

For sheer freak, though, I think Ken Jespersen, still another white-hunting friend of mine, has the capper. Ken was shooting around a lion-heavy place called Loitokitok on the Kenya-Tanganyika border. The client hit the lion, low and back, and it went into high grass. Ken and his gunbearer, a sturdy soul named

Wambua, followed it into the bush and all of a sudden Ken was *riding* the lion. It had gone to earth in an ant-bear hole completely covered by long yellow buffalo grass. Ken was standing astride the unseen hole when the lion got up, and Jespersen became the first Dane ever to do a bronco act with a full-grown male lion. The lion pitched him off, biting a horrid gash in his meat hand, and then went for Wambua. He was chewing dedicatedly on Wambua – who later spent months in a hospital in grave condition – when Ken regained his senses, recovered the gun which had been flung from his hand and shot the lion off the neck of his associate.

Jespersen showed up in Spain as my guest a little later, and when I saw the scar I said, jokingly: "And I suppose you call that a lion bite?" Ken looked at the red weal and said simply, "Yes. That's exactly what I would call it – a lion bite."

Little John Sutton, who won all the prizes last year for big elephant, buffalo, leopard, and even managed five bull bongo on the Kenya Aberdare slopes, is possibly as good a white hunter as is now alive, although he's no bigger than a strong minute. John not only managed to get stabbed in the hand by a "dead" bongo, but I think he lived through as frightening an experience with elephant as anybody I know.

Sometimes an elephant will pick out a person from a group to hate. In this case a Texas client wounded an elephant and Little John plunged into miserable bush to sort it out. "Miserable bush" is a tangle of thorn trees or some such in which you can't see your elephant until you run smack into its backside. Jonathan found that he was not tracking the elephant; the elephant was trailing him, sniffing at his scent with its trunk exactly as a bird dog works, and ignoring the other trackers. Finally, in dense scrub palm and bamboo, John couldn't elude his unseen enemy any longer and attempted the desperate device of hiding in some even thicker bush, hoping for a clearer shot at the wounded bull.

Now the bull, only slightly hurt, was screaming with rage and *pounding* with a massive trunk in every available cluster of cover which conceivably could be holding Sutton. John was naturally petrified as the thrashing trunk searched out his hidey-hole. But the noise and the pounding had one effect – as the elephant was beating the bushes close to John, he got a swift look at the screaming bull, head high, trunk upraised. Sutton, no lad to flinch in a clinch, took a long chance and brained the bull – shooting through the throat and up between the tusks into the brain as that great rubbery flail was literally raised over his head. I think perhaps John, a light drinker, had more than one *chota-peg* when he got back to camp that night.

The ultimate story on elephant, however, comes from Mozambique and my favorite hunter, Wally Johnson of Macombique Safarilandia. Wally was a professional ivory hunter for a lot of years when there was no limit on elephant in Portuguese East, and he is a very careful man in the bush.

Wally was elephant coursing in 1947, with a Portuguese sportsman along for the ride, and they came up on a big herd of bachelor bulls.

"There was an enormous body in the herd," Wally says, "but I couldn't see the tusks. There was another, smaller bull in front of him, so I took a shot at the smaller chap, who looked like a 60-pounder. He didn't drop, but he gave me a clear bash at the enormous bloke, who fell with a crash. The monster turned out to have no tusks at all, so I took off after the wounded fellow.

"The first chap separated from the herd, and I followed him up until we saw him on the plain. I got up to about 25 yards behind the wounded bull, walking slowly, waiting for him to turn so I could put a shot into his brain or heart."

Wally still gets excited when he tells the story.

"Although I was matching his pace, suddenly I saw his backside getting bigger and bigger. His bloody legs were going backward in perfect rhythm, but very, very fast! He knew he was being followed and was smart enough to know I probably wouldn't risk a shot up his bum. I was being *charged backward*!

"At the very last moment he swung his head and trunk around to take me and I dropped him with a brain shot. But if I hadn't noticed the increased speed of the backward charge he'd have had me for certain."

Soon afterward, an accident befell Wally Johnson that brings me back to my dead-leopard adventure and reminds me of an even more haunting one – for Johnson was severely tossed by a "dead" water-buck that got up and hoisted him with a horn in his crotch.

Anyhow, the closest squeak I ever had in the category of "dead" animals killing me still gives me nightmares. At the time I was shooting tigers in India's Central Province, cattle-killers were classed as vermin and it was legal to shoot at night from a tree *machan* over the body of the "natural" kill, as opposed to staked-out bait.

I was feeling very brave about tigers, having killed two huge ones by daylight the previous week. We had been off hunting blackbuck or bear or anything for fun, when word came that an enormous tiger had killed a full-grown domestic buffalo in the nearest village. The locals had thoughtfully constructed a hurried platform in a tree, and had moved the water buffalo's corpse to within shooting range. The tiger had been driven off the kill before feeding: it was a mortal cinch he would come back by night to collect his dinner.

My shikari and I climbed up the tree, using a homemade ladder, made ourselves as comfortable as possible on the *machan*, and settled down to let the mosquitoes chew us until the tiger came. We had a big flashlight, and I was shooting the same .470 with which I had stoned the other two daytime tigers.

I dozed and was wakened by munching sounds. We waited a good ten minutes for the beast to get well and truly stuck into his dinner, and then the shikari flashed on the light. We knew the tiger was enormous from his pugmarks, but I was not prepared for the blood-smeared head which turned slowly into the light. This tiger's head was as big as a bale of hay.

I held close on his neck and squeezed off. You could hear the bullet whonk, and the head fell forward on the rump of the buffalo. The body of the tiger never even twitched. This was a *real* rug. I started to give him the other barrel behind the shoulder for insurance, when the shikari grabbed my arm.

"No, no, Sahib," he said. "This tiger is dead and there's no use spoiling the skin. Anyhow there will be a joke on the others. If they hear only one shot they will think you have missed when we come in with this huge animal."

This all seemed very logical. I had a couple of nips out of the flask and smoked a couple of cigarettes while we waited for the boys to come with the ladder. I reflected that not even Jim Corbett could compare with me as a tiger shooter, and had still another drink. I ran for Prime Minister of India and was elected unanimously, and there I decided I wanted another look at my best and biggest tiger, the vastest tiger ever slain by hand of man. Fully twenty minutes had passed since I had plugged him behind the ear.

I flashed the light on and heard a mighty roar as I saw a striped tail disappear. My tiger had come back from the dead, and now between me and the *dak* bungalow I not only had a jungle full of cobras, but a wounded tiger as well. It would not be a very pleasant walk home in the dark.

I was thinking a variety of things; how in the daytime shooting I had sat down beside my dead tigers, lifted their heads and posed happily for pictures. I had sat *on* my dead tigers. If the boys had come faster with the rough ladder, I would have been down out of that bloody tree posing with this "dead" tiger. Oh brother!

I still dream about that tiger, the one that got away, and invariably I am sitting on him in the dream when he gets up to go.

Of course you know what happened. Shooting at night, and from the high angle of the tree, instead of smashing his vertebrae I merely touched the top, knocking him out with a sort of metal rabbit-punch, but not harming him seriously with the solid bullet which went straight on through. We hunted him seriously for two days, but he had quit bleeding within 100 yards or so.

Since then I have been a very cautious fellow. I shoot it once, and kill it, and shoot it twice, to kill it again, and sometimes I will fire a third and fourth bullet to re-kill it. And, like my leopard, it sometimes will *still* arise and chew on you. Because it is not really only the live animals which fight back. It is the dead ones that get up and kill you.

"Game Animals That Fight Back," *True*, February, 1954.

Dukie's Dangerous Deed

*M*r. Percival Evelyn McGunn leaned against the bar of the Norfolk Hotel in Nairobi and pounded with his glass. "Moussa!" he shouted in a whisper that, with a favorable wind, might have been heard in Mombasa. "The other half for the warden and me, you damned heathen!"

"*Yas*, Bwana Dukie," Moussa said, sloshing a generous dollop of gin into Mr. McGunn's glass, seasoning it slightly with pink, and then conferring a less lusty portion on Mr. McGunn's companion. The men clinked glasses; Mr. McGunn drank his gin in a gulp and wiped his bright-red guard mustache with the back of his hand.

"Continue, Warden," he said. "As always, I am at your service."

Mr. McGunn – called Dukie because of the Swahili word for gun, *bunduki* – was quite a sight to see this fine, dim day in the

131

moist grotto of the Norfolk's public room. He was wearing his safari-going, town-leaving costume, which was somewhat heroic. His tunic, fringed like a Yankee frontiersman's jacket, was of red goatskin, mottled with startling black and white patches. A broad crocodile cartridge belt encompassed his waist, and colobus-monkey-fur holsters of silky black and white held two enormous .45 Colt revolvers. It is not necessary to say that their handles were of hand-shot ivory.

Mr. McGunn's trousers were of pale-gold buckskin, tapered at the bottom and stuck into carved-leather cowboy boots. An apricot-silk ascot caressed his somewhat obvious Adam's apple. On the back of his head Mr. McGunn wore a brilliant white Stetson, a touch less than one yard wide across the brim. Its crown was girdled by a five-inch leopard-tail hatband.

As a professional hunter – and a popular one – for the firm of Farr & Browning, Safaris, Ltd., Dukie McGunn believed that a man owed a certain debt of glamour to his clients, who would be paying in the neighborhood of fifty quid a day for the privilege of being bitten by tsetse flies, of being frightened by rhino, and of providing Mr. McGunn's daily ration of a quart of gin. In the bush he would carefully place his Hollywood-hunter clothes in his lockbox, and scream for Juma, the headman, to lay out his shabby old green drill bush jacket with the bullet loops, and to change off his fine carven boots for a battered pair of sneakers. But right now Dukie McGunn was on stage, center. He was what Nairobi sarcastically called: Going on Safari into Trackless, Secret Bush, and the client must necessarily be stunned with admiration.

Sipping delicately at his drink, the warden said, "Look, McWeapon. I can tell from your getup that F. & B. has entrusted another sucker to your care at Heaven knows what margin of profit. I suppose you'll be going into the Masai?"

"Indeed, yes," said Mr. McGunn, hammering with his glass again and glaring over his red mustache at Moussa. "It's a photo-graphic safari chiefly. Some people from Chicago or Texas or a similar suburb of the United States. I believe the old boy manufactures padlocks or olemargarine, or is in oil. He wants to shoot a buffalo, and take pictures of himself being brave in front of the lions."

"You can do me a small service, if you will," the warden said. "I must be off to England, and I won't be able to get back into the Masai. My second fellow broke his leg the other day, and I've just got a message on the telephone from Narok that old Tiberius is on his last legs. He's taken to sneaking outside the fly area to clobber a few Masai cattle. Next you know he'll be working on the Masai themselves, and Government will want me to be shooting *all* my lions. Poor old beggar, I suppose he does want killing. I should have put him away the last time I saw him – he was feeble enough to warrant it – but I hadn't the heart. He's my special pet."

"Tiberius?" Dukie murmured. "Is he the big black, sort of mangy old boy that lives around Jagatiak? The one with the broken canine tooth and the scars on his rump?"

"No, man, no," the warden answered. "That's Hector. Tiberius is the ginger-maned one with the crooked front paw who lives at Egelok. You know the one I mean. He's the one that you can hand-feed for picture purposes. The one that'll jump in the back of a lorry if you shove a zebra haunch into it. I want you to shoot him for me, if you see the poor old fellow, but whatever you do, don't go walloping Hector. He isn't even ten years old."

"Of course," Dukie McGunn said. "Of course I remember Tiberius. He's the one that comes running when you fire a gun, looking for his dinner. I expect I've taken a thousand pictures of him since you people closed the fly area to cat shooting. Oh, oh. Here comes Paddle. I expect my new charges await without, panting for action.

"Have a drink, Paddle, if you've got the price of three," McGunn said to his apprentice hunter, Mr. Anthony Rowbottom, who had been cursed from earliest infancy with the nickname of Paddle. Even the natives as far away as Tabora in Tanganyika or Lokuta in Uganda knew him only as Bwana Paddle. Bwana Paddle was a tall, weedy blond youth of some twenty-three years. He executed the more menial chores of professional hunting for his master, Mr. McGunn, chores such as repairing broken axles or replacing spring leaves when the lorry leaped into a pig hole and wounded herself – such chores as Mr. McGunn felt unbecoming to the glamour of his station.

Young Mr. Rowbottom's one ambition was to complete his apprenticeship to Mr. McGunn and then obtain a status of senior hunter, with his personal rig in any location that was far from Mr. McGunn. Mr. McGunn had successfully blocked this ambition for two years. He said that these young chaps were altogether too keen; they wanted to be off on their own before they learned to tell a leopard's track from a hyena's, and he, Dukie, would take no part in such madness.

"They're ready, Dukie," Paddle said. "They've bought out the African Bootshop and all of Ahmed's fancy clothes. They've got nine cameras and at least eleven guns. One of them is a thirty-thirty Marlin carbine, although Heaven knows what they intend to shoot with it out here."

"What are their names?" Dukie asked, although he had known name, sex, pedigree and livelihood since a year and six months ago, when the safari was first booked.

"Maxwell," Paddle said. "John and Helen. He's about fifty. She's about thirty-five. Not a bad looker. He seems a pleasant enough bloke. Both of them mad to be off. Sitting outside in the Rover now, gnawing on their nails."

"I suppose we really must be off," Mr. McGunn said, draining his glass, hitching his holsters slightly forward and settling his Stetson a touch more dramatically on his brow. "Have a good leave, Warden. I'll stifle my finer sentiments and do poor Hector for you."

"Damn it, man," the warden said. "*Not* Hector. *Tiberius* – at *Egelok. Not* Jagatiak. Mind you make no mistake."

"Make a note of it young man," McGunn said to his assistant. He strode to the door, and his magnificence uplifted every tea-drinking head on the Norfolk veranda. At the age of forty-seven, although a trifle spindly in the shank and a bit watery of eye, Mr.

McGunn was some six foot of impressive man. It had often been said of him, among the hunters who gathered in the Regal Grill, the Mr. McGunn had invented himself on purpose. This was properly damned as professional jealousy by Mr. McGunn, when the report reached him. Because, in truth – in wet years or dry, long grass or short – if a really impressive elephant or a forty-eight-inch buff got collected by a client, it always seemed to be Mr. McGunn's client who collected it. Dukie was intolerant of mediocre heads, even if it meant occasionally slipping illegally across the road into a national park to collect a superb one.

It is a long, dusty, bumpy, uninteresting, uncomfortable drive from where the track turns off the tarmac of the Nakuru road to Narok, where the Masai Reserve actually begins. The lava dust drifts like snow and creeps into your teeth. Except for a few bedraggled Thomson's gazelles and an occasional Grant's gazelle, there is no game. For sixty horrible miles there is nothing to see but a few whistling thornbushes and an infrequent buzzard. For years, Dukie had used this four-hour interval to brief his clients on what he expected of them in the way of behavior, and to impress them with the notability of his own career. Dukie and Mrs. Maxwell were leading the way in his Land Rover, a kind of jeep which was as bedecked as Dukie himself, including a buffalo skull and horns mounted on the radiator screen. Paddle and Mr. Maxwell were following in another Rover, poaching Dukie's dust.

"And there I was," Dukie was saying, "flat on the ground on my – on my posterior. I had both hands on the rhino's horn, and both feet in his face. As the old devil was battering me along, hammering me about while I waited for someone to come and shoot it loose from me, all I could think of was that the horn was *longer* than I thought when I told the client to shoot it."

"My!" Mrs. Maxwell said admiringly. "And what finally happened?"

"Nothing very much," Dukie said modestly. "I suppose I must have worn it down a bit, from hanging onto its snout. It died of its wounds and collapsed into my lap. Took three native gunbearers and a lever-*cum*-fulcrum to pry the creature off me."

"Heavens!" said Mrs. Maxwell. "Oh, how awful. And what a dreadfully dangerous way to earn a living – professional hunting, I mean. Are you sure there's no danger for us with all these animals?"

"Not," said Mr. McGunn, threading his Rover over a boulder, "so long as you do as I say when we're actually in the bush and amongst the game. I've never lost a client yet." Mr. McGunn chortled loudly. "I must remember that one. Never lost a client yet. Jolly good, that?"

"Very," Mrs. Maxwell said. "May I light you a cigarette?"

Helen Maxwell gazed about the massive blue hills and the dusty plain of the Rift Valley. Over toward her right, Longonot, the crater, was wreathed beautifully in cloud and reddened by the afternoon sun. A bright blue jay flew across the track, perched in a thornbush and screamed at her. A brace of doves flew ahead of the Rover, fluttering to light in the dusty track and taking off again as the little hunting car bumped closer. The Wakamba gunbearers and a Swahili car boy were perched like monkeys on the mass of guns, cameras, lunchboxes and similar gear that was packed into the tiny back seat of the car. She sneaked another peek at the Africans.

One of the Akamaba, with huge holes in his ear lobes, lobes so big that he tucked them over the tops of his ears, caught her glance and smiled horribly, exposing sharply filed teeth.

"*Jambo, Mama*," the Wakamba said. "*Shauri gani?*"

"What's he mean, calling me mama?" she said rather indignantly.

"They call all white women mama," Dukie replied. "Anyhow, when that nice Mrs. Hollander looked out of the ladies' tent, a rhino was grazing between her and camp."

Mrs. Maxwell shuddered. Dukie glanced quickly at his new client, and was pleased. She was quite pretty. She was a little, pouter-pigeonish woman in her middle thirties, with a trim, plump figure, a turned-up nose, and very wide-set brown eyes. She had a bright yellow silk scarf tied 'round her wavy brown hair to keep out the dust, and wore a lady's Stetson, with the brim turned rakishly upward on one side and pinned there, after the fashion of the Australian army hats. Her safari clothes fitted her neatly and didn't do anything seriously wrong to her body. Dukie noticed her chin, while nicely rounded, had rather more determination to it than he himself fancied in females. I'll wager, he thought, that I know precisely who runs the Maxwell household.

Mrs. Maxwell looked at Dukie as he drove sternly along, speaking now of a native uprising, again of a witch doctor he had been forced to combat in black magic, again of the lion he had knocked unconscious with one punch, and the leopard he had fought off with a stalk of sugar cane. Helen Maxwell decided that he was rather a striking figure, with his roan mustache blowing upward in the breeze, his blue eyes squinting against the sun, and his Stetson upcurling in the wind like the hat of a pony-express rider at full gallop. Just a little more chin, perhaps, she thought, but on the whole an impressive man. And those stories. What a brave fellow he must be.

In the other jeep, John Maxwell was doing most of the talking while Paddle pushed the car along a half-mile behind his boss. Maxwell was a sturdy, red-cheeked man with gray hair and steel-rimmed spectacles. He came from Montclair, New Jersey, where he manufactured piston rings and lived in a house worth at least two hundred thousand dollars – if you counted his stamp collection and his wife's Meissen ware. He and Helen Maxwell had been married sixteen years. They had two children, a boy and a girl, both of whom were away at boarding school.

"It's the first real vacation – long vacation, that is – that we've ever had," John Maxwell said. "Of course, we've been to Europe a few times, and to Florida and Bermuda and Mexico, but never for more than a few weeks. I've been promising myself this trip a long time. I don't want to shoot very much, but I would rather like to go after a buffalo, to see if I'd be as scared as they say. I don't think I'd run. But I don't know."

"Some run, some don't," Paddle said. "Bloke never knows until the situation arises. Whether you run or don't run's got very little to do with your head or your heart. Your legs take over."

"Well, I'd like to find out for myself," Maxwell said. "This is wonderful country, isn't it? So *big*."

"You're in the M.M.B.A., now," Paddle said. "It's what we call Miles and Miles of Bloody Africa. See over the edge of the escarpment there, where she sweeps down? That'll be Narok. We'll stop for petrol and a Coke in the Indian *duka*, and then push on to camp. Dukie sent the lorry and the boys on ahead. We'll camp on the edge of the Loita plains, somewhere close to Majimoto, and see if we can't find you a leopard. Place is stiff with 'em.

It was not quite dark when the little convoy bumped across a plain and entered the green woods that rimmed the river. Juma, the head boy, had the camp nearly erected. Helen Maxwell thought it looked lovely, just like in the movies. The green sleeping tents were up. Even the little green ladies' room tent stood brave in the background. The mess tent, with two sides open to the breezes, was already stacked with provision boxes. A huge fire was burning brightly in the center of an inviting circle of canvas easy chairs. Tantalizing smells were beginning to come from another fire a good distance away, where old Aly, the cook, was fussing around his stove. Juma, dressed in a white *kanzu*, with a red-and-gold bolero jacket over it and a gold-and-white fez on his head, was bustling about the drink table, which looked beautiful with its bottles of whisky, gin, beer and assorted bright-colored fruit squashes.

"*Campi*," Duke said expansively, with a sweep of his arm, as he reined the Rover, bucking, to a halt. "Welcome to your new home, Mem-sahib Maxwell. Now, how about a wash, a spot of painkiller, and some *chakula?* Juma, *bathi!*"

Juma bowed and scuttled off to supervise the preparation of the baths. Dukie gestured at the drink table and Paddle mixed long limes all round. They sat in front of the fire, watching the sunset on the lovely mottled-yellow trunks of the fever trees, glowing rosy on the big boulders that littered the sandy river bed, shining dark red and purple on the distant hills. A small troop of impala, seeming bright gold and long-horned in the evening light, merged with a herd of Thomson's gazelle and a few zebras down by the thin trickle of water. Off in the bush there was a loud grunt, a scream, and a steady panting sound like the noise a crosscut saw makes when it passes through green wood. Dukie nodded knowingly.

"Leopard," he said. "Just belted a baboon. The grunt and the squeal was the baboon. That sawing sound was the leopard."

Helen Maxwell, after washing in the canvas tub, put on heavy pajamas, a robe and mosquito boots, and sat down to a rather magnificent meal, served with flourishes by Juma, Yussuf and Mohammed, the personal boys. She gasped with delight when Juma brought her dessert, which turned out to be crepes suzette.

But Helen Maxwell did not sleep that night. Hyenas ringed 'round the tents and roared, laughed, giggled, grunted, yelled, shouted and wept. The lions roared, no more than half a mile away. The zebras screamed. The birds clamored. The baboons cursed the leopards, and the leopards cursed the baboons. It was a horrible cacophony of unidentifiable sound, and Helen Maxwell shivered under her mosquito netting and wept a little. John Maxwell snored. Helen Maxwell, wife of sixteen years, hated John Maxwell. She hated Africa too, but mostly she hated John Maxwell for snoring while she wept.

The next morning she was still hating him, but not so much, and her temper improved with breakfast and a nap. By lunch she was beginning to enjoy herself, and by dinnertime, after a ride around the animal-cluttered plains, she was beginning to love the safari.

She rode with Dukie in the Rover, and marveled at the skill with which he steered it over rocks, around holes, up mountains and across water. She marveled at his knowledge of natural history, his identification of shrubs, animals, birds, and insects. She marveled at his running shot on a warthog, which he needed for leopard bait. Dukie shot it casually through the head at about two hundred yards.

He chose his leopard tree meticulously, although it seemed to Helen Maxwell to be much the same as any other of a thousand trees. He supervised the building of the brush blind with the assurance of an architect.

"The leopard won't come tonight," he said. "He'll come tomorrow. He'll feed a little then, and more the next night. On the third afternoon he'll have complete confidence in the kill, and we'll clobber him that day."

It was exactly as he said. The cat arrived on the third day at about five in the afternoon. The light was good enough for Helen Maxwell to shoot four or five minutes of color film before the big, beautiful golden cat stirred restlessly and then leaped to a higher, shaded fork, where he stood proudly erect and stared straight into the blind through cold, evil, killer's eyes. Helen thought that the devil would have eyes like that and shivered.

Dukie touched her husband on the arm. John Maxwell, shooting from a steady rest in a forked stick, fired. The bullet knocked the cat off the limb, but it hit the ground running and was away into the bush.

"Too bad," Dukie said. "You hit him, but you hit him too far back. You and the missus can wait in the Rover. I'll take two of the boys and nip into the bush and collect him. Matheke! *Toa* shottygun *na tia* buckshot."

The car boy drove up from where he had been waiting for the sound of the shot.

"*Na piga,*" Dukie said, unsnapping the barrels of the shotgun and checking the loads. "*Kuenda piga ku fa.* Where's the damn blood track?"

"Here, *bwana,*" the gunbearer said. "He went in over here."

"I wounded it," John Maxwell said. "Shouldn't I go in after it too?"

"I'd rather you didn't," Dukie said. "It's perishing thick in that stuff. Generally somebody gets scratched up when the cat comes, because when he comes he comes so fast you can barely see him. I'll have enough to do just looking after the boys and me. You and *mem-sahib* stay here, and I'll haul him out by the tail."

Looking pale and shaken, John Maxwell drank from the water bag and sat in the jeep. His wife sat beside him. Neither said anything. Dukie McGunn, following two gunbearers with the shotgun ready in his hands, plunged into the bush. He had been gone about twenty minutes when they heard the double roar of the shotgun. Ten minutes later he came out, one sleeve ripped to shreds and bloody streaks on his arm. The gunbearers were carrying the leopard, which had very little left in the way of a face.

"Sorry to spoil the trophy," Duke said, handing the shotgun to the car boy. "Blighter came in a hurry and I had to shoot at what I could see. Took a piece off my shoulder, at that. We'll just nip back and slap a little sulfa on the scratches. These animals have filthy claws, due to eating carrion."

John Maxwell looked at the dead leopard and then at his wife and then at Dukie McGunn. He said nothing.

It was the same with the buffalo, only worse. After they'd move off the Loita plains, they went up into the hills of the tsetse-fly area where buffalo hunting was permitted. Quite naturally shaken by a stampede of the enormous beasts, when Maxwell finally shot one he hit it aft, and away it went into the thorn. Dukie went after it and it charged him from behind a bush. He had to shoot its eye out at about six feet. John Maxwell did not speak to his wife, nor did his wife speak to John Maxwell for a day after that.

Helen Maxwell began to invent excuses not to hunt with her husband, even when they were taking pictures of lions. John Maxwell went out with Paddle. Helen went out, when she hunted at all, only with Dukie McGunn.

It was the lion incident that tore it. Dukie had driven up to within ten feet of a pride of lions, feeding on a zebra, and Helen was taking pictures when suddenly one of the lions got hostile and made a pass at the Land Rover, whose top had been jettisoned and whose doors had been taken off. The lion was practically in Helen Maxwell's lap when Dukie slapped it in the face with his hat and veered the jeep at flank speed with his other hand. They stopped later for a drink of water and Helen Maxwell walked deliberately around the car and kissed Dukie Maxwell firmly and completely in the middle of his guard mustache. Dukie nearly fainted.

"I think we'd best get along back to camp," Dukie said nervously. "I must go and see to the whatchamacallit."

"Yes," Helen Maxwell agreed. "By all means." All the way back to camp she stared at Dukie, who remained speechless. . . .

Dukie called Paddle into his tent after dinner.

"We've got to do something," he said. "The old girl's about to go moony on me. They come out from the city and it's all new and strange and glamorous. The husband does nearly everything wrong and looks silly. The professional does everything right, which ain't strange, Paddle, since all we are is outdoor mechanics anyhow. Then the old lady goes a little soft on the hunter, even though she's as nice as this *mem-sahib*, and the hunter gets nervous, and the client gets sorer and sorer. Then he either gets too brave and gets himself killed, trying to impress his wife, or what is more important he gets too brave and gets *you* or *me* killed. In any case, it's no good. We got to think of something, Paddle, because he's a nice type, is old John, and I don't want him to spend the rest of his life apologizing for this trip every time he and Helen have a family fight back home in Kansas, or wherever they live in America. You got any ideas?"

"Not I," said Paddle, cheerfully. "*You* are the senior hunter. I'm only the apprentice. I shall observe the master with the keenest of interest. Cherri-awfully-ho."

"Go to hell," Dukie said, and drank half a glass of water before he discovered it wasn't gin.

For a week the situation grew steadily worse. Shooting tensely now, Maxwell knocked the jaw off a zebra and they had to chase it; and while they did, he missed it half a dozen times and finally broke a hind leg. Helen Maxwell looked at him with great, scornful disgust. Maxwell became extremely taciturn, and the camp, once so jolly over the evening meal and the bright fire, was morose and taut. On several evenings Dukie and Paddle, lying in their tent, could hear the mutter of argument coming from their client's tent.

"It looks," Dukie said quietly, "as if the Bwana Maxwell is going to have a long, tough series of winters, if I know women. Every time he looks cross-eyed at a dressmaker's bill she's going to remind him of their lovely, lovely safari. Well, we've waited long enough. We will apply the drastic treatment. *You*, my lad, will. . . ."

The next morning Mr. McGunn announced that both of the Maxwells must ride with him in his jeep that day, as his assistant had to run over to Narok to see about the delicate state of the lorry's differential.

"I'll stay in camp with the boys," Helen Maxwell said crossly. "There must be at least one book here that I've read only once."

"If you don't mind, ma'am," Dukie replied, "I'd rather you didn't stay here alone. Snakes, you know, and the odd rhino. Safe enough if Paddle's here to keep an eye open, but I'd never forgive myself if a cobra crawled into your tent with me away and nobody here to administer the antivenom.

"We'll drive up past Egelok," Dukie continued. "There's a herd of big buff up there I want to look at. One monster bull, if somebody hasn't shot him."

They were tooling along in the clean, dewy morning when Dukie stopped the jeep and pointed. A big, fat topi bull was dozing under a thorn.

"I wish you'd get out and wallop that antelope," Dukie said to John Maxwell. "We need some camp meat."

Maxwell nodded glumly, accepted the .30-06, stalked up to a bush and shot the big antelope quite precisely through the shoulder.

"Jolly nice shooting, *bwana*," said Mr. McGunn. "Smack on the button. We'll just let the innards out of the chap and stuff him in the back of the Rover and hunt on a bit. I remember some wonderful lions about here. Tame as kittens. Make ruddy fine pictures. Hurry up with that topi, Matheke. I want you to go with me to look for those buff." He turned back to the Maxwells and said, "I'll leave the thirty-oh-six for you people. Loose it off if you need me."

Dukie picked up his heavy double rifle by the barrels and swung off, leaving the Maxwells alone in the jeep. The gunbearer went on ahead of Dukie. The Maxwells looked at each other and said nothing at all. John Maxwell was thinking what a dreadful, horrid bust this safari had turned out to be when he heard his wife scream.

A lion, a huge, big-maned beast, growling, swung heavy-shouldered out of the bush and charged for Dukie McGunn. Dukie let out a banshee screech, dropped the gun, and tore straight to the closest tree, which he scurried up like a leopard in a hurry. The lion swerved and headed in great bounds for the car. To Helen Maxwell, the animal's mouth was a fiery furnace, its head as big as a locomotive. John Maxwell whirled, grabbed the .30-06 and slammed in a shell. He fired just as the lion left the ground in a gigantic leap at the car. The lion dropped like a stone with his vast head a foot or so from Helen Maxwell's in-drawn legs. Helen Maxwell fainted, and John Maxwell's hands were shaking when he fired again in the *coup de grâce*. It took the lion in the forehead.

Dukie shinnied down out of the tree.

"Marvelous shooting, old boy," he said. "And just in the nick of time, too. Most men would have missed him or wounded him, and somebody would certainly have got killed."

Helen Maxwell, deadly pale, had revived. She looked at Dukie with bitter dislike.

"You had your damn nerve leaving us here alone in this zoo," she said. "All that talk about these lions being harmless as kittens! If it hadn't been for John – " She began to weep. Her husband put his arm around her.

"We'll go back to camp," Dukie said, "and I'll come back with the boys and skin him out. He's a little past prime, but a lovely trophy. I'll have to square it with the Game Department though; we're not supposed to shoot them here. And then I reckon we'd best head back to Nairobi as soon as possible.

Dukie left the Maxwells talking animatedly in camp. Helen Maxwell's eyes were warm with admiration for John Maxwell. She looked scornfully at Dukie McGunn, who had run away and climbed a tree in the face of danger.

Dukie drove back to the lion, sprawling dead and rumpled. The lion was thin, mangy, scarred and fly-bitten. One foot was crippled from an old fight. Most of his teeth were gone, and he had a cataract over one eye.

"Poor old boy," Dukie said aloud. "Poor, sad old beggar. Poor old Tiberius. You'll never pose for another picture, but the hyenas would have had you in a couple of weeks anyhow. I certainly felt a skunk when I planted that topi carcass in the back of the jeep, and you came bounding up for your dinner, all full of hope and high purpose." Dukie cupped his hands and yelled: "Okay, Paddle, you can come down now. The city-folk are safe in camp."

"Very nice, my boy," said Mr. McGunn. "Very, very nice timing. For a second I thought Maxwell wasn't going to shoot at all – not that poor old Tiberius here would have hurt them any – but if Friend Maxwell hadn't shot, our little charade would have certainly soured. And we would not, as the saying goes, have been drinking their grog any longer. And the old lady would never have forgiven him *or* me. Or you, for that matter."

"It was nothing at all," said Master Rowbottom. "I had enough gun up that tree to put the quietus on an elephant. It was merely a matter of shooting the poor old blighter in the ear as he jumped. I don't suppose I was more than a hundredth-second behind Maxwell's shot. Poor old Tiberius, coming out for his free lunch and instead he gets clobbered in the head."

Dukie reached into the Rover glove compartment and hauled out a bottle of gin. He took a long swig and handed the bottle to Paddle.

"Son," he said, "when you have been around clients as long as I have, you will have learned to treat them like another kind of wild animal, to put yourself in their place. As long as we had to shoot poor old Tiberius for the warden anyhow, I couldn't see any harm making him play cupid in the process. You know, Paddle, when you've been at this a bit longer, you'll realize that it ain't the buffalo in the bush that collects the hunters. It is women on safari. And I have managed to remain unshot and a bachelor for forty-seven years. See you do the same."

"Yes, sir," Paddle Rowbottom said devoutly. "Every day I learn something new."

"Dukie's Dangerous Deed," *Collier's*, January, 1954.

A Leopard In The Rain

*C*ast month, you'll recall, we chewed over the business of luck and confidence and full-stream effort as all-important factors in hunting and fishing, based on the Old Man's injunction to "Hit 'em where they ain't," à la the late Willie Keeler. I hinted that this homely and inexact axiom applied to big game as well as to North Carolina bobwhite and buck deer in other people's backyards.

You probably have read that leopard shooting is sometimes a matter of luck. There was one classic safari that was out looking for leopard for a dozen years, or some such, and when I first started going to Africa they would guarantee you almost anything else *but* leopard and, of course, the Kenya mountain bongo.

This is not a leopard story. It is a kind of story about mind over matter, and the leopard is incidental. Last November I was briefly out in Kenya on the dreary business of book writing, with no idea of hunting. But the hard work got finished faster than I expected, and all of a sudden I had a ten-day hole in the schedule with nothing much to do; so I conceived the idea of a short safari.

Loud and raucous laughter greeted my idea. The short rains had set in. The Masai was closed. The Northern Frontier was closed. Tanganyika was soaking. You couldn't get over the Aberdare from the Kinangop to the Mount Kenya area. Something else was closed to birds. It was raining in blue sheets in Nairobi, and back roads were closed down toward the coast, Mombasa way.

Then I ran into an amiable Dane named Ken Jespersen, a white hunter who was just back off safari. Ken looked about as sour on the town as I did.

"You want to go on safari?" I asked. "You look pretty browned off and loose-ended."

"Sure," said the good Knut. "But where? You can't even get to Limuru in this rain." Limuru is a suburb. "Everything's closed down tight. We're tucked in for the rains."

"Let's go to the Game Department and see," said I, still stubborn. "Maybe there's *something*."

We went to the Game Department, after consulting with some more of the bored pros who were just coming in for the rainy layoff, and sure enough, there was some unbooked land about five hours' drive from Nairobi on the Kenya-Tanganyika border close to the national park at Amboseli.

"That's a real nice place if we can get there," Ken said. "Let's go."

We rassled up some short-order gear and sent a hopeful telegram to Ken's headman in the little town of Machakos, where he was visiting his wives and goats, and another hopeful message to the long-suffering Metheke, without whom I feel naked in the bush.

We departed Nairobi in the downpour, and as we created a bow wave in the general direction of Machakos it rained more and more and more, until the stubborn determination began to drain off both us. There is only forty miles of blacktop in that direction, after which it is a matter of mud, dust, and hope for the best.

About fifty miles out of Nairobi in the direction of Mount Kilimanjaro there is a little one-street, half-horse town called Sultan Hamud, and it was there we were supposed to collect the safari crew, if any. About fifteen miles away from Sultan Hamud the rain stopped as if it had been chopped off by a giant cleaver. Behind us the sky was purple-solid with rain. Ahead of us the sky was sweetly blue and puffballed with jovial-looking clouds.

Miraculously, the boys were awaiting us at Sultan Hamud. But the face on Mr. Jafferali, who runs the general store, was sadly long. He said it had been raining fit to drown giraffes in our direction and we'd never make it. Truck on top of truck had been mired, he said, and the road was closed by the order of the Road Department, the Game Department, the National Parks, and Ngai himself from his perch on top of Kilimanjaro. So we said goodby tearfully to Mr. Jafferali and went hunting anyhow. Let Mr. Jafferali gloom it up on his own time.

It *had* been raining; there was no doubt. That area can be drier, dustier, and more prolifically tick-bearing than most parts of Kenya. It has largely been neglected as a hunting ground, being only a five-hour easy drive from the center of Nairobi on generally good roads. I don't know why it has been overlooked; it is an open controlled area, listed on the bookings map in the Game Department, and it collects a goodly spillover of animals from Tsavo National Park and Kimania Swamp. Common sense says it has to have lion, leopard, buffalo, and elephant to shoot, plus all the ordinary antelopes and gazelles and birds. Rhino, too, but they're closed to shooting in those parts.

We made the full trip, including a pause for a picnic lunch, in about five hours, and had plenty of time to get the tents up and the camp settled before supper. We slept soundly and arose in the nippy dawn, and there was Kilimanjaro and her sister mountain, Mwenzi, standing out sharp and bright against the blue, practically edging into the mess tent. During the night I'd heard lion and leopard hunting up and down the little river on whose edge we camped. On the way in, animals had flashed ghostily across the track, blinded by the Land-Rover's lights. The place was vibrant with game.

The rains had settled the dust and painted the plain with billiard-table green; the thorn was greening up too, and the air was moist and blossomy like April in England. We rambled slowly out of camp, twisting along easily with the river, and ran into traffic jams of game – tame as only African game can be in the morning on new grass after a long drought.

Herds of golden impala were feeding close to camp. There were clusters of zebra and big coveys of ostriches and armies of guinea fowl. The big, fat, yellow-necked francolin flapped and squawked and scratched in the track, sand grouse carved their jet trails in the skies, and the tall thorn trees erupted big blue pigeons. Lesser kudu bounded across the track, and we saw gerenuk rearing on their hind legs to browse. On the higher plains were regiments of Grant's and Thomson's gazelles and fleets of big, dumb kongoni. Isolated herds of oryx seemed tame, and in the yellow high-grassed swamps you could see the sliding hummocks that were elephant. A cow rhino and her grown calf chased us; convoys of warthog trotted primly along with their antennae proudly high. The air was like hard cider on the high plains, the view superb.

I looked at Jespersen and smirked. Jespersen smirked back. We had blundered into a kind of miracle. It was evidently raining on four sides of us, and most of the country was immobilized. But we were in a momentarily dry oasis, where just enough rain had fallen to make it all sweet and fresh and lovely. We had not come trophy shooting or to run up a record number of kills. We had just wanted to get out into God's good air, and with the help of Ngai and a little stubbornness, we had.

But if we'd wanted to kill extensively we could have shot the ticket. There were elephant every day, and buffalo in the hills, and the place was populous with lion and leopard. We saw rhino constantly.

I was collecting zebra hides for a friend; so we shot some zebra with a little .244 Holland & Holland, which is the most remarkably flat rifle I have ever fired. I am no great shakes as a marksman, but Jespersen pulled the eye out of kongoni at 416 paced yards, aiming with no compensation through a 2 1/2 x 8X Bausch and Lomb scope, and he called the eye. It was the right eye, as a matter of fact.

As usual I went mad over my two weakest spots, birds and leopard. I don't think I ever saw more guinea fowl except possibly in Somalia. For the pot, spur fowl and sand grouse were equally sporty and frequent. And the place was simply stiff with leopard.

We put up three kills and had leopard feeding on all three in a couple of days. I scared two of the cats off two different kills, because they were females, and shot the third one on the last day. There was a fourth leopard – an enormous chap – on one of the other kills, but he made off with a whole impala the day before we left and I hadn't time to wait for him to revisit us. From his claw marks on the tree and his pug marks on the ground, he must have been as big as a lioness.

The day I shot the leopard it rained, the first rain we'd had. It began to clobber up pretty good on all sides of us – time for us to depart. When we pulled the cat out of the dripping bush, Jespersen said: "You know, I was never on a safari when we got a leopard in the rain. I had some idea that they wouldn't come to a bait in the rain. But then," he added thoughtfully, "I have never before hunted with a client who was damn fool enough to sit in a leopard blind in the driving rain."

Over the last dozen years I have been a dozen times to Africa, and have hunted in India, Spain, England, Australia, New Zealand, and the United States. I think I can say in all honesty that I never had a finer hunting trip – if hunting is not to be construed as quantitative collection – then we managed on this bobtailed safari.

We had pulled off a seemingly impossible feat: we had miraculously cheated the weather and come upon a magic circle of sunshine and centrally gathered wildlife that stayed perfect for the time we were there. We had seen thousands of head of game each day, and had stalked up to within patting distance of several groups of elephant. We had shot no trophy but a leopard, and we had scared two away on purpose as unfit. We had eaten well, hobnobbed amiably with the natives, and explored the country. Though we might very well have shot out the license on the permissibles, we didn't. We didn't drink much, an occasional beer or a glass of wine with meals. Every day was a picnic, which is what I think hunting should be – a joyous picnic with a serious basic intent.

It was raining very strongly behind us when we left, and the Masai were bringing their cattle up out of the swamps to graze the high hills. We could see the roads becoming impassable behind us.

But it didn't rain *on* us until after we'd paid off the boys at Sultan Hamud and were hightailing for town on the blacktop. Then we ran into the same purple, pouring skies, and when we landed in Nairobi it was just as miserable and dank and drenched as when we'd left.

"Where've you guys been?" people asked us when we rolled in, sunburned and smug.

"Safari," we said.

"But *where*?" they asked.

"Oh, just outside of town," we said. "It's really quite easy if you know how."

It isn't easy, even if you know how, but Willie Keeler's point about hitting them where they ain't still holds strong in a strange league. If you want it badly enough, and are willing to gamble on it, quite often the Gentleman who sits on the Mountain will stretch down a helpful hand. I will admit it was luck that Jespersen and I found about the only plot of hunting ground where it wasn't raining in Kenya during those ten delightful days, but you'll have to admit that we'd never had known it wasn't raining there if we hadn't launched off into the wild blue improbable.

Of such things are happy endings made, but even the luckiest hunter doesn't find his promised land unless he stirs off his dead fundament to go look for it. You shoot very few leopard in the moving-picture houses and bar-rooms, even in Nairobi, when it's raining.

"A Leopard in the Rain," *Field & Stream*, July, 1961.

Far-Out Safari

*T*he number-one boy, Manolo, was suddenly a whirling, twisting, leaping demon. He was wearing a gray baboon-hide cloak and a pair of bushbuck horns on his head. War rattles clanked on his piston-pounding legs and he flourished a wildebeest-tail fly whisk, embroidered with magic beads. He had clamped a war whistle between his teeth, and occasionally blew piercing blasts. Another chap – the cook, I think – was blowing mightily on a kudu horn. Another – perhaps the room boy? – was dressed in leopardskin and rattles, and was tumbling madly on the ground. Africans of all shapes and sizes were leaping and stamping to as wicked a multiple drumbeat as ever announced the first serving of boiled missionary.

It seems now that I, wearing bare feet and a red *kikoi*, a kind of African sarong, was dancing as well, and the frug had nothing on what I was performing in the way of wiggle and stomp. Now the man with the baboonskin and the rattles and the horns was dusting out the spirits with his whisk, and suddenly I was sitting cross-legged under a female nyalaskin with a small black boy, a token human sacrifice, eating some nauseous mess of mealie meal and guinea fowl, and the wickedly horned gentleman was brushing the evil spirits off *me*.

The chanting grew stronger, the dancers leaped higher, the drums beat louder, the spirits were all about us, and then the head witch doctor bit me on the neck to let the Devil out. I was really not expecting to be gnawed.

Satan now properly exorcised, I continued to sit under the hide with the small boy while the witch doctor rolled the bones, and the dark chorus chanted response to his invocation. The bones were composed of knucklebones of leopard, lion and warthog: crocodile toe bones, tortoise shells, cowrie shells and old coins.

This was *kush-kush*, a kind of Black Mass with which one begins a safari in Portuguese East Africa – a divination of what's to come. They feel very strongly about *kush-kush* out there, and witch doctors do a thriving business, rather like psychiatrists back home.

It appeared from the prognosis that we would see lions, but would not shoot one, because the major lions in the area were the ancestors of one Faif Medica, a poacher-turned-warden, and a considerable *kush-kush* man himself. We would see many buffalos, and would shoot two at once. It was not the rainy season, but heavy rains would fall. We would find honey. We must expect to see many poacher-crippled animals. But we would have enormous success on safari – at first – and then the unseasonable rains would halt us, because the frogs had told the *kush-kush* man so.

Then the *kush-kusher* walloped me over the skull with his whisk and everybody carried me around the room in a thunder of drums, to a tremendous conga lurch, and it was announced that my name was *Baas* Leopard. (I had been chewed up by a leopard two years ago, and my arm was still in a sling when I came to Mozambique the first time.) My hunting partners were Ben Wright, president of *This Week*, and Walker Stone, editor-in-chief of the Scripps-Howard Newspaper Alliance. They thought all this mumbo jumbo mildly amusing.

The first thing Wright shot was a one-eyed warthog. The next victim was a very long-horned greater kudu who had been crippled in a poaching snare. The next was a very sick sable antelope bull, on his last legs from an old arrow wound. All were fine trophies.

Wright shot a buffalo bull, and nailed it with the first bullet. It fell, but appeared to get up, and I checked in with the collaboration bullet, because night was falling and you don't chase wounded Cape buffalos after dark.

Two dead buffalo bulls lay on the ground. Another had come swiftly back and appeared to be the first one getting up and heading for thorn. I had shot the carbon copy.

Stone and Wright shot most of the major trophies in a couple of days, and I hauled in near-record kudu and nyala, as an afterthought. Wright collected an unlikely, accidental leopard, possibly in honor of me and my new name.

After three days the heavens wept and it rained for a solid week. I finally had a word with my gunbearer, Luis, also a *kush-kush* practitioner of repute, and he evidently stopped the rains. The moon filled and the weather was lovely and the shooting was fine. We found the honey, all right; a bee stung me between the eyes and I couldn't see for three days.

Stone wore "lucky beans" in his hat, and didn't get stung. He collected four gallons of honey, and left some for the honey guide, the bird which leads you to the hive. If you don't leave honey for the guide, next time out he leads you to a snake. I believe it.

I do not say that you need the services of a witch doctor and a *kush-kush* ceremony to go hunting in Africa today, but it sure helps.

Like the old gray mare, safari today ain't like she used to be. Today you just can't jump into a Jeep and go whistling off to wallop the nearest inoffensive creative. You may have to travel far, and you have to figure on everything from uncertain weather to politics and outright native warfare. The winds of change, of which Mr. Macmillan and Mr. Macleod spoke so breezily, have switched the whole safari picture in black Africa. In recent years a two-way radio meant communications with town headquarters. In Kenya at least, the possession of a piece of complicated machinery today is apt to get you shot for a spy by some ambitious ward heeler bucking for sergeant. Vast areas close without warning, due to game shortages, flood and native battles; and rules change according to the whim of newly emerged nations. Once-wide-open territories, such as Kenya and Tanganyika, are now operated on the "block system," which means you have to book months in advance, sometimes, and are restricted to your own area. In the Portuguese African countries, Mozambique and Angola, the shooting country is gobbled by concessions, or *coutadas*, under private management. Poaching has drained some portions of Kenya and Tanganyika, and the wardens are empowered arbitrarily to close and open such areas. I know several sections of Masailand which haven't been really shot over in fourteen years, but the poachers have been very busy.

This piece is being written in Mozambique, one of the last strongholds of lush animal life and smiling natives. But my outfitters have had nine recent cancellations. I asked why.

"Every time some bloody wog in the Congo or in Whozitsville rubs out another wog, it makes the papers, and puts the clients off their stroke," my hunter, a profane South African, said. "You've got this bloody madwoman Alice Lenshina with that cult in Rhodesia, killing off people right and left, and you've got the rebels kicking hell out of the army in the Congo. Most of *you people*" – he looked at me with disdain – "potential clients, I mean, think that Africa is about the size of New York. I mean to say, have you ever been murdered on your last three safaris here?"

"Only by the garlic in the food," I murmured. "And by the conversation of your last female client."

But it is very true that the areas are shrinking, as self-determination rears its nationalistic banner. Mozambique, Angola – if you don't run into a massacre – Bechuanaland and a portion of Southern Rhodesia are the best bets. Chad, I'm told, is good, but there are few fancy frills to be had in hunters or equipment, in the classic sense of romantic white hunter, good tentage, a well-filled chop box and evening cocktails in front of the fire. The Congo – forget it. You never know which native is on first base in the government, or who is making war on whom for what. At this writing the battles are brisk.

I used to do safari on horseback, with camels carrying such vital supplies as water and booze to keep your system safe from harmful irritants. Hunting African elephants on horseback is a dicey business, at best, because once in a while you have to get off and haul him up the nearest escarpment. Horses, generally speaking, are no damn good – particularly when an old gentleman rhino boils out of a bush in a testy temper.

The elephant-*cum*-horse-*cum*-camel safari was about as far out as today's plush operation, with the sanitary toilets and the built-in mosquito nets, as a fellow could find. But you can't do that anymore – at least not in Kenya. The Northern Frontier, where the big Jumbos with the big teeth live, is closed to hunting. It is closed because the Somalis, who live in northern Kenya figure that they dwell in an extension of Somalia, and they keep shooting up the locals in the name of lebensraum. You have some trouble on the Ethiopian border, too. A bunch of gay cats called Gelubba can't go courting until they hand the father of the potential bride a set of fresh testicles – somebody else's testicles – to prove that they're worthy to come a-wooing with a flower stuck in the wig. This is discouraging to the innocent bystander who might reckon that a man comes equipped with only one set of crown jewels.

Last time I was in the Northern Frontier (NFD, it's called), I thought I'd got myself mixed up in a TV serial. Everybody was furious at everybody else. The Gelubba were pummeling the Turkana up near Lake Rudolf. The Rendille were pounding the hell out of the Samburu, who, in return, were pounding hell out of the Rendille. The Merus were coming down the hill to steal Somali cattle, and the Somalis were defending themselves with old Arab blunderbusses and tin swords. I personally got involved in a knife fight with a flock of Somali camel jockeys who wanted my water. (The fight ended unspectacularly. My companion, a white hunter, cooled my adversaries with a flashlight. It was a very large flashlight.)

But everywhere in East Africa the air was full of iron.On the Uganda-Kenya border, the Suk and the Karamojong engaged in no less than 260 full-scale battles in a year. The Masai and the Wakamba were filling one another full of poisoned arrows and spears in border cattle rustlings. My own boys, Wakamba, when we were in the Masai, spent all their spare time making bows and arrows and stripping the dead animals of sinew for bowstrings. The best bow wood grows poetically in the Masai country, and the Kamba were arming to kill Masai.

Over the last dozen years, I have been on possibly twenty safaris. That's to say, I've hunted twice in India, once in Alaska, four times in Mozambique, once in Australia, once in New Zealand and about ten times in Uganda, Kenya and Tanganyika. I have shot three elephants of over a hundred pounds per tusk, killed a couple of lions and attended the deaths of a dozen others. I lost count on leopards – maybe twenty – and have no idea about buffaloes; maybe a hundred. The small game – zebra, impala, Thomson's gazelle, Grant's gazelle, wildebeest, gerenuk, oryx, duiker – in general, camp meat, must run into a thousand. I have shot three tigers, been severely mauled by a leopard, shot gaur and water buffalo, cheetah cat and chital deer, wild dogs and hyenas and guinea fowl and sand grouse and bustard and francolin (all white meat, even the legs, a lovely bird, the francolin), and I have had cerebral malaria, infectious mononucleosis and have been poisoned by tsetse flies and maddened by mosquitoes. I have walked a thousand miles, Jeeped a hundred thousand, and have rung up another hundred thousand in light planes on home-made airstrips in deep bush. I have slept in tents, as well as rondawels and native huts, and I have also slept on the ground in the pouring rain. I have eaten elephant, snake and fried grubworms. I have drunk native beer, palm wine and a tasty mixture of blood, milk, cow urine and wood ash.

This is not meant to be construed as personal triumph, but only to lay platform for the statement that two thirds of what you read about safaris, and hear about safaris, is sheer cock and purest bull.

There is a simple formula to successful safari. First, you must have enough money to go first-class. You do not wait until you get to Mozambique or Nairobi to choose your hunter, on the off-chance they will undercut one another in bidding for the job. You do that, and you wind up with some reformed locust-control type, and all he will get you is lost. What you do is ask somebody who has been out before to recommend a reputable firm and an established hunter, or you pick up a sporting magazine and check the safari advertisements. Prices are nearly the same on most safari outfits, and most of the good firms have competent hunters, with steady staffs and stout equipment.

What you want is comfort; not unnecessary hardship, because even on the lushest, plushest safari, there will be discomfort enough. That's to say, you will crawl through bush, walk endless miles, bump interminable on trackless terrain, be scorched by sun, frozen by morning wind, be bitten by every bug ever created, go to the can in the bush, be rained on, be frightened out of your wits, and bored to distraction in the long waits and perpetual dusty journeying.

With all these negatives going against you, what you really don't need is a white hunter who is frightened of game, has no sense of direction, doesn't know the country, can't judge trophy heads, tries to sleep with your girlfriend and has employed a surly gunbearer and a lousy cook. You don't need a white hunter who can't fix anything that happens to a car, a gun or a camera – and believe me, something is always breaking down on safari, whether it's a car ruining its bearings, a scope jumping suddenly out of focus, or a camera with its innards full of sand, water or just plain contrariness.

The white hunter should be most of the things contained in the boy-scout code – kind, courteous, thoughtful, able, inventive, amusing, undrunk, brave and, above all things, competent at running an outfit that will average twelve natives for a small safari, and up to thirty for a big one. His skinners should be able to skin well, so the trophies won't be ruined. The personal boys should have washed everything you drop on the floor twenty minutes after you dropped it. The head boy and his assistant should be immaculate in uniform, body and performance. The gunbearers should be able to bear guns, track and skin – and also keep the guns oiled, the ammo sorted, and the hunting car washed clean of yesterday's blood. The *cho*-boy, the sweeper, should keep the lavatories sanitary, and the boy who fills your shower or canvas bathtub should hold the number of frogs, newts, shrimps, scorpions and baby alligators to a bare minimum.

The tentage, if it's that kind of safari, should be stout and waterproof. If it's like the one I'm on now, the permanent camp dwellings – whitewashed rondawels with peaked straw tops and plaster walls – should be as well tended as a good hotel room. There should be soft toilet paper and Kleenex and a first-class dispensary, as well as the Red Cross box that contains snake-bite treatment and like that. Everybody should have at least two flashlights, as well as pressure lamps, and the first time the hunter says: "We had some last week but we just ran out of it," shoot him. Hunters are nearly always running out of something, including gin and ammunition.

You cannot have too much gin or ammunition. The only thing drier on safari than a dry throat is a dry gun. The best part of safari is to be found at night, sitting around the fire with a drink, telling and listening to a lot of lies, and rehashing the day's heroism. To this aspect of the trip, alcohol is as necessary as firewood. Most good white hunters are rotund with a fund of anecdotes, plus a positive wealth of folk, animal and flora lore. They should be encouraged to talk as well as to drink. Most good ones drink copiously and hold it adequately, and after all, you are paying for the booze. When the hunter stops drinking your gin and eats privately in his tent, you might as well pack it in.

The hunter-client relationship is as ticklish as any I know. The "good" client is a man or woman who comes out to enjoy the trip, and who does not want to kill too much, or to shoot inferior trophies. Quite frequently mild men and mousy women become suddenly blood mad, and want to squeeze the last drop. They rise at three A.M. and await the dawn impatiently, so they can begin the day's murder. They keep lists of what they've shot and what they plan to shoot, down to the last dik-dik on the ticket, and resent any moment of daylight that is not punctuated by rifle blast. The good hunters despise clients of this stripe, as they hate braggarts who do not perform well, as they loathe boasters who run when the buffalo charges or the leopard gets up from his deathbed for one last pass. One gentleman just left here, after shooting everything, including hippo and crocodile, lion, and eland, tiny oribi gazelle and ugly

wildebeest. He left his wife in camp, where she talked all the innocent bystanders into trauma, while he relentlessly milked every
bloody hour from the day. He has shot everything, everywhere, and
is careless of trophy. All he wants is to see death, and go on to
assassinate something else. As he left after a month, he tipped his
hunter a dollar.

A good hunter should never let a client shoot anything that isn't
a superior representative of its species. I have known one – now
delicensed – who would cheerfully allow the shooter to kill anything, regardless of size, horn length, mane, sex or species. He also
slept with his clients' women. Before he was unfrocked for some
peculiar business with illegal elephant shooting, he achieved his
lifelong triumph. He took fifteen women on safari, rewarded one
for shooting a buffalo by bedding her behind an anthill while the
boys carved up the other carcass, and then, later, achieved a reverse
triumph when his wife invaded another lady's tent – just as our
friend's robe fell off while he was embracing the lady. The safari
ended rather suddenly, and so did the marriage.

A tip to the uninitiated has to do with hunting friends, both male
and lady. Under no circumstances should two friends who have only
known each other in cities, professionally or cocktailwise, embark
on a first safari. Competition breeds temper, and the two Toots Shor
buddies are apt to wind up as deadly enemies when one gent's
leopard is bigger and spottier than the other fellow's; one lion shag-
gier, one buffalo wider, one kudu longer. We had a recent example
of two doctors here in Mozambique; they came out arm in arm,
friends to the death. In a few days, when Jack shot something that
Charlie hadn't collected, they quit speaking. Then Charlie knocked
off something that Jack wanted but couldn't find, and suddenly they
requested to hunt out of separate camps. They went off separately,
and will hate each other all their lives because Jack's sable is shorter
or Charlie's nyala is thicker. The only time two men should hunt
together in Africa is when they've had a vast experience in mutual
hunting in Pennsylvania or South Carolina, and even then it's dicey.

As for women: Something strange happens to women under an

African moon. Hemingway wrote it well in *The Short Happy Life of Francis Macomber.* Momma comes out, perfectly contented with Poppa. Poppa is showing off in front of Momma – particularly if Momma is a younger, second or third spouse, or perhaps just a girl-friend that Poppa has fetched to romance under the velvet canopy of African sky, spiced with stars and slashed by a big butter at moon. *Tragedy.*

Poppa's pure hell in the paper-box business, but he starts trying to compete with the outdoor mechanic, the white hunter. The white hunter is usually young, always strong, generally charming and very competent at his work, which is chasing things, tracking things, killing things and fixing things. He is full of wise words and anecdotes.

Momma sees the hunter patch up a busted Land Rover with chewing gum and string. Momma sees the hunter go boldly into the bush after a leopard that Poppa has gutshot. Momma sees Rock Hunter stand spraddled in the face of a charging wounded buffalo because Poppa has also gutshot the bull. Momma sees Poppa run, stumble and fall, then watches Rock Hunter save his life by shoving the barrel of his rifle in the buffalo's eye. Momma sees Poppa red-faced and sweating, falling behind, tripping over the grass withes, complaining about the flies and the bugs, getting his fingers stuck in the rifle, missing what he should hit, hitting what he should miss, like the one cow buffalo in a whole herd of bulls.

Momma forgets that Poppa is very big in the paper-box busi-ness, that he belongs to six clubs, that they have a duplex in New York, a country home in Connecticut, Meissen china, and three cars, including a Cadillac. She just sees this little city man trying to compete with a Rock Hunter type, who does everything well because he's done it all his life. She does not pause to reflect that Rock Hunter would be a bum in the paper-box business, couldn't get into the club, and would be thrown out of Twenty One for being badly dressed. In shorts and bullet loops, under that papaya slice of moon, with hyenas calling, lions roaring, fire bright and Poppa down in the tent with a sprained back, Rock Hunter is purest *romance.*

Whether or not Rock Hunter takes advantage of the lady when she flings herself into his arms and murmurs, "Darling, take me now, whistling thorns and all," Momma will never feel the same about Poppa again. She may not hate Poppa when they get back to The Colony and the paper-box factory and the home in Greenwich, but when Poppa folds her in his flabby embrace she will close her eyes and see Rock Hunter, not Poppa.

What Poppa *should* remember, if he *does* bring Momma, is that Poppa is old enough to be rich enough to afford a safari, and that Poppa doesn't know his rifle from a rhino, and that Poppa shouldn't try to compete with some young yahoo who was breast fed by a lioness and who would be lost in any place that didn't have trees in it. Poppa should walk slow, shoot slow, and let Rock Hunter do the work. In this fashion a certain amount of dignity is maintained, and Momma should be forcefully impressed with the fact that Poppa is not Tarzan, but only Big Daddy from the paper-box circuit, out in Africa to have some fun, not to compete in a rural Olympics with some young Adonis who is all legs and nine-tenths muscle.

We had a rather sad example of this husband diminishment here the other day. Momma was well-preserved thirtyish. Poppa was not-so-well-preserved sixtyish. Poppa was slow to shoot, so Momma would take the gun away from him and do it herself. Momma would also laugh heartily when Poppa missed something, and remark to the world that Poppa was too old for this kind of work. It gave the locals some rather odd ideas about American marital relationships. Once I saw a lady command her husband to *shoot that lion,* which Poppa had shirked three times, or *else*, and this in front of six other people at the mess table. At last count, relations were still strained.

It is quite possible that the Portuguese territories, Mozambique and Angola offer more diversified game than any other areas in Africa. Mozambique will give you about twenty species for a license cost of $107, plus extras for a second head, which can be bought very reasonably on a coupon system. Mozambique will give you elephant, leopard and lion in addition to the three top trophies – sable, kudu and nyala. If you're a pig fancier, they have the best and biggest warthogs I've ever seen, and in great profusion. To me – I'm a pig nut – there is nothing more emotionally stirring than a big pig with fifteen inches of ivory sticking out of each side of his face. The fifty-mile-an-hour chase over log-and-pig-hole-booby-trapped terrain is thrilling, if you can manage to stay inside your doorless Jeep (I got unloaded three times last year). The warthog is *not* ugly. He's beautiful, and the tusks, silver-mounted with bottle opener and corkscrew, make great bar implements, but it's a tough way to furnish a bar. When you've come to a screeching halt you have to dash madly on foot after 300 pounds of armed animal who dearly loves to fight back with the ripping knives he wears in his face.

Angola offers you bigger and fewer sables, smaller and fewer kudus, and has more and better lions and leopards and elephants. In addition, it has roan antelopes, mostly prohibited in Africa, sitatungas, sassabies, and the red lechwes, all exotic, if smaller, antelopes which are hard to come by in most of the other shooting territories. The best source of information on Angola, as well as other African areas, is a book by Robert Lee, called *Safari Today* (The Stackpole Company), which is really a bible on far-out African hunting, if subject to sudden change due to wind and political weather.

Sudan, a practically unshot area, offers bongo, giant eland, Nubian ibex, Mrs. Grey's lechwe, white-eared kob and lelwel hartebeest – all unusual trophies, and mostly peculiar to the area – as well as most of the common stuff. In Bechuanaland, these are giant oryx, the needle-horned prototype of the ancient unicorn, plus the sable-kudu-lion-leopard-elephant axis.

But for my money, the Portuguese possessions – Mozambique and Angola – are streets ahead of any other shooting area. White hunters are a nickel a gross in Kenya. With the exception of a handful, the good ones have left town out of prudence. The remainders are mostly reformed locust-project boys who call themselves hunters. The old warriors such as Hemingway's hero, Phil Percival, are either dead or debilitated. The modern classics had much to do with killing Mau Mau, and the Mau Mau, beginning with the prime minister, Mr. Kenyatta, is *government* these days. So the modern heroes, such as Harry Selby, gave up their homes and took their wives and children away. Selby is hunting out of Bechuanaland, and can still be booked via the firm of Ker and Downey, which is hanging on by its fingernails in Nairobi. (Neither Donald Ker nor Syd Downey takes shooting safaris anymore. The firm is owned by a man named Jack Block, who also runs the Norfolk and New Stanley hotels.)

Currently I am making my fourth safari to Mozambique in a period of two years. It is expensive – $3,500 for three weeks for one client, and $30 a day for a nonshooting companion, plus the usual extras of ammunition, booze, private air transport from either Beira or Lourenco Marques, cigarettes, and suchlike nuisances as tips to the assorted staff and the white hunters. Disregarding air fare from wherever you are, and taxidermy in its final stages, I reckon three weeks in Mozambique will cost you a flat $5,000.

This trip was prepared by the firm of Mozambique Safarilandia, whose anchor man is an Australian who never saw Australia. Wally Johnson was conceived in Australia, born in South Africa, and is a Portuguese resident. Wally is First Hunter, Chief of Camp, and the best hunter and tracker I ever knew. He looks as much like a white hunter as I look like Fred Astaire. Wally is fiftyish, fat, bald, short, red-faced, and his mustache is a blond wisp. His conversation is generously laced with Australian, South African, Zulu, Changaan and kitchen Kafir profanity. But around the fire, after a hard day, when the gin pours, he is a master raconteur, and his narratives are delivered in almost B.B.C. English. Wally is well worth the trip, and also the money. But there are extras, such as young Walter Jr., 23, who is nearly as good a hunter as his father. Walter, Jr., is a literate, practical, well-educated young man who has chosen hunting as a profession over tempting offers as an electrical engineer in Germany and elsewhere. He is strong enough to play fullback for the New York Giants, and has a snub nose and a smile guaranteed to steal any female companion you might bring along. He also shot his first elephant when he was nine.

The major exotic member of Mozambique Safarilandia is a

German named George Dedek, who is also worth the price of admission. George sports a monocle, carries an umbrella and cuts his hair with a comb with scissors in it. George is meticulous; the umbrella wears a bulb that can be used either as an oral spray or an enema. When he goes even for one day into the bush, he carries tent, chair, nylon rope and Zenith radio whose antenna can also be used for a fishing rod. He smokes a Jaeger pipe with a cover on it, and speaks fluent English, German, Changaan, high Coastal Swahili, and French.

The rest of the hunting personnel – there must be about nine, according to the size of my bar bill – is a mixed bag of South African, Rhodesian and Portuguese. Outstanding is a Portuguese nobleman named Manoel Posser de Andrade, whose grandfather was once president of Portugal. Manoel is a pleasant blond chap in his mid-40s, who will tell you with a smile, in purest Oxonion, "I was a gentleman once who could afford to hire safaris. But I resemble my father too closely. Slow horses and fast women have made a white hunter out of me. Whisky helped." Manoel is a fine hunter, a pleasant companion, and a gentleman of the old European tradition from his hat to his rawhide boots.

This particular concession comprises about 36,000 square kilometers. It has everything from elephants to anteaters. Its general face is that of Connecticut in the fall. No bugs, except in the rainy season. Snakes, yes, but not many. The only snake I've seen in four trips was an eighteen-foot python that they brought into camp to play with.

The elephants here are nothing in the tooth department, but on a twin concession on the Limpopo, a day's drive away, there are some quite decent bulls. Last shot was ninety pounds per tusk, which is good even for the old days when the NFD was open in Kenya. But the Limpopo concession is mostly dense bush or ironwood and mopane, the most unpleasant bush I've ever hunted in. It seizes your car, hits it in the chin, wallops it in the stomach, and then rabbit-punches it as you pass, all blows accompanied by horrifying noise. Two hours in mopane and you're ripe for the psychiatrist. But the animals love it.

The country here on the Save river, close by Lake Zenave and only forty-five minutes by air to Beira, the second biggest city, is gorgeously alive with fauna, beautifully bright with flowers, stately with trees, and as noble in its spaciousness as an English deer park. The air is crisp and windy; the nights are cool and the days are never very hot, although the sun is warming after the morning fog lifts.

There are lions and leopards here, in fairly short supply, but they can be obtained by hard work and clever baiting. The Cape buffalo is here in lavish force, and is easily come by. The standard – waterbuck, eland, bushbuck, reedbuck, oribi, wildebeest, zebra, impala, duiker, hartebeest – are almost embarrassingly profuse, and it is not uncommon to see a thousand animals in a day. Fishing is good, and you can also shoot crocodiles and hippos while you wait for the tigerfish to strike.

But the big deal is something almost impossible to encounter these days – the big three. That would be sable, that noble black antelope with the arched stiff-maned neck and the haughty head with the great backsweeping sabered horns. The sable is as big as a horse and ranks as the world's top trophy. Then there is nyala, of the bushbuck family, a most amazing animal as big as a quarter horse, with a white mane up top, bongo-type horns with ivory tips, a white-striped black body and a black undermane, orange legs and almost literally a purple goatee. You could shoot him for camp meat if you were allowed more than one to a customer.

The most spectacular of the trophy animals, although he is not so hard to find as sable, is the greater kudu, which has generally been regarded as the Grail of African hunting. He is grayish brown in hide, which is barred by white stripes. He has a full mane on his underneck, white chevrons on his nose, and white spots on his cheeks. The horns are double-curled, colored like walnut meats and tipped with ivory. He is about the size of a racehorse, with long legs and a fluffy white tail. The record kudu of the world came from here: seventy-two inches around the curves. Shootable is fifty; very good is anything over fifty. The best I've ever shot was just the other day – fifty-six inches – which is notable, and even more notable were the braggadocio-building conditions under which he died. It was very thick mopane-ironwood bush, and all I could see was his neck. I broke that neck with a tiny 100-grain bullet from a pipsqueak gun, a Holland & Holland tailor-made .244, which isn't much bigger than a hopped-up .22.

This rifle, I must say, has changed my entire concept of weaponry. The Kenya boys tend heavily to brutish double rifles and solid bullets. There is actually nothing that can't be killed with a Winchester .375 – and very little that can't be put down permanently with my .244. That's to say, I have killed a forty-one-inch sable with it, and the record here is forty-four inches. The sable was shot at a good 300 yards, and last year I stoned an enormous kudu at about 400 yards with a bullet no bigger than a sharpened point of a pencil. A waterbuck is as big as a mule; I must have killed a score over the last few years with this kickless marvel of machinery. Nyala – here go the braggies again – half a dozen, and the last was twenty-nine inches, almost the local record.

I've shot a bull buffalo, weighing something just under a ton, with my mild marvel. You have to hold tight, but a hit between the eyes or behind the ear, or even behind the shoulder, will induce him to wind that last sad bellow. The old-time white hunter wouldn't go up against a buffalo with anything much less than a .470 double, which throws a bullet as big as a cucumber and kicks like home-cultured gin.

Except for elephant, and possibly rhino, the solid bullet is really part of the buggy-whip age. Winchester's Silvertip, which I think to be the best bullet ever mass-produced, is deadly in the .30-06 and murderous in the .375. You can hear a solid bullet whistle as it passes clean through a buffalo, but the Silvertip, which mushrooms perfectly and penetrates deeply, will knock him over like a bowling strike.

The trouble, I think, about new hunters and their guns is that they've read too many articles by hand-loading gun nuts, seen too much advertising and read too many books by amateur safari hands.

Too many guns, like the legendary cooks, spoil the broth. The ammunition gets mixed up, the weights of the guns change according to caliber, and the shooter never really becomes comfortable with his rifle. In this respect – comfort – a rifle is very much like a woman.

During the time I wore leopard-skin hatbands, carried everything from canteens to scout axes, had an elephant hair bracelet on my wrist and affected tailor-made safari jackets, I owned weapons for all occasions and was pretty lousy with all of them. The .450-400 double balanced differently from the .30-06, which had a different feel from the .375, which was an unlikely neighbor of the .316 (I read about that one, bought it, and can't remember ever hitting anything with it), and the .316 took my mind off the .220 Swift, which is useless for Africa. And when I got around to the varying gauges of shotguns, I was never sure whether I was shooting the .410 or the 20 or the burly 12.

Over the years I have graduated to tennis shoes or desert boots, shorts, a beret or a bandanna to keep my scant hair out of my eyes, any shirt with pockets, no socks, no underwear – underpants gall you during a long day's drive in a Jeep or thirty miles on a horse – and I have chopped my armory down to a minimum.

The little .244 is good enough for anything except elephant and rhino. I keep a battered .375 as an insurance gun for big stuff. I shoot a feather-light 20-gauge shotgun, and that's it. There is a big double somewhere, and I vaguely remember a Hornet or a Swift. God knows what's happened to all the assorted shotguns; most likely I gave them away.

If I had to settle for just one weapon, I'd choose the .375. Put a solid in it, and you can kill an elephant or a rhino. You can also shoot a bird without damaging the carcass, because the bullet goes clean through. With expansible bullets, you can shoot anything else in the animal world and drop it in its tracks.

The most important single aspect of a successful safari anywhere, apart from the presence of client, money, game, gun and hunter, is weather. In any country – apart from New Zealand, and even the Kiwis have better seasons than others – you have to find out when it starts raining and when it stops. The game moves according to rain, and the most pleasant time to hunt is just after the long rains, in May when the roads are passable again. In most hunting country, you can't move from here to there in the rains, because the vehicles are permanently mired, and the game retires to thick bush. Living is miserable, and the trip useless. I once saw a movie company miscalculate rains in Kenya, and the entire cast, including a tame lion, sat around for three months without shooting a foot of film. And when you've got stars drawing pay, technicians drawing pay, and everybody drunk, sore and sick, you make no movie. Even the tame lion had rheumatism, and the extra cost ran into millions. The same applies to safari; nobody ever shot anything worthwhile sitting in a dripping tent.

For certain animals the best time is the tail end of the dry season, when there's no water in the ponds and pools, and animals congregate around the few remaining water holes. The weather is hot and miserable, and the grass burnt black. The country is ugly, but the big boys – elephant, notably – hang around what water's left. And you can catch the cats, as well. They are staying pretty well nailed in order to prey on the antelopes and gazelles, which have to patronize the only crap game in town. For serious hunters – elephant, leopard, buffalo – the last of the long hot summer is ideal. And in India (no, Virginia, there are no tigers in Africa), the hot season is far and away the best.

I have had several odd experiences with weather manipulation. As a pretty good witch doctor – *kush-kush*, *machawi*, *mundumugu*, voodoo, what you please – I once made some Mau Mau-type medicine because it hadn't rained in two years. The ceremony involved a human skull, an arch of thorns, a slain goat and some judiciously sprinkled gunpowder to make the fire flare. I suppose my medicine was stronger than I knew. A tornado came and blew my camp flat, and it rained solidly for two years. I left the country. I had no Luis to lift the spell.

Most first-timers overload themselves with kit. It takes a very horny hoof to hunt in tennis shoes, and a sore-footed hunter can't hunt. The best boot in the world, I think, is the Russell "Bird Shooter," and its nine-inch version is light, waterproof and guaranteed not to chafe, even on its first wearing. It has nonskid soles and also keeps the mosquitoes and tsetse flies off your ankles. All you need is one pair of boots and something light for slopping around camp after the shower's had and the gin pours.

We used to cool our booze in canvas *garibas* or *chaguls* – canvas bags for water and canvas boxes for the hard drink – and allow evaporation to do the work. Now any respectable safari firm has refrigerators, gas or kerosene, for mobile use, and dynamo-fed monsters for the main camp. The outfitter will supply the booze at cost, in Kenya at least, but it's a good idea to give him an early idea of what wines and spirits you think you'll need, and also how many cigarettes you think you'll require.

You can have hunting clothes made overnight by Indian tailors, or buy them off the rack in most African towns of any size. They cost less than the air freight, and you give them to the boys at the end of the safari anyhow. Two suits, jacket and pants, are plenty, because everything is washed, dried and ironed on the day you drop it on the floor or ground sheet.

What people don't generally realize is that Africa can be bitterly cold, in some sections, in some seasons. I always stock a woolly bathrobe – you'll wear that over pajamas around camp at night, after you've bathed – a cashmere sweater and one close-hugging suede windbreaker. The sweater under the windbreaker keeps you warm up top, and I like a couple of pairs of corduroy pants for camp wear or for days when your khaki isn't warm enough in the early morning. In a pinch, you can always use your robe for an overcoat.

Forget the floppy double terai sombrero that the old hunters used to affect. It just blows off in the jeep or is scraped off in the bush. The commando beret keeps my bald spot cool. An English squire cap such as John Huston fancies is as good; a baseball-type billed job is excellent.

Underwear, socks, handkerchiefs – a bare minimum, because

they get washed every day, too. I preach not in the interest of economy, but only because you'll be lugging your gear around in a small tin safari box, and space is precious, whether it's a shooting brake or hired aircraft to tote you over the landscape.

Don't depend on any outfitters to remember bug dope. Most white hunters are salted from years of being bitten, and in the festive hysteria of getting out of town, little things get forgotten. It doesn't happen often, but on one occasion, a couple of white hunters got taken in farewell festivity and actually forgot the *guns*. Another lost a loaded truck, but that was exceptional, too. A small check list helps.

If you're traveling with baggage, keep a firm eye on it. I wound up on safari once wearing a business suit and a Homburg due to some ticketing mix-up which sent my gear to Léopoldville when I was getting off in Beira. I spent the entire month in makeshift clothing, and this was by no means my first safari.

If you send your guns and gear out ahead, ship the stuff at least three months in advance, and demand a cabled affirmation of their arrival. In recent years I have made at least two lifelong friends by lending my weapons because their artillery was tied up in a strike in Mombasa.

Do not discount the light plane, even if it costs a few hundred bucks more. Game areas are often hundreds of miles apart, and it is pound-foolish to waste days eating dust to travel from a sable or kudu area to an elephant area, when you can shoot the ground safari on ahead to bump and rattle and break axles and have flats while you take it easy for a day or so and then arrive at the next airfield in an hour or less. African bush pilots are the best I've seen, and nearly every area has an airstrip. And if it hasn't, your hunter will make one by merely smoothing the anthills, filling in the pig holes, tracing the strip with his Jeep, and lighting a greenwood fire to advise the pilot on the way of the wind.

And don't think you're cheating yourself of an experience by not traveling overland. Most of what you pass through is as dull as Delaware, if you're not actually on a highway, and you'll see more of the country – and the animals – en route by chartered aircraft.

There is one word to the unwary on cameras. You can hunt *or* you can take pictures. But you cannot hunt *and* take pictures, except possibly after the animal's dead. Permanent enmities have begun because somebody snapped a picture just as the rifleman was taking aim, and maneuvering into ideal lens positions is guaranteed to spook any trophy animal. But if you *are* taking pictures and scorn shooting, four cameras are ideal. One should always be full of color, one of black and white. There should be one cine, preferably with a zoom. And as important as any is the new Polaroid, which also shoots color. This is *kush-kush* of a high order, and impresses the native any amount. The locals are always being promised pictures and rarely receive them. To be able to cook up a color print in a minute is very big *mouti,* and often leads to valuable cooperation. It also gives the shooter the pleasure of seeing himself standing on the neck of what he has just belted with his gun. If I were a camera hunter, I'd take *five*, because one is a cinch to go sick on you, from dust or concussion.

In the lens line, any good swiftly detachable telescope for a heavy rifle is useful, for if you wound a dangerous animal and have to follow him into thick bush, a scoped rifle is useless for quick shooting at close range. You simply can't find the animal in it fast enough to keep him off your neck.

For your light rifle, I'd fancy a bolt-on permanent model, as you'll be taking much longer shots at much smaller beasts. The finest I know is the Bausch & Lomb Balvar, which adorns my little .244. It's a variable job, and spins up from 2.5 to 8 power. At its extreme magnification, you get practically twenty-inch-television views of the prey. I once saw white hunter Harry Selby kill a jackal with this gun and this scope at 750 measured yards! Of course, he was holding a touch high . . .

I have not dwelt on the intangible plus of safari, no matter where you take it. There is no computing the wine of morning air, the elephant you track for twenty miles only to find he has just one tusk; the six sable bulls you don't shoot because you hope to see a better one; the roaring of the lions outside camp; the whoops of the hyenas and the scary night sounds you will never identify; the brilliant birds and the daily dramas – a cow buffalo protecting her newly dropped calf from five lions, or a pride of twenty-seven lions tumbling like kittens – elephants making Japanese straw hats for themselves from grass because the sun's too hot; the taste of that first drink after you come bone sore to camp; the feeling of utter peaceful exhaustion after you've showered; the daily rehash and the steep tales of olden times around the campfire; the sleep that needs no pills; and finally, the sweet sadness you feel as you leave, bug-bitten and thorn-scarred, when you think you may never see it all again.

That you have to work out for yourself. But it may explain why I've been coming back at least once a year since I first saw Mount Kenya bare her snaggled tooth to the freshly laundered morning air of green Kenya, and watched the snows grow heavy on Kilimanjaro. There is something of safari – the leopard's snarl and the baboon's curse; the leaping golden impala and the scarlet desert rose; the yellow waxy acacias with their umbrella tops; the great blue lakes and the angry, barren, mountain-strewn deserts of the north – that you will not be able to find on TV or even in church. If you're lucky, you'll find it in yourself.

"Far-Out Safari," *Playboy*, March, 1965.
Editor's Note: This piece was included in the limited edition of Michael McIntosh's book, *Robert Ruark's Africa*, but this is its first appearance in any regular edition of a book.

New Zealand Trout

*I*f a hunter or a fisherman died and went to heaven, he would be likely to view the place disparagingly if he had ever been fortunate enough to visit New Zealand first. There is a deep-blue volcanic lake called Taupo, on North Island, four hours' drive from Wellington, that I believe has everything in it a fisherman never dreamed of before. I was not a chronically afflicted angler when I first went there. I was an addict when I left.

Taupo is huge and icy cold, and is fed from the Stern Mountains by rivers and little streams. It is, I think, unique, since a man can take a rod and fish any way at all, combining what he likes best of both salt- and fresh-water fishing techniques. On this lake it is possible to troll with a spoon, to whip a mountain stream, to fish the outlet of a river, to fly-fish from a moored boat or a launch, or to surf-cast with a fly rod. And the answer is an unbelievable catch of rainbow and brown trout. The records on rainbow and brown, respectively, are over thirty pounds each.

Nobody can buy or lease fishing rights in New Zealand. The Maoris who live around Lake Taupo fish free, since they were there a little ahead of Captain Cook and company. But even a foreigner can skim the cream of fishing for six months for a license of six pounds, New Zealand fashion, or less than $18.

The country's Maori tribesmen are probably the most dedicated fisherfolk in the world. While there, I ran into one old gentleman, a

Maori chieftain, who was eighty years old. I would say that he has not missed more than ten years of his eighty years, allowing for sickness, death and celebration, of flipping flies into the deep pools that form where Waitahanui spills into the lake. It was almost unbelievable to watch, as a pure duffer with a fly rod, but these old boys get heavy-rod surf-casting distance out of a tapered line with a bucktail fly.

I saw here more fishing courtesy than anywhere, ever before. When one of the big rainbows would rise and smack the fly, every fisherman in the path of the working fish immediately reeled in and waited respectfully while the fighting angler wore down his fish. In the time I watched there was never a snarl or a crossed line. And I might mention that anything under six pounds got gently and lovingly released.

This is fishing, of course, for people who do not own cars or boats, and who just wish to pick up the rod and the creel and amble outside town. A man with a little more ambitious budget can sample slightly more exotic fare. The first leg of my watery safari was with Alan Hall, a game ranger, and Jim Storey, the skipper of the *Lady Pat*, a commodious launch that was my home for a couple of days on Taupo.

I wet the first line in a little stream emptying into the Bay of Whakapio, in the northern part of Lake Taupo. It was a sparkling rill that gurgled and chuckled down a sheer volcanic mountain, spilling into unbelievably blue, clear water. At the pool where the stream fed the lake, the pink-sided rainbows and the heavy-bellied browns fought each other for a chance at making an amateur look wonderful. I was averaging about a maximum twenty feet on casts, when I got them out at all without taking a piece of ear along with the fly, but it was enough for the trout. The second cast fetched a six-pound rainbow.

My chaperone Hall and I had accumulated about six rainbows, from six to ten pounds each, when we heard a holler from the *Lady Pat,* moored a couple hundred yards offshore, and observed the skipper, Mr. Storey, having his own difficulties. Jim had merely flipped a fly off the stern sheets of his little yacht, and was engrossed with something that seemed unwilling to come to net.

We paddled back and encouraged Captain Storey verbally, and eventually he hauled about six pounds of the prettiest brownie you ever saw out of the sparking blue depths of Taupo. It was a midget, of course, for the records, but Storey is a considerable cook in his peanut-sized galley, and it was coming on suppertime. The fish got to looking – and smelling – even prettier when Storey took off his captain's hat and approached the skillet.

The thing about the high-mountain lakes of New Zealand is that there isn't any legal time, really, when the fishing's bad. After chow we went night-fishing off Whangamata, and the fish bit. Alan Hall took me out in a dinghy and sort of fiddled around while I let my fly swim behind the little boat, and the fish bit. We got up early the next day and trolled with a plug – and this is murder – because the fish bit. You couldn't make 'em stop biting. We never caught any big ones, because the biggest rainbow was only twelve pounds, and we netted no brownie bigger than ten pounds.

But I wouldn't exactly call it a wasted night. Hall is the strongest little man I know – he's got a nineteen-inch neck from carrying packs over South Island Mountains – and I am not exactly feeble. But less than a dozen fish would have us bowed and bent.

Run-of-the-mill fish on Taupo will average out at about eight pounds and, if my memory's right, the record fish are in the small-whale category. The explanation is simple, and yet it isn't, since they can't marshal any real scientific facts to backstop the suppositions. The rainbows and the brownies were imported, and have thrived, as has everything else that was imported to New Zealand. In the beginning there seems to have been nothing much but birds on the islands – birds and a three-eyed dragon – until the importing started. There was obviously some sort of extra vitamin accumulation, over the centuries, on which the late-arriving fish and the animals thrived.

There are no native animals, for instance, on New Zealand's two big islands, but you will find bigger wapiti than in Wyoming, bigger moose than in Canada, bigger stag than in the Carpathian hills, bigger tahr, bigger chamois, bigger Scottish red deer, bigger axis spotted deer, than in any of their native heaths. Deer, rabbits, opossum – even Canada geese – are accounted a menace, and a bounty is paid you for shooting them. As thrived the fauna, so thrived the fish. Catching a fish is never a problem. Catching *many* fish is never a problem. The only problem is how long you'll have to fish to catch a rainbow of more than twenty-five pounds. It is almost like the deer hunting. I shot three Scottish red deer in an hour and a half, but I saw twenty-seven, and never left the road around the manmade forest – 200 by 50 miles of it – at Kaingaroa. This was literally between fishing forays, because Hall said his freeze-box was lacking meat, and he lives off his guns.

The Wairakei-Rotorua district is literally a paradise set inside paradise. There are a great many steaming thermal springs, and you can snatch a trout out of a brook so cold that it numbs your wrists when you unhook the fish, and then you can walk a rod and drop the trout in a spring so hot that it'll boil him.

The water of Lake Taupo is colder, bluer and clearer than any volcanic lake I ever saw – and this I can promise you, because I took an early-morning plunge and they had to remove me with a boathook from Taupo's icy embrace. It does not react similarly on the trout. They like it cold.

The chief thing about Taupo fishing is that it is so easy and so cheap. The Tourist Department runs a fine hotel in the vicinity of Taupo, and there are many other commercial lodges in the area where an ardent angler can fish himself to death for a couple of bucks a day. Launch hire is cheap, and in two days on the lake a man can kill enough fish to make him ashamed of himself and still stay within the law.

And the laws are loose enough to satisfy even a hog. Angling is illegal only from 11 P.M. to 5 A.M. Minimum lawful size of fish is fourteen inches. Maximum daily bag is eight fish per person. Only artificial flies and lures are allowed. There are a few closed waters, and you're not to have more than one rod assembled. That's about all the restrictions there are.

There are practically no bugs to gnaw you, because one of New Zealand's game-control problems is that there aren't enough biting insects to make the spread of effective game-control diseases such as myxomatosis feasible. The sun is warm in the daytime, and you burn easy in the thin, clear mountain air. But the hot thermal springs all around give you a fine athletic-club refuge from the late chill, and their sulphurous content is supposed to cure everything except chronic orneriness sponsored by an acute hatred of fun.

There is not a lot of night life in New Zealand, because people eat dinner when the sun's still high and go to bed early. It is an outdoor country that does not depend on contrived entertainment to keep the citizens happy and healthy.

But if you like to fish, you can't beat it. You can't beat it for the fish you catch or the people you fish with. And if you don't like the small stuff, like the twenty-pound rainbows, savage in the freezing waters, or the burly browns, you can always fish off the coast and land yourself a marlin bigger than the late Zane Grey's, or pop over to the North Island and shoot some geese, chamois, Asian tahr, moose, boar, elk, stag, or simply fall down and bust your neck in a crevasse if you happen to be ski-happy.

Your footloose correspondent will be heading back to New Zealand shortly, and this time he will be a touch more skillful with a fly rod. The only thing about the trip I plan to change is the incidence of catching myself by the ear, on the hook, and also I don't plan to do any swimming in Lake Taupo. Once was enough, and from now on I'd rather be dirty than frozen.

"New Zealand Trout," *Field & Stream*, July, 1955.

The Tiger Doesn't Stand A Chance

*T*he Royal Bengal tiger is a very canny animal, with a couple of major exceptions. He will pay small attention to game if there are cattle about, because a sambar stag is wary and speedy, and a big gaur, or wild bison, may just get his dander up and tread on the tiger. The chital deer is only a mouthful, and a wild pig isn't even an hors d'oeuvre. So the tiger kills cattle – cattle being construed as either native bullocks or the domesticated buffaloes. If he lives long enough as a cattle lifter, he will become a man-killer, because someday a herdsman will get between the tiger and his prey. Once he's tasted human flesh he is a John Dillinger or a Pretty Boy Floyd in a beautiful double-striped coat. He is almost unkillable as a man-eater, because he will not return to a bait, and very rarely can be beaten by drivers, since he has no fear of man.

The tiger is still the king of the jungle beasts, if you forget the African elephant, and has lost nothing in the way of compact ferocity and cunning. A hundred miles south from the Suphkar area, in Central India, one single tiger has killed more than 150 natives, and is still killing. In another camp, a tiger killed a woman a dozen miles away from where we had a drink. The daily toll on cattle amongst the herds of the Gonds and Baigas – aboriginal agriculturists – is the same as in the days of Kipling. A tiger in the area I shot over was recently seen to kill seven oxen just for fun, and on another occasion, five horses – just for fun. A mature bullock is worth about 150 rupees, or three months' wages for the local. The second, big, fierce-whiskered marauder that I shot had cost one skinny little black aborigine a half-year's income when the tiger clobbered a bull

181

and a buffalo for his morning's sport. But the tiger's taste for easy meals is hurrying his extinction.

Tigers are classed as vermin in Central India of today, and may be shot in any quantities, by day or by night. They may be shot more easily and comfortably than white-tailed deer in Pennsylvania, as witness the fact that I shot three in ten days. And so a new industry has arisen in India – commercial shoots in the lands where viceroys and rajas and maharajas once controlled the royal sport of tiger slaying.

The tiger and the panther have house-cat tendencies, and you will find tigers in areas which might not yield a rabbit. There has been very little shooting in India since before World War II, and the tiger crop is both bumper and bumptious. There were at least thirteen mature tigers feeding in my ten-mile-square shooting block.

It has always been possible for a man with enough money and sufficient political or social connections to organize a tiger hunt, but it was a chancy business, wide open to error. Today any man with sufficient cash may order up a tiger as coolly as he'd buy a rug from a department store. By merely writing a firm called Allwyn Cooper, Ltd., of Nagpur, India, and enclosing a check for half the tariff, an amateur shooter can definitely specify that the playroom fireplace will boast a hand-shot rug. That or your money back.

In terms of modern money, a tiger for the suburban den is not hopelessly expensive. Mr. V. C. Shukla, the director of Allwyn Cooper, charges $1,000 for a ten-day shikar, $1,878 for twenty days, or $2,715 for thirty days. With average luck, a man should shoot two tigers per week. The outfitting firm guarantees one tiger to be shown within shooting distance, which is well under forty yards.

The blanket fee covers food, transportation, servants, hunters, beater, shelter and sundries, from the time you step off the aircraft or train in Nagpur until they shove you aboard your vehicle when you leave. Nagpur is two hours by air from either Calcutta or Bombay. The only extras are liquor, cigarettes and ammunition. You don't even have to bother with your own guns. The firm has double express rifles, shotguns and peashooters on hand. You may tip your personal servants or not, as you wish, and they don't sneer if you don't tip.

A similar deal has recently been inaugurated by Maharaja of Cooch-Behar, at about the same prices, except that Coochie provides pad elephants and social glitter as well. His hunt centers in Assam, another area so populous with tigers that it's difficult to keep them out of the pantry. In Cooch-Behar's shoot, the tigers are collected from elephant back, there being some slight danger of a sprained ankle if you happen to tumble off the elephant.

Taking the tiger the easy way is about as dangerous as going against a rabbit in a Sherman tank. The worst thing that can happen to the shooter is that he'll miss the tiger or wound him. In case of wounding him, a covey of buffaloes are summoned, and the huge, stupid animals plow through the jungle on the tiger's blood spoor, and set up an unholy clamor when the wounded animal is at hand. Tiger's apt to be dead by the time he's found, but if he isn't, somebody, amply bulwarked by the buffaloes, will pop him with a finishing shot.

The mechanics of short-order tigers are quite simple. Your out-fitting firm rents a piece of land, called a "block," from the government. With this rental come the facilities of the government's rest houses, or dak bungalows, plus the incidental services of the game and forest rangers. The local tribes, living in small villages under a *mukia-dom*, or headman, are part of the package. These tribes provide the scouts and the beaters and the baits.

It is only two hours by train from Nagpur to Gondia – after a couple of days of well-tended relaxation in a private house – and then a four-hour drive to where, with luck, you will shoot a tiger the first or second day. Though Central India is dust-dry, there can be a very cold and dry martini waiting in the bearer's hand when he greets you as his new master. Special permission must be obtained for liquor permits, but you can get enough to float a cruiser if you want it.

There is no monkeying with licenses or red tape. The tiniest detail is laid on in advance, from guns to chutney. After Shukla gets you settled down, the camp manager takes over and makes a career of running your life according to your whim. Your whim extends from morning tea to nightcap in the brisk, crisp air, and you exercise your whim with a clap of the hands.

Our first camp looked more like a private home on the grounds of an expensive Westchester country club than a hunting camp in the middle of India's Central Provinces.

A fat white kerosene-fed refrigerator squatted comfortably in the corner of the dak bungalow, contentedly turning out ice cubes, manufacturing ice cream and maintaining a heavy bead on the beer bottles. It looked like a modern idol in the shady interior of the rest house which had been extending hospitality to wayfarers since 1910.

The dak bungalow was a huge house on a hill, a huge house with huge *punkahs* – the human-operated fans – on its ceilings, a broad veranda, big bathrooms, bedrooms and sitting rooms. On the veranda, long, low Indian deck chairs with foot-rests made loafing a distinct pleasure. Tall, straight, evergreen trees, looking something like poplars, formed a cool background for the shocking scarlet blooms of the *samal* trees. A pine forest lent a lovely scent to the dry and gentle breeze, with an occasional whiff of tuberose to sweeten the aromatic pine smell. At one side of the dak bungalow was a badminton court. In front, in a tall proud grove of *sal* trees, you could see a concrete platform for dancing and picnics. On the smooth road in front of the hill cottage, long convoys of bullock-and-buffalo carts took teak logs out to the mills. Somewhere in the wood a peacock uttered his nasal imitation of a human attempt at a catcall. The coloration of the forests and the crispness of the 2500-foot atmosphere more suggested New England in early autumn than the Madhya Pradesh of India in the spring.

This country-club approach to a lovely rug can be very pleasant apart from the hunting. For one thing, the food is excellent. We enjoyed a first and second cook, with excellent personal attendants, *dhobis* – washermen – camp managers, assistant camp managers, and what seemed to be about half the government of Central India dropping in to help. Biram Singh, the government forest officer, and the game ranger gave friendly and helpful advice to the head shikari. The massed eminence of Nagpur throws a party for the newcomers on arrival day, and in my case the Raja Bahadur of Khairagarh gave a pleasant personal lunch. India is beginning to take its American visitors very seriously.

You can eat Indian, American or British. We mixed the three, and a typical meal might have contained a Madrasi curry, cold peacock with salad, and roasted sambar steaks. There was plenty of such humble hunting grub as ham and eggs, there were American soft drinks as well as German beer in the refrigerator, and a man who felt strongly about cereal, orange juice, bananas and cream in the morning had same.

We covered ground with jeeps and Land Rovers, furnished with chauffeur. A box of soft drinks, beer, ice cubes, sandwiches and fruit was regulation equipment. I never touched a gun or any other piece of equipment until I was ready to shoot the gun or drink out of the canteen. When the *memsahib* went along, a couple of bearers carried inflated cushions and a small rubber mattress, so she could be comfortable.

Always the organization was ahead of you. The head shikari – in my case Khan Sahib Jamshed Butt, a Punjabi with a Turkish wrestler's mustache – sends out fleets of local shikaris to look for tiger pug marks or the signs of a natural kill, usually wheeling vultures. They report to him daily. When the tiger is discovered the bait is tied. Baits are living animals – buffalo calves – which are staked out in areas tigers are known to frequent. The animal is left out for the night only. If the tiger kills him, he will seize him and drag him off to a piece of thick jungle, feed on him all night, and lay up beside the carcass until about three p.m. You can tell quite easily when the tiger is on the kill, because the vultures and the carrion kites circle and slide slowly in the sky. When the tiger has left the kill, the birds slant down with a rattling rush of wind through their feathers, to feed on the baron's repast.

The perversity of tigers is such that they will generally ignore a planted bait to go and kill a non-intended animal, thereby providing what is called a "natural" kill. On a natural kill the killer inevitably returns to feed at night, and a man sitting in a tree with a gun and a flashlight can usually collect him before eight P.M. For no known reason, though, a tiger rarely returns to a deliberately staked bait. In any case, when the tiger kills he is generally self-anchored in the area for about twenty-four hours after the act. So he becomes beatable.

Estimating, from the position of the kill, where the tiger is likely to be, about sixty local natives set out to drive him. The beat is the rough shape of a horseshoe, with the open end narrowing to a small funnel. Thirty men plow through the jungle, beating on drums, shouting and whacking the boles of trees with their ax handles, driving the tiger toward the shooter.

The thirty stoppers are the important people in the beat. They are men placed in carefully selected trees, forming a corridor down which the beaters drive the tiger. The corridor narrows at the end. The shooter is at the open end of the funnel. The stopper's function is merely to clap hands when the tiger, routed from his after-dinner nap, starts to move, generally no more than 200 yards ahead of the beaters. If the tiger starts to "go through," a hair-breadth dash through the long lines of the corridors, the stoppers set up a rhythmic handclap and so direct him ahead to the shooter. About the only time you lose a shot at a tiger is when the beaters don't spot a break-through move early, and then fail to arrest it with their patty-caking. We lost one tiger when a holiday hangover dulled the perception of the stoppers. The tiger took off.

You are probably wondering now about the shooter. Well, the shooter is in one of two places. He is either roosting in a tree, on a platform called a *machan*, or, if he can shoot, he is sitting on the ground. If you are frightened of tigers, they will build you a *machan* so high that you need an oxygen mask to live in it. If you are not afraid of tigers, the *machan* may not be more than six to ten feet off the ground, in easy range of an angry tiger's flailing forepaws and three-inch fangs – since a big rooster tiger can jump several times his length, and usually measures from nine to ten feet from tail to tip. The main purpose of the *machan* is to give you a visual field of fire in high grass and brush. Shooting on the ground is actually easier if the underbrush is sparse.

Mostly the tiger will come slowly and carefully, putting his big feet down gently and casing the neighborhood. Where the wind is makes no difference. The tiger has practically no ability to smell. He sees beautifully and he hears fantastically, but he couldn't locate a skunk in a rose garden if he depended on his nose. A few days before this was written, a friend of mine named Charlie Vorm, hunting down the road a piece, shot a mature male tiger three hours after arrival at the shooting block. The tiger walked out of the bush and passed directly under Charlie's *machan*. Charlie pointed his gun straight down and shot him in the back of the neck.

If you're as lucky as I was, you see your first one on the gallop. You could hear the tiger roar when the beaters stirred him from a full-paunched sleep. He was mad. He was real mad. Some butch with a gun he couldn't aim properly had hit the tiger in the hind leg a long time ago, and the tiger is never a fool. He associates ancient hurt with drums and the "*oho-o-o-o-oho-o-o*" the beaters make, and he always knows that there's both hurt and humans at the narrow end of the horn he's supposed to roll out of. This tiger would be maybe fourteen, fifteen years old, according to his splayed pug marks in the powdery soil alongside the place where the wall-eyed, wailing buffalo was staked out as temptation.

You could hear the steady clap-clap of the stoppers as they tried to keep His Evil Highness, Shere Khan, on the straight and unpleasant path to overdue extinction. Then you saw the sudden tawny flash, heard the murderous growl again, and a broad golden arrow, barred in black, as big as a horse and as powerful as a rocket, tore straight at you. His head was old and scarred and bearded and evil and full of fangs. His ruff stood off from his face like spikes. He was making twenty feet with his jumps. He was a tough old he-tiger in a hurry.

I threw the gun to my face and followed the huge cat through the tawny bush that hid his hide, and then I laid a big .470 slug into his shoulder at the top of a leap. You had to lead him like a duck, because he would be going that fast. You could hear the bullet hit, and see the shocking impact.

The tiger crashed like a plane in sharply arrested flight. He spun on his tail and the other barrel of the big double rifle tenderized him. How you shot or where you shot, you never really know, except that if you've done it very much, you always concentrate on a pin-point target area with heart and bone as your object.

Now he was done and dead in the long yellow grasses, but then he wasn't dead, and he roared and started to go away, although he was already heart-shot and spine-busted and shoulder-smashed. It took that extra knock for the neck, and there was your first tiger, dead and as broad across the rump as a zebra, his legs spraddled frogwise and even his tail looking as big as a telephone pole.

Elapsed time: forty-five minutes from door of dak bungalow to tiger to door of dak bungalow.

Of course, I sat up fruitless hours after others, and wasted a lot of time on panthers and bears and similar truck, and was allowed to shoot from the ground – a compliment – and suffered after other game. But it you just want to shoot a tiger, you don't even have to be able to shoot. Your shikari will shoot it for you. The rest of the day you can spend reading, sleeping, working or getting quietly squiffled – a pastime which is not unknown on these expeditions.

The Indian shikari has very few of the skills which make African hunting so exciting, even if you don't shoot. It is nearly impossible really to hunt a tiger, as, say, one hunts elephant or rhino or leopard or Cape buffalo in Kenya. You can't really track him, and he won't play in the open spaces, so, unless you bait him or drive him, you just don't get him. Maybe old Jim Corbett and some of his contemporaries could tackle the tiger on his own ground and track him to his lair. I don't know anybody in India today who can collect Shere Khan unless he's baited and shot from a pit or a *machan*, or driven and shot from elephants, or driven and shot in an organized beat. The supreme thrill, I think, is to take him in a beat, from the ground, with no blind, so that the tiger boils out with a horrid yowl, and there you are, all alone with the tiger. I have never included myself in the category of compulsively brave people, like bullfighters, and so can say that when a tiger whips through the bushes, making more noise than any lion, he is the most impressive sight I ever saw.

Nor is the evening expedition unfraught with tension. You go just at dusk to the jungle and situate yourself in a tree. To get to that tree you must walk maybe a mile in the dark, living jungle, stumbling and falling, and wondering if any cobras heard the word lately that a new sucker was about. When you're in the tree, you can't talk, smoke, drink, think or even breathe very loudly. You wait; you listen.

A jungle at night is compounded of all the noises destined to convince you that when you die you will proceed straight to hell. All the bad things you ever did come home to haunt you. You were never before so conscious of noises. A sambar's belling sounds like a railroad gun going off. I heard a tree fall one night and the H-bomb was quiet by comparison. The things that go quietly "clonk" frighten you, and even the dusky conversation of a raven has more variation than a ventriloquist's repertoire. The bellbirds and the peacocks and the barking deer and the locusts and the crickets turn the night into a kind of Doré version of hell. The leopards help, and so do the monkeys.

But when the tiger comes there is no noise until he passes. He comes in a way the devil would come. Sneakily, quietly and with evil intent. If it's moony, you can see the slip of his shadow, crossing the barest patch of open ground. If it isn't moonlit, you just don't see him at all. You only know he's there because he's ripping, tearing, pulling at the prone beast he killed yesterday or early today. The first ten minutes of making him happy and content on his kill, I believe, is the tensest time in a hunter's life.

You must sit, unbreathing, while he familiarizes himself with his dinner. Then you must sneak your gun into shooting position. Then you must, quietly, carefully, noiselessly, adjust your light. And then you must wait some more until the old demon below is so firmly stuck into his food that a rocket wouldn't bother him. Then you slip the catch on the light and you hope to shoot him almost simultaneously as he glares upward into the sudden stream of man-made moonlight. It's no good shooting him except fatally, because nobody ever had a second shot at a wounded tiger at night if the tiger was hale enough to move his legs.

Every hunter has his one, big shameful mistake, and I made mine on the tiger at night. It was very possibly the biggest and oldest tiger in the neighborhood, to judge from his pug marks. And when I saw him in the tongue of light, later, he seemed bigger than the last, which was within an inch of the record for those parts.

I did everything fine on this beast. I gave him the ten minutes to feed. I walloped him carefully through the neck. He melted like snow in the spring. He never even moved his head off the rump of the animal on which he was feeding.

"That's enough, sahib," said Mr. Khan Sahib Jamshed Butt, Gentleman Shikari. "Don't shoot again."

Khan Sahib is fifty-two. He has accompanied the death of 400 tigers, and has shot 153 alone. This was the first time Khan Sahib Jamshed Butt ever violated the inviolable rule of bestowing the finisher even if the beast is finished. Over a period of years I have hunted everything from Cape buffaloes to African elephants, and never failed to kick in the extra pop as precaution when dealing with dangerous game.

But two Stateside friends were waiting in easy earshot. We already had two tigers, a gaur, a couple of sambar, a chital, some pigs and other things in the bag. We were very big and very brave and very proud, because The Presence, meaning me, had been shooting everything through the neck vertebrae. We were swanking it up. Khan Sahib and I gave and received congratulations and smoked a couple of cigarettes. We could hear the boys coming to collect the tiger and help us down out of the tree.

So there was a blood-curdling growl below us, some fifteen minutes later, and we flipped the light on the dead tiger just in time to see the dead tiger's tail disappear into the high yellow grasses. We knew he had to be dead within a hundred yards. He wasn't. We spoored him two days. He quit bleeding inside of half a mile, which told a simple tale. In aiming for the neck, I had merely creased his spine and stunned him. The bullet had gone through without expanding or breaking bone, and the tiger actually was no more hurt than if somebody had shoved a hatpin through the fleshy part of his neck, but close enough to touch the spinal nerve and still him momentarily. Neither Khan Sahib nor I will ever get over this one that got away – and the only reason I tell it is that when I arrived in Kenya a little later, the story had already preceded me as a source of shame.

There was no real reason to grieve, because the two earlier fine he-cats were already in the pickling solution. Messrs. Jack Roach of Houston, and Charlie Vorm of Indiana, had theirs, as had everybody else who had visited the area. And there were still rampaging tigers to spare. Khan Sahib and I proceeded profanely back to camp, where Vorm, Roach and mamma were waiting for the hero's return. They were dressed in a style which might have admitted them to the 21 Club.

"There's been a panther rustling around the back door," the lady said. "I suppose you missed the tiger. You only shot once."

"That's right," I said. "I only shot once. Comes of hunting in a damn suburb."

"The Tiger Doesn't Stand a Chance," *Saturday Evening Post*, October 30, 1954.

My Last Safari

*T*his was a very important trip for me. Although I didn't know it at the time, this was my last safari – in Kenya, anyhow, which to me was second home. In a very short time a certain amount of emerging-African-nationalist displeasure with my work would make me a "prohibited immigrant." I was having my last real look at the land I loved most.

The weather of the country was topsy turvied. It affected even the birds. There had always been birds at Maji Moto in the Masai country. Now there were no birds at Maji Moto. The extensive floods had wrecked their laying cycle or rotted their feed or something. And the elephant were acting most peculiarly, too, way up here on the Northern Frontier.

After the long rains, I had seen the elephant at Ngornit and on the plains well outside Illaut making Japanese hats for themselves out of bales of hay. It is quite a staggering sight to watch a herd of a couple of hundred African elephant scything great swatches of high grass with their trunks and clapping the hay on their heads to fend off the smiting sun, tugging and pulling at the straw bonnets like women primping in front of a mirror. Elephant, more than any of the other African animals, held a special fascination for me. This was the first time I had seen the haberdashery operation. The explanation finally was simple, because an elephant is a mysterious but intensely practical beast.

Mostly, elephant will come daily out of the dry riverbeds, where the water lurks below the surface of the sand, to forage on the plains, returning to the palm-shaded *lugas* when the heat of midday becomes unbearable. Contrary to general belief, an elephant's skin is

193

quite sensitive to irritation. A fairly common sight is to see a whole congregation of Jumbos tearing off branches, clasping them in the fists of their trunks and swishing the leafy limbs over their shoulder and backs to drive off the flies. When the bugs are really very bad, and surface water is available, they will coat themselves completely with mud.

But it is a long walk to water – sometimes elephant have to graze an area of as much as 100 miles out from certain water, since they carry a reserve tank in their oddly constructed stomachs. Occasionally after rains a yellow, gourdish sort of fruit the size of a squash, with blunt spikes, grows on rambling green vines over the high, lava-rocked plateaus of the Northern Kenya country. The pulpy gourds contain enough moisture to satisfy both food and thirst. So these Jumbos were merely saving wear and tear on their feet. The yellow gourds were providing the water: all the elephant had to solve was the sun. They solved the sun by making hats. Simple, when you think of it simply.

I had been fascinated for weeks, sitting on a high blue hill in the Samburu country, with powerful telescopes mounted on tripods, scanning the countryside and looking for a big bull with bigger tusks than any I'd ever shot before.

I had heard that elephant breed only at night. That isn't so. We saw several instances of breeding in broad daylight, with the bull mounting the cow in the approved barnyard fashion. We saw the tiny calves nursing, butting at their mothers. We also saw a whole fleet of the big beasts sitting on their backsides in order to slide down a steep hill.

We saw an elephant kindergarten, which is not too rare: one old dry cow baby-sitting a whole flock of youngsters of assorted sizes and whacking them irritably with her trunk when the play got too boisterous. We saw, as well, an elephant christening (this for the first time) in which the proud papa stands astride the new heir, shaking hands trunkwise with all the uncles and aunts and god-parents and family friends, accepting congratulations freely and all but handing out cigars. There is much milling about and trumpeting, and the father stands athwart the body of his new baby for the most practical of reasons: He doesn't want Junior to get stomped by old Uncle Henry, who might be a little high on palm toddy.

I knew that elephant talked with each other, using a gentle prodding of trunks for emphasis and having a real conversation with a gurgling noise that is commonly mistaken for belly-rumble. I knew that they would return sometimes to a dead relative and cover his body with brush, all the while screeching the heavens down, and that they would do the same thing when they killed a person. I had seen elephant walking along the bottom of a river, using their uptilted trunks as snorkels. And I had heard about this radar-communication business. But I hadn't seen it until now.

For two weeks we sat on hills and watched maybe 1,500 elephant, covering a space of perhaps fifty miles from horizon to horizon. We saw the same beasts again and again – the one-tusker young bull, the cow with the crooked teeth, the same biggish bulls of perhaps eighty-five to ninety pounds per tusk. They slid like great black slugs through the tall, yellowed grasses. There was no major exodus or ingress of elephant for those two weeks.

But one day a signal spread from Illaut to Ngornit. How it spread no man can say, because some elephant were as much as fifty miles from the others. But spread it did, and we had the unusual sight of seeing a mass logistical movement that would have shamed a crack army corps. Companies were formed, and within the companies, platoons. Sergeants fell out to march beside the squads, dropping back to whack a laggard across the backside with a trunk, used now like a baton. The columns merged and fell into route step, with the sergeants – old cows – cursing and batting at the irregulars in the ranks and the older bulls forming companies on their own, to one side and usually ahead of the procession.

One day we had 1,500 elephants to watch. The next day we had nothing but fast-drying pyramids of droppings, deep footprints and pushed-over trees to indicate that there had ever been an elephant in the area. Don't ask me how the signal was made; Harry Selby, a white hunter who has studied elephant all is life, doesn't know either. And this was the first time Harry had ever seen elephant making straw hats.

Until recently no white man had ever hunted this Samburu country, which lies in northwestern Kenya with Mount Marsabit to the east and Lake Rudolf and Ol Kalou westering ahead.

The hunting blocks of the Samburu had just been opened – and opened only to foot, horse and camel safaris. The old ivory killers had never favored it; it was too tough a country to make it worth the foot-slogging pain. Your Karamojo Bells and similar freebooters pillaged the Lado Enclave or the outer lips of the Congo. That is soft country there, and easy to get the ivory out of. This Samburu was sheer murder, a vast wasteland of dry riverbeds and carelessly strewn mountains, as if God had got tired of packing and thrown away His excess baggage. This was the land of the migrant graziers – the Samburu, a Masai tribal off-shoot which wandered north when the classic Masai were English-colonial, shifted south from the Laikipia plains of Central Kenya and resettled in the land that bears their name now. These were the people whose god sat on Mount Kenya – these were the people who spoke names like Ololokwe and Serarua and Seralippi and who frequently crossed a big, brown, twisty river named Uaso Nyero. These people know the lean, mane-less desert lion and the rangy, hungry leopard. These people counted their wealth in the only kind of riches worth having in that country – spotted Boran cattle, high-humped and durable, and tawny camels untold – the only wealth that carries itself.

The Samburu are lovely people – Nilotic, Hamitic in origin, with carved hawk noses and gorgeous bodies. The men are more beautiful than the women, but they would sling a spear clean through you if you accused them of being effeminate just because they hold hands when they walk, paint their faces in thick red ocher and spend more time on their hairdos than the average affluent female New Yorker. They are happy people, robust on a diet of blood and milk curdled by wood ash and cow urine. They are unemerged. The uplifters would not know where to start with them because they want nothing they do not own – space which includes blurred blue hills and angry red mountains and wicked flood-slashed riverbeds, and the odd "Somali canary," the fawn-colored, striped-spined donkey, to carry their meager pots and the hides with which they roof their little wickiups of mud and cow dung and wattle ribs.

In years before, I had been close to this part of the country – by car around its edges, and over it in planes. But this was the first time that what had been called "national parks" had been open to hunting. I'd known that the place was going to be legalized for hunting as part of a scheme to plow back some license money to the local tribes – a scheme to attempt to educate the African in game conservation.

So now I was here, one of the first white men to hunt legally in this area since God made the earth. The impact was shocking: Every time I did something even as simple as disappearing behind a bush, it was the first time it had ever been done by an *auslander.* Each thornbush and scrubby tree was as much mine as if I were Adam; each elephant, each rhino, my own personal pet. The enormity staggered me.

So did the horses. I am not afraid of elephant, rhino or lion, but horses frighten me, and all of a sudden I had to hunt wild elephant on horseback; dodge unsophisticated rhino on horseback.

We had moved from a camp on a dry riverbed called Keno, moving the whole safari afoot, ahorse and acamel fifteen miles away to another dry riverbed called Ireri. We rode our steeds over the baked ground in the smiting heat – with me looking picturesque as all hell in an Arab rag head dress – and made camp on the snow-white sand of Ireri. The *luga* – dry riverbed – was very narrow, and the bush alongside it was very sinisterly black and thick. The camels trudged placidly along with their shock-absorber ankles squishing up and down and our noble nags managed almost to keep up with the parade. A dozen of our African safari hands walked, while two white hunters rode these scraggly ponies.

It happened as swiftly as this – snap! There was a trumpeting screech, and where there had been only horses and men there was now a charging elephant, boiling full ahead from some greenery no more than twenty-five yards from our thoroughfare. Rather fortunately the elephant went for the pedestrian natives, who managed to scramble straight up the sheer wall of an escarpment almost as swiftly as we got off the horses and dragged them up the other side of the mountain. By the time the screaming elephant had lost a close view of the three Africans, the other visitors had made it up the hill on foot with the gee-gees reluctantly in tow. One thing I learned about horses on this trip is that a horse isn't worth a damn in an emergency. You have to carry *him*.

The noisy elephant had disappeared in dense bush, and it looked like an elephant who might have a couple of unannounced relatives. We went all the way up to the top of the frowning scarp and swept the bush with glasses. Before long a double dozen elephant appeared like brown anthills in the redundant verdure. And they were mostly cows with tiny calves – as close a synonym for suicide as anything I ever met in narrow corners. We spent the best part of the day on that mountain. Game Department restrictions allow only one elephant license for the entire party in the Samburu area, and it appeared to all of us that a testy sort named Rodney Elliot, warden for the out-flung miles, would take unkindly to the idea that a dozen or more elephant had been slain in self-defense.

We had threshed the area relentlessly for weeks – Keno, Ireri, Ngornit – and now we were fine-combing Illaut. When Illaut was finished we were finished.

So when a streakily daubed Samburu warrior sauntered into camp with news of two enormous bull elephants still at the water at Illaut we struck the camp at Ngornit and whistled up the camels, which complained noisily and bitterly as usual. The Somali ponies just looked dispirited. We merely looked skeptical. Most native game reports are useless.

But there *was* an elephant in the area of Illaut – not two, not ninety, but one. He was a bull, and he was old, very old. His big fresh tracks were corrugated by age, and you could tell by the concentration of his waste that he foraged close by the scanty water in the blinding white sands of the *luga*.

So there was this elephant at Illaut, and Selby and I were drinking coffee in our tentless camp in the middle of the *luga* when Areng, the plum-black Turkana horse wrangler, marched up to the table pushing a scared ten-year-old Samburu-Rendille girl ahead of him.

"This *ndito*, this maiden, says she was off looking for strayed goats this morning, and she was charged by a very big elephant with very big teeth," said our one-eyed horse-wrangling genius, Areng. "It sounds like the bull of the local loose talk and of the big footprints."

Selby and I grunted. The longer one lives in Africa, the more one grunts. One grunts or one coos or one changes his voice from bass to falsetto to denote shadings of assent, dissent or skepticism – enthusiasm, despair, disbelief. We grunted skeptically. But you always run out your hits in Africa.

We jogged the nags to a little hill and climbed it just as the sun began to paint the stern blue mountains and the sere brown stretch of the scorched wasteland. Selby and Metheke had the glasses and they began to search the terrain.

Metheke is a Wakamba gunbearer, and I have hunted with him for a dozen years. He is possibly the keenest sportsman I know, and above all he respects big elephants with big teeth. They scoured the land with the glasses, and suddenly both Africans – white Selby, black Metheke – began to coo.

They turned, beaming, twinlike despite the disparity of race and color, merged soulfully in true hunters' delight. They handed me the binoculars and pointed. Something filled the binoculars, and suddenly I began to coo too.

"Ah-ah-ah-ah-ah-ah-ah-*eee*!" I crooned, and almost fell off the boulder on which, apelike, I was perched in the crisp breeze of an early Kenya morning. Then we all slid down the hill and kicked the horses into a trot.

The old man was terribly, awfully old. He had lived too long – much too long. Quite possibly he had seen more than one century switch – the 18th change over to the 19th, the 19th to the 20th. Nobody will ever know accurately just how long a wild elephant lives. In zoos his life-length is an average man's three-score-and-ten span. Twenty-one to grow up. Twenty-one to fight and breed. Twenty-one to teach his wisdom to the young bulls, and ten or twenty more to brood and die. In Africa you would have to follow him on his many thousand miles of aimless meandering from Ethiopia to Rhodesia to check him, to watch him grow huge and fight and breed and finally become outcast, and you would still never know if it was the same elephant if you had a hundred years to follow his plod. From the look of him, our old gentleman was at least 150 years old.

For many, many years he had been prison-pent. He had lived on this dry river luga named Illaut. As long as the oldest native around the waterhole could remember, he had lived near Illaut. He came to drink daily at the waterhole a few hundred yards away from the only crap game in town – the one-room Somali general store, called *dukah* in East Africa. He was so far gone in ignobility that he no longer minded drinking with goats and donkeys. He did not even try to murder people anymore, because people and goats and sheep were really all he had to associate with.

The old bull was decades past his last breeding. He was long exiled from the world of other elephants. Likely one of his own sons had kicked him out. In any case, his memory of women and palm toddy was dim and possibly exaggerated. The young bulls no longer came to him for counsel, although his accumulated wisdom was vast. He had long since run through his repertoire of jokes and no longer found listeners for the chest-rumbling, trunk-probing, nostalgic tales of the good old days before the white man came with guns – the quiet days before the iron birds ripped the heavens apart with rude noises on their way to Ethopia. Somehow the skies had been bluer in those days, and you could count on the seasons. Now the weather, like everything else, had gone bloody well mad. Three straight years of drought, for instance – and then it rained until it fair washed the country away, the Tana pouring red with eroded earth as it swept Kenya's lifeblood forty miles out into the Indian Ocean.

He was more than a little deaf, of course, and certainly his eyesight was clouded by the years. His great ears, which once clapped like giant hands as he shook them irritably at the little hold-me-close flies or smacked thunderously against his head in harsh anger as he lofted his trunk and screamed in a charge, now hung in pathetic tatters; now his ears swung limp and shredded, and flapped only feebly as he waved them. Over his entire back a green mossy excrescence had grown. He was as barnacled as an old turtle or an ancient saltwater piling. He was wrinkled excessively, and perhaps he had lost three tons of weight from his original seven. He carried his tusks awkwardly as if they were too ponderous for his head, too heavy to tote in comfort now that all the counterbalancing weight had left his behind. How he'd reached this great age without breaking one or both tusks in this harsh, stone-studded country, with the full thirty years of routine fights, was one of God's mysteries. But there they were, great ivory parentheses stretching low and out and upward from his pendulous nether lip. Age had made him visually ridiculous; he wore a warrior's heavy weapons on his front end, and no single hair survived on his obscenely naked tail.

There would be curious growths in his belly that old elephants frequently have, like the hair balls one finds in the stomach of a crocodile or big catfish. Ants would have trammeled the length of his trunk; certainly his feet would be cracked and wincing on the lava rocks of his self-imposed prison. You could tell this from the ridged tracks of his pad marks that covered ten miles of country outside the water area. Old gentlemen's feet always hurt, and the pain is apt to make the owner tempery.

He swayed from side to side now and grumbled to himself, as old men will, and the burden of his complaint rode clear on the wind as we walked close – carelessly close – leaving the Somali ponies tethered to a thorn tree. The old bull had been a flashy traveling man in his time – all the way from the high blue hills of Ethiopia through Tanganyika and then into the Rhodesias, traversing the miles and miles of bloody Africa as he followed the dom palms whose red nuts he adored – as he occasionally ravished a maize field, as he whimsically butted over a railway train or upended a water tank or, just for the hell of it, swung his trunk like a rubbery scythe to wreck a native village. Cows had touched him tentatively with their trunks in girlish admiration; he had smelled the blood of a close cousin as he took out his tusks from a gut-spilling belly. Sycophants had swarmed around him – young *askaris* eager for the knowledge he had amply to give; stooges to fetch and carry and always to heed his wit and wisdom.

But now he was very much all alone, chained by necessity to the creaking rocking chair of the limitations of old age. All the cows and calves and younger bulls were long gone. They had tolerated his presence in the area, even though he had become a bore with his stories of old slave caravans and regiments of spear-hunters. The country had played out. It had rained again on the other side of the mountain and everybody has whistled off, following the fresh green that thrust upward under the rim of the escarpment. Everybody had gone but the old bull. He was too feeble to trek with them. His head was heavy, and his feet hurt.

Now he stood sadly alone, because he could not leave certain water for an uncertain excursion for food. And he was starving himself, because he had eaten the country clear. But he would not travel the usual two-day, 200-mile grazing distance of a younger bull. He had grazed his land rock-hard, and his tracks were imprinted atop each other. His dung abraded on itself in piles and was scattered by the passage of his own feet. He had made tracks enough for 200 elephant, and they were all his own.

Soon he would die. Unless the rains came almost immediately to green his prison yards, he would die of senile decay and the lack of nourishment – and, most of all, of purest boredom. The boredom was the worst of all the ills, and he would be glad to see the finish of it all.

There he stood now, pathetically magnificent on the slope of a sere brown rise, with the morning sun red behind him. There he stood against a cruel blue hill, his enormous curving tusks a monument to himself and to the Africa that was – the Africa that had changed, was changing, would forevermore change until nothing beloved of it was left.

"Poor old beggar," the white hunter Selby said. "Poor, poor old boy."

We had come there to shoot an elephant in an untouched, savage land, a land unmarked by tires, unseen by tourists. I did not weep when I shot the old bull twice through the heart and he crumpled to his creaking knees. In retrospect, yes, of course I would weep – but only as a respectful gesture to another age. When the old bull fell with a mighty crash, much of what I loved best of the old Africa died with him.

Now he lay stiff-legged in the bright morning sun, his age-blackened tusks looming huge in his oddly small dead face. Quite soon the chief skinner, wizened old Katunga, who is as ancient a man as the bull was an elephant, would come with his assistants carefully to hack the great teeth from the sunken old head.

Katunga would croon "Eeeeeech" in ecstatic, piping falsetto when he saw them and would take exta care in drawing them from the skull. For Katunga it may have been his thousandth, perhaps his two-thousandth, elephant, for he is older than Philip Percival, to whom he first came as 'prentice when both were boys in Africa, and Philip was nudging hard now on his eighties. Katunga was along when Philip took Hemingway on his first safari many, many, years ago.

Katunga would be careful, because he knows that elephantine immortality dwells in the tusks and that the tusks are paper-thin inside the head, where the nerve cavity extends from head through tooth. A clumsy blow with the ax can shatter that delicate ivory, and one tusk was already split, for the old bull had fallen with an enormous crash. It split because it was soft and old and full of grainy fissures which had widened as age had dried the ivory.

Katunga would be very careful, because when he died, and his Wakamba family tossed him out to the hyenas, he would not want someone to split the tusks of his memory as the best skinner in the world – the best skinner, the best lover, the best drinker, the best talker and, in his bandy-legged way, the best man *he* ever met. At 80 Katunga still ran ahead of a camel caravan, singing: he finished a twenty-mile walk in the smiting sun at a gallop and jeered at his younger colleagues, men half his age, whose tails were dragging at the end. Katunga is a man – I heard him once tell a congregation that he was the best man in camp and that he could defeat them all with words apart from blows. He has told me that when he dies and the safaris pass Machakos the white bwanas will say, "Here lived King Katunga." and I know he is right. A man who thinks himself a king is often right.

Katunga is as much a part of the dead elephant as the vultures which are still sliding, circling slowly, on stiffened wings in the freshly laundered Kenya sky – as much a part as the jackals and hyenas which will contest with the vultures for the rights to the monarch's mortal remains. But there is more to it than Katunga. There is now the business of handing out the reward.

The reward of 100 shillings is always paid to the local native who first brings news of a big elephant, and this is a very big elephant, well over 100 pounds per tusk. And the reward in this case goes to a little prepubescent Samburu maid, the *ndito* who was off seeking strayed goats in the early dawn when she stumbled on the big elephant.

Her name is Lukumai, the local equivalent of Mary, and her little brown face peeps from a huge mound of beads that covers her neck and shoulders like a cape. She goes bare to the waist, over a kirtle of skin, and her legs and arms are tightly wrapped in coils of copper wire. She is shy; she weeps before she smiles when she poses with me and the dead elephant for Selby's camera.

She has earned the reward – more money than she can possibly comprehend, if she understands money at all. But just watch the vultures try to take it from her – watch the sophisticated African jackal at work with his still-unemerging savage sister.

First it is Salah, the snidely handsome camel-wrangler, a good man with camels but devious about money.

"Her father is in Marsabit," says Salah. "Her father is my brother. She will only waste the money or lose it. The people in the *dukah* will cheat her. Give me the money and I will give it to my brother when I see him after his return from Marsabit."

Selby and I look at Salaha. He is pure Somali – a black Semite, with a face like Errol Flynn's. He is a Mohammedan, and the chance of his being related to a Samburu maiden's father is roughly the same as that of Jackie Kennedy's tracing her ancestry through Eskimos. I laugh. I summon up my best Swahili.

"You bloody liar," says I. "Go maltreat the camels. The camels are your brother. Go have congress with the donkeys. The asses are your wives."

Salah doesn't quit easy.

"Well, perhaps the little girl's father is not my *true* brother," says he. "Not *mama moja* – not the same mother. But we are such friends that we are *like* brothers. I will mind the money for the little girl until her father, who is like my brother in my love for him, gets back."

Now Selby laughs.

"Your mother was a hyena, and your brother was a jackal," says Selby. "Go away from my sight and talk to your mother and your brother."

Salah dies hard.

"Well," he says, "perhaps the little girl's father is not my close friend, but at least I (heavily accented) told her to go and look for the elephant. It was my doing that she found it. I deserve the reward, for she is only a *mwanamuki* – a she-thing."

Now I snort.

"*Shaitan* will wrap you in pigskin through eternity for your lies," say I.

Salah retreats now. Enter Big Brother. He is painted like something out of a New Orleans Saturday night. He wears a red skirt and is ostentatiously moody in his handling of his spear.

"I am the *Ndito's* true brother," he says. "*Mama moja*, but different father. I will guard her money for her." He smirks, the family honor accounted for, responsibility established. We were weary of Africans by now. It was beginning to resemble the United Nations. It took less than twenty paces for Big Brother to relieve Little Sister of her loot. Selby shrugged.

"That gives you some idea of the political future," he said

sourly. "Let's go weigh the tusks."

There is nothing really so conclusive as shooting a big elephant. I made a swift summary: In ten years I had shot three elephants, for a gross tusk weight of 600 pounds plus, or an average of better than 100 pounds per tusk. I know one very fine professional hunter who has never fetched in a 100-pound elephant in thirty-five years of hard hunting. This last chap was 108 one side, 106 on the other. He had looked bigger because of his bodily desiccation, but anything over 100 is a lot of tooth.

We permitted the boys in camp to rough us up a little out of jubilation and the scent of a tip at the end of safari.

Eventually we became motorized again, and I must say it came as a shock to have wheels under us. You have just carved a new country for yourself out of raw bush. Your first tracks have become roads. You have built bridges and cut passes through steel *dongas*. You have felled trees and moved rocks, and the whole outback has become home.

And now you have to say good-bye to the green-rimmed dry riverbeds, the purpling hills and the great sweep of rolling plain. You sit for hours in front of the last campfire and wonder if you will ever do it again. We did not regret the elephant; the only way to keep him with us always was to shoot him, and we had shot him very well.

"I guess we've tied the ribbon on it," I finally said to Selby. "I guess we've wrapped it up."

"We never did shoot that biggest buffalo in the Masai," Selby said, "And the Masai is kind of on the way home, too."

"I don't particularly want to shoot him," I said. "I just want to see him in the Masai. I've grown accustomed to the country."

"It has a way of growing on one," Harry Selby said. "It's a pity we don't own it any more, isn't it?"

"My Last Safari," *Saturday Evening Post*, April 27, 1963

PART FOUR

Poor Man's Hemingway On Papa

Poor Man's Hemingway On Papa

*L*ate in his life Ruark would suggest that both he and Ernest Hemingway were "embarrassed by the title 'poor man's Hemingway.' " By the same token though, he was a great admirer of Papa, aped both his writing style and lifestyle to a considerable degree, and the parallels between their careers are in some ways striking. Both wrote exceptionally well on Africa and were deeply moved by their experiences on the continent. Arguably the finest work each produced was inspired by Africa – *Horn of the Hunter* in Ruark's case and *The Green Hills of Africa* for Hemingway. Hemingway committed suicide as his powers began to slip, and for all practical purposes Ruark did the same, with alcohol being the instrument of a slow but certain death.

The two men were also remarkably similar in appearance. They could have passed for brothers or even twins, and had their hairstyles and facial hair been worn in the same fashion, there is no question incidents of mistaken identity would have been commonplace. There was a certain raw crudeness about Ruark and Hemingway, and each individual cultivated a macho image, drank far too much, could be exceptionally difficult and loved sport. Indeed, the parallels could be extended almost indefinitely, and it is a bit surprising that some literary critic hasn't undertaken exactly that sort of exercise.

For present purposes though, what matters most is that Ruark was quite fond of Hemingway, thought highly of much of his work, and undoubtedly secretly envied him. By his own account, "I was a reasonably good friend and a great admirer of Ernest Hemingway. We corresponded occasionally, once got notably drunk in Pamplona, and had a lot of mutual friends." Papa's death moved Ruark deeply, perhaps the more so because he had had ample indication his days were limited unless he quit hitting the booze (which he could not do). Here we gain a bit of insight into their relationship along with Ruark's reaction when he received word of Hemingway's suicide. His tribute is strange, but there can be no denying, as Ruark said, "Hemingway taught me a great many things."

Ernest Was Very Simple

*B*aragoi, Kenya – I strongly suspect that the human vultures at home have pretty well picked over the old man's bones by now, with what amounts to ghoulish glee, and the man that was Ernest Hemingway has been scattered all over the plain.

I have no way of knowing what has been said of Hemingway and his death. There are no newspapers on this dry river bed called Keno. There are only strolling elephants and sudden rushing rhino and, always, the circling vultures.

I suppose that everyone's had his whack, and by now Ernest's reputation as a man has been carved up in all the literary saloons and cocktail parties. He was always an object of contention alive – dead they will probably succeed in separating the writer from the man, and the man from the myth. And they will forget the basic Hemingway, who was really a very simple fellow who combined vibrant writer with lusty man and made a myth of the whole.

Hemingway's simplicity was his secret weapon. People were always seeking deep meaning in the man's work, and writing in their own personal allegories. They tried to interpret the work in terms of the man, and the other way 'round. I have heard it said that his hairchestedness was a pose, and that his preoccupation with tragic maiming and death was indicative of all sorts of hidden things in the man ranging from success or failure as a lover to a crippled son to the fact that his much-loved father committed suicide and Hemingway never got over it.

211

Most of this focus on what somebody once called "furbearing authorship" was as false as the various interpretations of his work by chinless intellectuals who walked vicariously through the old boy's whiskers. Actually, a stinging accusation might be that Ernest Hemingway suffered from a delusion that he was Ernest Hemingway, which was dead right.

Hemingway did have hair on his chest. He was as strong as a bull. He liked booze and women and men and good food and sunlight and hunting and fishing and bullfighting and talking and profanity and dirty jokes and making love and, above everything else, he liked writing about things the way they are, which is simple. That's what threw so many of the aficionados. The simple approach was construed as mysticism.

All the things that he did which got him the "he-man" reputation were really simple almost to the point of savage innocence, and it was finally poetically apt that he died simply of a bullet. I can't imagine that he greatly enjoyed being pawed over as a sick man for the last few years. He never really enjoyed being pawed over as a well man.

There was a lot of ham in Hemingway, as there is ham in any good writer. You cannot dramatize other people without dramatizing yourself. A writing man must of bitter necessity be acutely conscious of himself in relation to the things in the world in which he moves. But that is the simple conceit of childhood, in which the most frequently baby word is "me." Any author is all "me," or he wouldn't be an author.

But phony, Hemingway was not, and poseur he was not. He did not shoot lions and leopards because he was searching for the answer to life. He shot lions and leopards because he bloody well liked to hunt and shoot, and the killing was a neat punctuation mark at the end of the intricate and fascinating process of hunting. He always assumed that death was at the end of any struggle, life included, and the fact that he faced the simple necessity of dying when he wrote got him a reputation for being morbid, cruel, twisted, all easy tags that envious incompetents festoon on successful competents.

Danger fascinated him, which led him to big game and wars

and bullfights and their inevitable bloody finish. But it was not a carefully compounded affectation, any more than his beard was an affectation. He grew a beard because he had a benign skin disease which made shaving painful and impractical. He liked the profane company of full-grown men because they did the things he liked to do and spoke of the things he liked to talk about.

He was an immensely kind man, a nonpatronizing man, and he was easily wounded and sometimes cruel as a child in his dismissal of people he regarded as phony or pretentious or crashingly dull. He was fonder of peasants than of kings, and he liked his rough wine out of a goatskin bota as well as a vintage press in a crystal goblet.

I do not think he personally attempted to justify the image of masculinity and tender tragic realism which he pioneered as a modern writer. He merely did things first, and they were interesting things because nobody else was doing them. He traveled extensively before it became an international disease. He shot in Africa before it became infested with package tours. He learned about bulls before bullfighting became a fashionable passion with college kids and society tramps and frustrated old maids.

He was a creature of perfect timing in a changing century, and he got out of it with the same timing. He repeated to me in Pamplona one time his favorite saying, which was that nobody but bullfighters ever lived their lives all the way up.

Hemingway lived his life all the way up so long as he had the tools. He kept on doing what he liked to do until he couldn't do it any more. Then he quit doing it, accidentally or not.

"Ernest Was Very Simple," *New York World Telegram and Sun*, August 4, 1961.

Papa's Death Reaches Africa

*N*airobi, Kenya – The plane shuddered as it lurched down the strip at Hola. The strip was grass-bearded and full of pigholes; with the coming of self-determination in Kenya, the Mau Mau prisoners, who used to keep the airfield operable, are mostly all free and busy playing politics here in Nairobi.

The pilot took off on one of the more violent bumps, and as he banked steeply and headed for the clouds, you could see the Tana River twisting slow and yellow to your left. On the right below, there were a few scabby patches of green remaining from the irrigation scheme which had made the dry northern frontier bloom.

Then we were prisoned in the gray cotton-wool of cloud. Flying blindly, the man in the front seat turned his head to me and sighed sharply when the plane fought its way into the clear, high air which became suddenly smooth.

As the pilot leveled, away to the left in the far distance the white-wigged head of Kilimanjaro and her sister Mawenzi, appeared dimly. Kilimanjaro's round skull was only lightly capped by the snows. Kenya has suffered a lengthy drought and famine is on the land.

"That's Kilimanjaro," I said to the tenderfoot in the front seat. "On good days you can see Kim and also Mount Kenya over to the west. The Kukuyu say God sits on Mount Kenya; the Masai claim that God lives on Kilimanjaro."

215

We flew on quietly into the blue, and Kilimanjaro was looking sharper and darker in the distance. A low drift of white cloud filled the sag between the tallest mountain and sister Mawenzi.

"That's higher than Mount Kenya?" the man asked.

"Yep. Kili's something like 19,650. Kenya is only about 17,000 and a half."

"Is it true what Hemingway wrote, that they found a leopard frozen stiff on Kilimanjaro, as he said in the preface to that short story? Is it possible they've found elephants in the snows as well?"

"Certainly Hemingway was right when he quoted the Masai as saying nobody knew what the leopard was seeking at that altitude. Hemingway got a lot of mileage out of that old mountain."

The man in the front seat said he had a lot of mileage out of Africa: as a matter of fact, there's an awful lot of mileage in Africa. I said enough to go around.

"I never believed this country could be like you people write it," the man in the front seat said. "After three weeks, I believe it now, and that kudu I shot yesterday, when the whole thing seemed to be finished, I know what Hemingway felt like when he made a Holy Grail out of kudu in the green hills of Africa. I believe it all now. I've seen the green hills of Africa personally."

"It's true, all right," I said. "You just have to see it to believe it. Once you believe it, you keep coming back to see if it's still true and still there."

The man laughed quietly and happily. Kilimanjaro was bulking larger as the distance shortened. "I guess none of us really know what we are seeking at this altitude," he said.

We altered course and slid in through the cloud cover to a greasy landing in Nairobi. The people at the airfield had a newspaper. "Your friend Hemingway just shot himself," the flying service fellow said. "See here."

He handed me the paper and I read that Mary Hemingway had issued a statement saying that Ernest had shot himself while cleaning a gun preparatory to a hunting trip.

It is a very difficult trick to shoot yourself with a loaded gun while cleaning it, because any old hunter like Hemingway would know that you cannot clean a gun while a shell is in the chamber. But one often reads of such accidents in the papers.

"Papa's Death Reaches Africa," *New York World Telegram and Sun*, August 4, 1961.

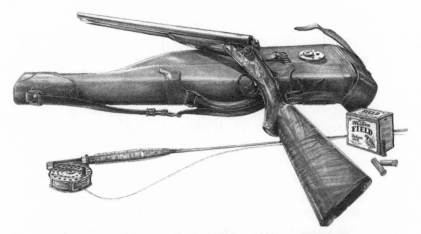

Papa Had No Use For Sham

I was in Africa when Ernest Hemingway died last summer, and I supposed the shock was doubled by the fact that I had flown close to Kilimanjaro just before I got the news of his death. I hunted hard for three weeks in new country, and I couldn't get Hemingway out of my head. We were friends; I greatly admired some of his work. But we were not close friends, nor did I think his work was flawless. Still he preyed on my mind, and it wasn't until I shot a very old elephant that I sort of got rid of brooding about Papa.

What bothered me, I think, was that both Hemingway and Negley Farson had died more or less by their own hands in the last year. Farson didn't actually kill himself – he wore himself out just living hard and free. But to me, both writers stood for something that we seem to be running shorter and shorter on – a simple appreciation of the things that *Field & Stream* has stood for over so many years. I am talking of manhood, and the uncontrived joy that man has always derived from hunting and fishing and camping and firelight and a reeking pipe.

I expect nobody ever wrote better of hunting and fishing than Hemingway or Farson. Certainly few traveled more broadly or lived more fully, if recklessly and sometimes foolishly. These two lived hard, hunted hard, and roved hard. I would not say that an early association with the outdoors made the men into the literary giants they became. But I believe that Hemingway could not have written the bulk of his best without early introduction to rod and rifle, and certainly Farson's *The Way of a Transgressor* was veined with the man's love for the outdoors and its creatures.

Hemingway had it, too, even when it was a secondary theme to a major work. Never had the love of man for God and the outdoors been so beautifully delineated until he wrote *Big Two-Hearted River*. Never had the respect for life and death and the dignity of man been more strikingly shown than in *The Old Man and the Sea*. Hemingway's heroes were mainly simple men and good men, and their instincts were direct and uncomplicated.

It seems to me that we have been losing, and are losing, a great deal of this simplicity of approach to man's natural instincts in a baffling world of nauseating cant and hypocrisy and contrived complications. We have had so much steam heat and air conditioning that we have forgotten wood fires and fresh air.

It is the fashion of the literati to speak knowingly and loftily of the "art" of a Hemingway, the "significance" of a Hemingway, and blandly ignore the fact that he was being neither arty nor sophisticated in most of his writings, but was merely worshipping at the shrine of wood and water, men and women, animals and birds, wine and bread and onions and cheese – worshipping as an antidote to the predestination of all his pieces to end in disaster.

Papa gave such people short shrift. He hung his game heads and fish on his walls and put the memories in his books, and at the end was considered by a considerable arty segment to be old hat. Kipling, too, has fallen into disrepute, and there is some criticism of Herman Melville for spending too much time fretting about whales. There is also the off chance that the publishers of Mark Twain will have to clean up Huck Finn someday to make him suitable for modern consumption.

I had flown into Nairobi the day Hemingway's death was announced, and I wrote a couple of quick pieces for the papers before I plunged into a howling wilderness on a horse-and-camel safari. Some mail arrived via a native bearer with the well-known cleft stick, including a letter addressed to "Robert Ruark, Associated Press, ANYWHERE." It found me sixty miles northeast of a place called Baragoi. I think it is a good letter. "Sir: I heard this great writer died at the end of my vacation, and while the vacation entailed the burial of a relative, the loss of Papa hit me much deeper. The loss of this man couldn't have been worse if he were my own father. For this person, while on my list for his friendship with Castro, gave me the whole world. He gave those of us who love hunting and life adventure in Spain, Africa, Cuba, and the beautiful Upper Peninsula. He gave those of us who will never have the money or the guts to take a chance in a world where we could catch those big trout, drive through shell bursts.

"And we loved him, not especially as a man we didn't and couldn't know, but as a man who lived life and wrote of it; first, to tell the story, and second, to make money. We will miss him, and if in the course of toasting the greats I get a wet cheek, it won't be a crying jag. It will be a tear for the old man who taught me that men aren't made at Yale or Harvard, but at the end of a .303, fly rod, or behind a dirty red cape.

"So now it is up to you, my good friend of the pats, trout, and Africa. You can take us back to the days of the single 16 and grandfathers who loved the fields for the brown, hot sand, scurrying things, and God's crops, and had no thoughts of subdivisions, water rates, P.T.A., and child psychology.

"You are the only one left, good friend. Help us to take our sons out to the fields and streams. They might die in a hydrogen hell next week, but give them meanwhile the howling of monkeys stirred by leopards, the trumpeting of elephants, or even the Masai tourist dances.

"It's up to you. You can give us the dark continent humanly, or baby food. May you always make enough money to tell the baby food editors to go to hell."

It seems to me that the writer of this letter, whose name I have withheld, has put together a pretty sound obituary of Hemingway, and has summed up my own point pretty neatly. And he can bet his bottom dollar on one thing. I will never be so broke I won't be able to tell the baby food editors to go to hell.

"Papa Had No Use for Sham," *Field & Stream*, October, 1961.

PART FIVE

Ruark On Ruark

Ruark On Ruark

*T*o some extent, virtually all of Ruark's writing was autobiographical in nature. His stories of coming of age in a sporting environment, as delineated in "The Old Man and the Boy" series, are obvious and the best-known example. Similarly, *Horn of the Hunter* and *Use Enough Gun* are reflections of his experiences in Africa and Asia. Even in much of his fiction though, Ruark the man shines through. *Poor No More* is his tribute to having arrived, financially speaking, but the keen eye, aware of the man and looking for reflections of his complex character, will also find grist for the biographical mill elsewhere.

Nowhere, though, does Ruark reveal more of himself than in the introspective piece printed here. It is, to use the phrase Ruark employed in describing the kind of journalism that first earned him recognition, "belt-level stuff." Published in his final years (in *True*, September, 1963) when Ruark was already all too painfully aware that there were no more intimations of immortality for him, "The Man I Know Best" is a moving, even compelling autobiographical statement. It tells us a great deal about the insecurity and braggadocio he had always known and exhibited, but in the lengthy essay we also see revelations of a softer, gentler and more likable Ruark. When he says "he works hard at his trade" he is telling the truth, and even his suggestion that "the man I know best is about as good a writer as we have around in the current flock" while unquestionably egotistical, is not far wide of the mark.

To read this forthright essay, redolent of a troubled soul still in many senses in search of itself, may not be to understand the man fully. Nonetheless, it is a remarkable piece, until now largely ignored; and it enables us to delve beneath the surface and get close to the real Ruark. "The Man I Know Best" saw the published light of day when his end was less than two years distant, and it is a fitting way, along with an introspective piece from earlier years, to end this collection of Ruark's lost work.

The Man I Know Best

*T*here's no doubt about it. I felt myself to be one hell of a fellow. Here I was just past 40, and I had it made. I was home and dried. I had roved the world, and made it pay big. I had a vastly syndicated column, and I was my own boss. I had put my literary courage on the block for everybody to take a swing at, and had come up with a monumental bestseller in my first serious novel effort, a book about the Mau Mau uprising in Kenya called *Something of Value*. It made Book-of-the-Month first crack, and my agent had sold it to the movies for more hundreds of thousands than the combined Ruarks had ever made since we stopped painting our faces blue. I owned a paid-for, beautiful villa in Spain's Costa Brava, a town house in Barcelona, an English secretary, the best cook in Europe, a long-term magazine contract, a fine paperback deal, a hand-shot tiger on the wall, two of the heaviest elephant tusks ever extracted forcibly from an old bull, a couple of admiring dogs and money in four banks. I had a closet full of fancy Italian clothes, and literally, a mink-trimmed jockstrap. Headwaiters in all the better saloons everywhere burnt incense when I came into sight.

And I had this Rolls Royce, a lovely, gleaming new Silver Cloud. Prince Rainier gave Grace Kelly RXK-1 for a wedding present. Little Rob from North Carolina had RXK-2. It was the only new model Rolls-Royce in Spain, and none had arrived as yet in America.

I will not say I was unbearable. I was just plain Saturday-night-Texas rich, and I wanted to share it with the world. Not the riches – just me and my condition of vulgar affluence, not to mention my vast accomplishment as a white hunter, lover and big liver.

It is to be borne in mind here that I was a boy bootlegger and a

227

boarding-house hustler to pay for my college education, and that I attended the University of North Carolina from 1931 to 1935, the most dismal depths of the big depression. I went through college on one shiny-seated suit and about two pairs of shoes, and when I got legally sprung, nobody wanted to hire a 19-year-old college graduate to do anything at all, for any wage whatsoever. I had been hungry, God knows, in college. Jobs had been various: country weekly, $10 a week; ordinary seaman, merchant marine, $10 a week; detail boy, *Washington Post*, $14 a week; copyboy, *Washington Star*, $12 a week; copyboy, *Washington News*, $15 a week. And about two years after Mrs. Roosevelt told me in Chapel Hill that the weight of the world rested squarely on my brave young shoulders, I was a sports writer at $25 a week.

Since I had hitch-hiked out of North Carolina, to enjoy a fraudulent stint with the WPA in Washington in 1935, I decided I wanted to go back to North Carolina in high style twenty-odd years later. I had not been much of a John Held, Jr., swain in college; the income was not up to movies and soda pop and the other vital necessities of courtship, and anyhow, I was too young for the big girls. But I had enjoyed the friendship of quite a few tolerant, non-commercial lassies, and I was eager to verify my early judgment of women. I figured I had class even then, on one suit and no money at all.

Now I had this Rolls, and all these gorgeous clothes, and I had been a *Newsweek* cover story, and a *Life* profile and oh, my! The premiere of the movie that MGM had made from my book, all full of Rock Hudson, Dana Wynter, Sydney Poitier and other goodies, was just about to be sprung in New York.

So you know I just had to go to New York, wearing my fancy Brioni duds, and just as naturally such a stylish chap could not depend on local transportation in New York. A fine-feathered fellow such as myself had to take his brand spanking new Rolls Royce Silver Cloud, all bought and paid for, with him from Spain to New York to impress the peasants. Naturally.

Naturally we had a party for about 200 people upstairs at the Twenty-One Club, attended at least two special showings of

Something of Value and took bows, and smirked, and drank too much with too many people, and then went off to Washington to peacock some more before the old home folks; and, finally, decided to carpetbag a bit and invade the Southern brier patches whence I had hitch-hiked so many years ago. I was going to stop off and check on the old girl friends, to see if they'd married well (and they had; each owned a strapping husband, lived close by the golf course, possessed two cars and had at least two sons playing fullback at Carolina or Duke) and then I was going to descend on my home-town, Wilmington, in a veritable fiery cloud of triumphant horses and chariots like Elijah, an earlier prophet.

Well, sir, the Rolls and I swept triumphantly into the seaboard town in which I was unable to get a job even as a copyboy on the local paper, and my triumphs rode ahead of me, like a police escort. (Perhaps it was a police escort. At that moment I wouldn't have put it past me to have hired one.)

I pressed some calls on some people, and some nice folk from my misty past decided to throw me a cocktail party. It was an excellent party, full of uncut whisky and uncut Southern accents. Dressed in something extraordinarily tasty in the way of Italian silk, I was shimmering around the garden with a julep in my hand when I heard two soft Southern female voices floating like melted marshmallow from behind an oleander bush. It was Miss Sarah Sue Somebody talking to Miss Dimity Ann Somebody Else.

"I swear," Miss Sarah Sue was saying to Miss Dimity Ann, "I swear to John. I don't believe a word of it!"

"What don't you believe a word of, sugah?" asks Miss Dimity Ann.

"Bobby, that's what I don't believe a word of. I don't care how good they say Bobby's doing; I don't care if he did have his picture on that magazine cover, right spang between Prince Philip and President Eisenhowuh, I don't care if he is a big book author and lives in Spain and all!"

"What don't you care, sweetness?"

"Well," said Miss Sarah Sue, vehemently. "He can't be doin' as good as everybody says, or he wouldn't have come back home after all these years *in that old beat-up Pierce Arrow!*"

Move over, Tom Wolfe, I said to myself. *It's true. You can't go home again.* Shortly thereafter I crated up the old beat-up Pierce – I mean I packed up the gleaming new Silver Cloud, and we caught the first boat back to Spain. No prophet, except possibly Elijah, achieves honor in his own hometown.

Quite apart from not achieving honor, I was delighted to be coming back unfettered to Wilmington, North Carolina. I had dabbled in bootlegging in college, and I suppose I might even have been a pimp if the fee were sufficient to pay the college tuition. And certainly, decidedly, my first overt act on graduation from the University in 1936 was to embark on a life of crime, with my sheepskin still stuffed in a hip-pocket. My last clear memory of Wilmington was the spiteful buzz of .45 slugs past my ear, and the angry splat of softnosed bullets on the stalks as I fled from policemen through a cornfield. Jail contained me on my first night of graduation, not three hours after Mrs. Roosevelt had told us that the weight of the world rested on our stout young shoulders.

In all fairness to the criminal – *me* – I was drunk.

I had achieved my load from eminently practical intent. Graduation exercises are usually extremely long, excessively windy. We were a big class, and the ceremonies were held in the football stadium. Each candidate for honorable expulsion was assigned a seat on an alphabetical basis.

It happened that my best friends – George Rowe, Nick Powell, Jim Queen, were ranged alongside Ruark. Being of an inventive turn, we had paid a sneaky visit to the stadium in the afternoon, and installed a crock commonly used for the manufacture of homebrew. This crock we filled with a delectable concoction of medical alcohol – Rowe was a medical student, and he probably drained it off a subject – and grapefruit juice. We then obtained lengths of tubing and stuck them in our pockets.

When the orators cranked up to fullest frenzy, we inserted the lengths of tubing into the crock, led the tubes under our scholar's gowns, and proceeded to get beautifully fried while Mrs. Roosevelt did her star turn and the lengthy business of parceling out diplomas occurred. Powell, now a distinguished lawyer, had an Oriental cast to his eyes and cheekbones. When he lurched up for his sheepskin, mortarboard askew and tassel hanging down his back, Nick looked like a young, drunk Chinaman.

We left Chapel Hill and headed home to Wilmington. About 2 A.M., in the outskirts of my hometown, we ran out of gas. None of us had any money, but we had those loving tubes from which we had sucked sustenance. A brilliant thought occurred simultaneously to our grain-alcohol-activated young minds. We would find a car and siphon out some gas, as our first official act of enterprise in the wide world outside learning.

We walked right smack into a police plant.

We had no way of knowing that gasoline stealing had been prevalent in the neighborhood, and half the town's cops were staked out in the oleander bushes. Somebody cried halt, the gay graduates fled, and the cops opened fire. It sounded like a movie gang war. I was coursing through the corn field, with the slugs whizzing and splatting closer, when the thought occurred that Mrs. Roosevelt had really not intended me to start wearing the world's burdens on a back with a Colt .45 slug in it. I chickened out. I surrendered.

I was taken in handcuffs to the jailhouse, and slung into a cell. Next morning, on proper identification, my family's reputation for civic decency got me sprang, and the nice sergeant falsified the blotter. My friend Queen, I later learned, had chased a big dog out of his house and had spent the evening literally in the doghouse.

A bit of compassion on the part of the cops detoured me around a life of crime, and in a few days I started off in the newspaper business in a miserable little hamlet called Hamlet. As the dreary weeks wore on, I often bitterly regretted that I had not stuck to gasoline-stealing as a career.

It seems to me that this vignette, when joined to another, is more or less the story of what makes Robert run. I'm a chronic loser, even when I'm winning.

Along about 1940, I was as brash a coward as ever wrote sports (a subject about which I knew nothing, but it was the first job that paid more than $15 a week which anybody offered me). I was young, and stupid, and afraid that I would soon be joining the other nineteen failures which a Mr. Rocky Riley, the sports editor, had sacked ahead of me in the last calendar year.

So I wrote tough. I knocked everything and everybody. I wore my hat in the office – Rocky wore his hat in the office – and I talked out of the corner of my mouth. Rocky talked out of the corner of *his* mouth. I wore wide-brimmed hats and an air of perpetual belligerence, which is to say I would brace the subject with a copy of the city edition in my hand on the off-chance the victim wanted to make something out of it. This took a deal of cowardly courage, for what I wanted to do, after Riley hung one of his inflammatory headlines on the story, was to slink off to another state and cover garden parties.

There was a big, loudmouthed, sloppy-jowled South Carolina pitcher, an itinerant hard-ball thrower named Louis Norman Newsom, otherwise known as Buck or Bobo. Buck had been on and off the Washington Senators, and elsewhere, several times, but now he was having a dandy year, and was winning thirteen straight for the Detroit Tigers, whom he was pitching to a pennant.

Buck had some sort of altercation with an old man in the Shoreham lobby, possibly while full of beer, the night before he was scheduled to pitch against Washington. As a hard-news sportswriter, I wrote a snotty piece about old Bobo.

When I got out to the ballpark, the first thing I heard was that Newsom was gunning for me; that he planned to eviscerate me after rending me hip from thigh.

This was an unpleasing thing to hear, because Mr. Newsom, in excellent physical condition at the same time, stood six two or three and weighed a hard 230 pounds. Hiding my cowardice, I decided to go gunning for Newsom, just like Gary Cooper. I went into the Tiger dressing room, and there was old Bobo dressing for the game and drinking a coke.

I walked over to his locker and said:

"I hear you're looking for me, Buck," exactly like something out of a TV Western.

Buck looked up and spoke in rotund tones. You could have heard him in Hartsville, South Carolina. They learn to cuss early in Hartsville, South Carolina, long before they whup their fathers.

"Why you this, that and those!" said Mr. Newsom, touching briefly on an Oedipus relationship with my mother, and equipping my entire family escutcheon with canine quarterings.

A big guy from a rival paper, whom I didn't particularly worship, was leaning on the door jamb, taking in all the profanity, and laughing his head off. Ordinarily I'd have said something like: "Oh, for Christ's sake come off it, Bobo, you old bastard," and that would have been the end of it. But the newspaperman's laughter, translated into a need for violence. My stomach contracted.

So I hauled off and poked Newsom in the jaw with my best punch, and I swear he didn't even drop the coke he was drinking! That cured me immediately of any delusions of being Joe Louis, but a merry scramble followed, in which everybody fell over benches. Happily two fine gentlemen named Hank Greenberg and Birdie Tebbets, rather more civilized than the average Southern ballplayer, eventually saved me from being devoured by the Tigers, who did not take kindly to people who slung punches at Newsom, who was leading them toward the first light in many a dark year.

That afternoon, Bobo, bless him and God rest his beer-sodden soul, was superb. He pitched a one-hitter, won the game 1-0, and personally struck the triple on which he scored his only run.

I dutifully recorded that triumph for the sports final, and was picking up my portable when a disgruntled Washington Fan – a gambler, I think – stopped in front of me at my pew in the open-to-the-public press box.

"Why don't you take a punch at some of our bums once in a while. Ruark?" he snarled.

Then he picked up my portable and hit me over the head with it.

It seems to me, in retrospect, that I have been hit over the head with a typewriter ever since.

The man I know best might be called the most humbly-grateful-arrogantly-brave-cowardly-laughingly-sad-introverted-extrovert I ever encountered. He is a timid swashbuckler, a hail-fellow who is frightened of nearly all human encounters, a former dashing news paperman who had to force himself to interview people, a wishful devilish dog with women who is sweatingly unsure of himself on the brink of any fresh encounter with a female under the age of 70.

He is at this writing a balding 47 years old, with an extra 20 years of hard living on his battered chassis. His arteries have already begun to harden, and his liver is dejected, if not downright disconsolate. He looks fat but thinks of himself as thin. Since childhood he has always embraced himself with an aura of self-importance. The man I know best conveys an impression of toughness, boldness, brashness. Inside he is a writhing mass of timidities, softnesses and insecurities.

He is not a handsome man. His forehead is too high, his frontal bones too prominent, his nose too big and crooked. His ears are large and outflanged, and he has always, even when physically thin after illness, owned a double chin. He has practically no eyelashes, and a beard which shows greenish gray. His mustache, which he has worn since his teens, is invariably ragged and sort of multicolored. His shoulders are too wide, too square, and his neck grows oddly from them, making the best of tailoring appear to have been hurled at him in a fit of rage. No suit he wears ever appears to be pressed.

Yet the man I know best *feels* handsome, to such point that he is often adjudged handsome by women, who invariably hate him by reputation, like him on sight, and sometimes love him later. He prefers the society of women to the company of men. He can turn his charm on or off at whim if the audience is worth the effort. In this respect our man is pure phony, because when he is completely sincere he is apt to labor his points, and earnestness drips off him like sweat.

The man I know best talks too much, but with the partial justification that he *has* got a tremendous backlog of things to talk about. He gives the impression of being a phony until a check actually reveals that he has done the things he has said he's done.

The man I know best is a phony in the sense that an actor is a phony; Peter O'Toole is not really Lawrence of Arabia, but he makes you believe momentarily that he is Lawrence of Arabia. But the man I know best is a completely valid, truthful man in a sense of achievement. What he says he will do he will do within the limits of Kismet.

The man I know best conveys a first impression of falseness because his conversation is larded with unlikely names, places and achievements. It will develop that over a period of nearly thirty years as a professional writer, his life has been intertwined with these names, places and achievements. But this first appearance of shooting-a-line works adversely on a man who might mention Bernard Baruch, Bing Crosby, Winston Churchill, Lena Horne, Louis Armstrong, Glenn McCarthy, Tom Mboya, Tallulah Bankhead, the Duke of Edinburgh, Mae West, Richard Nixon, Lillian Gish, Ava Gardner, Joe DiMaggio, Lucky Luciano, Toots Shor, J. Edgar Hoover, Carol Burnett, Dick Gregory, Ann Sheridan, Spyros Skouras, Walter Winchell, Leonard Lyons, Dinah Shore, Ernest Hemingway, John Steinbeck, Joe Louis and Joe E. Lewis, Richard Burton, John Huston, Clint Murchison, Cardinal Spellman, a wild lion named Meggie, Carmen Franco, Jimmy Stewart and Joe Bushkin in the same context with the savage tribes of New Guinea; the outback of Australia; tiger shooting in India; being mauled by a leopard; owning a castle in Spain; living out of a flat in London; having a working knowledge of two leper colonies; making the Book-of-the-Month Club with two of his last three novels; setting an all-time high for a movie sale; being kicked out of Kenya for his last novel; chasing Luciano out of the hemisphere and temporarily busting up the international drug traffic; helping Frank Sinatra lose his voice; entertaining the Duke of Windsor in his Spanish home; of using a two-million air-mile placque for a paperweight; of having spent three years in all theaters of war as gunnery officer, press censor and finally, outranking a Fleet Admiral of the British Navy in matters of security; of having averaged four columns a week for the past seventeen years for a syndication that hovers around 180 newspapers; of having written over 600 magazine pieces for slick magazines since the end of World War II; of having helped frustrate a revolution in Venezuela; of having earned a couple of million dollars with two fingers on a typewriter; of having written ten books, most of which were best sellers; of having sold his first original unpublished screenplay for $100,000, and having been in thick bush after dangerous animals ranging from Mau Mau gangsters to sick Cape buffalo to wounded leopards.

This multiplicity of living has its wryly amusing moments. Twice the man I know best has been accused of not being himself. Once was in Hong Kong, at the Peninsula Hotel, I was having a drink with a former Hong Kong police chief, when a decidedly colonial type, his guardee mustache mingling with the hairs in his beaky nose, stopped off at the table, and was introduced to me.

Beaky Nose sat down and stared at me through his monocle. "Ruark . . . Ruark . . . odd name, that," he growled in a chest tone which could only date back to Poona, 1902. "You'd not by any chance be any remote connection to that johnnie who wrote that book, would you? Something – *Something of Value* or some such name. To do with the Mau Mau in Kenya. Bloody, *bloody* book."

"Why yes, sir," said I. "In point of fact, I'm the johnnie who wrote that bloody, *bloody* book."

Beaky Nose speared me with a basilisk stare, and rose hurriedly from the table, knocking over his pink gin. He addressed my host.

"I must warn you," he said, "this man's an imposter. It's well known that the Ruark who wrote *Something of Value* is a retired major from the Indian Army who is now raising tea in Limuru in Kenya. Good *day,* sah!" And off he stalked. My host looked at me and shrugged. I laughed, because a short time before something similar had occurred in Sydney, Australia.

I was nursing a small warm Scotch in the guest's lounge of the Hotel Australia on Castlereigh Street in Sydney, waiting for some appointment or other, when a chap across the way seemed to be trying to stare me into the floor. The unblinking gaze finally rasped my nerves, so I got up and walked over to the man.

"Something wrong with my necktie?" I asked. "My fly open? Or what? What's all this in aid of?"

"Oh," he stammered. "Oh, I am frightfully sorry. But for a moment I thought you might be Robert Ruark. But that's obviously impossible, isn't it, because the Ruark I know lives in Nairobi. He's a white hunter, or something to do with the Game Department."

Oh, boy, I thought wearily. *Wilmington, North Carolina, we done come a far piece from home.*

The man I know best is no free-loader. What I have always sought in commercial facility is the maximum of service, an easy friendship with the owner, and the right to raise hell if anything goes wrong. You can only do this by paying your own way. I have used the Twenty-One Club literally as a country store for the best part of twenty years, and have never been insulted by a proffered subsidy.

Perhaps I carry this sensitivity too far. On the publicity which I have given East Africa, over the last dozen years, in column, magazine, book and movie, you could almost call me the father of the postwar safari trade in Kenya and Tanganyika. It was popularly supposed that either I was riding free with the safari firms or that I actually had a piece of the safari business, since my best friend in Kenya ran one of the two best outfits. In point of bitter fact, Harry Selby's and Jack Block's account books will show that I paid the top-going rates for my pleasant research, even though it is customary to deliver freebies to the outdoor writers of prestige magazines. I don't want any bloody freebie. It would have stolen my vested interest in a country I love and robbed my trophies of dignity.

I will lend money to friends, but I never feel quite the same about them after, and when I borrow I borrow from banks, and pay interest. I also have the hard horrors of being houseguest. I love to have company in my own home, but to be at the mercy of the host's whim gives me an acute rash. Perhaps it is selfish of me, but as the late editor, John Sorrells, once said: "I stay in hotels because I like to break wind out loud."

As a little fat kid I used to cry as I fought, and was generally sick to my stomach later. And I fought a lot. I had to. I was a Junior, and as a result was called Bobby. Except for Grandma, who called me "Rosebud." My middle name was Chester, and "Chester" is hilarious in the South. Also I was a bookish brat, with a massively overdeveloped imagination. Laboring under those weighty imposts, you had to fight to stay level with the louts who read only at gunpoint and who much preferred the barbarities of the athletic fields to a walk in the woods with a slim volume or possibly a shotgun.

I suspect I got to be a loner very early, because I really did not *like* the society of children. I don't think I was ever anything but an adult as a child. I didn't give a damn for ordinary sports – possibly because I was clumsy and slow, but mostly because I never liked to do anything with a herd. I was always several years ahead of myself in school, because of an improbable IQ, something called "achievement tests," and the schools' habit of skipping smart children upward. With the hard-muscled, pimply members of the mob, I was just a little fat kid who was too bright with the books. I was reading Shakespeare for fun at 10, and this is no way to become popular with a bunch of young thugs who liked to tin-can dogs and turpentine cats when they were not breaking windows or beating up colored kids.

So I fought from necessity in the schoolyards at recess. I fought my way home from school. But be damned if I was going to spend every afternoon fighting for fun. We lived well out of town where there was always the sound of quail sweetly calling, and the rustle of rabbits in the brush. In the summers I either went to Southport, a little seaport hamlet, to stay with my maternal grandparents, or else we had a cottage on Wrightsville Sound. Quite easily and naturally I got into the book-bird-dog-and-boat business, and became a hardened recluse well before I sprouted pubic hair.

My imagination – having fed on Dickens, Melville, Edgar Rice Burroughs, Robert Louis Stevenson, and Ernest Thompson Seton – often left me feeling like a hero of high adventure stories.

The only trouble was that nobody else knew how good I was. To the rest of the world I was that same fat kid with the cowlick who didn't like to play baseball seven days a week. Sometimes, today, when I read certain book reviews or scan the column mail, I get the feeling that the rest of the world still hasn't got the message, and that I am still the little fat kid with the cowlick.

This feeling of insecurity has led to all sorts of unnecessary, nonsensical excesses. I did not really want to shoot my first lion, and I was terrified when I braced him, close aboard, my second day on my first safari. I was even more terrified of my first Cape buffalo, staring at me eyeball to eyeball. Each time, after I shot the animals competently, I went behind a bush and was just as competently sick to my stomach.

Nothing in the war terrified me so much as walking up to my first elephant, and I was reasonably terrified during the war. But to skulk around flimsy bushes with seven tons of screeching fury heading in your direction at a fast gallop – *well*. I look at the tusks in front of the fireplace now and I know I couldn't have run from that elephant. I know I killed it, but I still don't believe I did it, any more than I believe that Harry Selby and I once charged a herd of stampeding buffalo because there was nothing else to do, and stopped the stampede long enough to shoot the lead bull.

It is really a terrible thing to be chronically frightened, to such a point that you must constantly prove that you're not. One lives with the feeling that no matter what you've done, what you've got, that some day the whole world will get wise to your weakness and come to take everything away. I have been living with the idea of getting fired ever since I got my first real job, and in the back of my mind was always the thought: "Well, I can always go back to sea"; or, "I can sell the Spanish place"; or, "I can go back to reading copy."

It is not mock humility which makes me say I never understood why people pay money to read what I write. I know they do. For years after I first came to New York to take over the old Heywood Broun column spot, I would sneak a peek at the *World-Telegram's* split page, to see if my picture were at the top. If the half-column cut was there, I heaved a sigh of relief, because I always half-suspected they wouldn't run the piece that day. On the few days they *didn't* use the piece, I was dumbly desolate, and would wonder if my luck had finally run out on me.

This distrust of fortune – and I am as superstitious as any Kikuyu witchdoctor living in a welter of ancestral ghosts – must have come from the early formative years of privation. We were deeply bitten by the depression: the family fell apart, old traditions went out the window, the pianos were sold, and my immediate family never recovered. I barged off to college, on my own, as a knicker-bockered child of 15, and on my first night in the dormitory, my roommate an athlete, went stark raving mad and tried to kill me. I got rescued by some jockstrap-scholarship athletes down the hall, just as this muscular nut decided he was Abraham and I was Isaac. He was a divinity student and a basketball player, and I have cared very little for either religion or basketball since. (I wrote this episode in a novel called *Poor No More,* and everybody commented on the fertility of my imagination.)

This was quite a bruising experience for a 15-year-old with no money, but was little more upsetting than the next roommate they foisted on me in dear old Grimes Dormitory. This was a rich and pampered esthete who was the most fantastic liar I ever encountered. A nutty athlete and a rich pansy, consecutively, were a bit much for the kid from Wilmington.

College was a four-year nightmare of financial embarrassment and real frustration. I was about three years younger than anybody in my class. My folks were described, bitterly, as "bad pay," and I was in hock to everybody. I was taken into a fraternity on the cuff, a sort of poor relation, and that bothered me. I could neither dress nor spend in the same league with the good brethren, and believe me, in 1932 nobody had much money. My roommate was rich on an allowance of $10 a month, which was exactly $10 more than I had. I think that phase of my life is basically responsible for my overeager-ness in check-grabbing; for an insistence on more than adequate supply of everything from clothes to whisky: for the Rolls-Royce in the backyard, and for almost a psychopathic set against being given *anything,* even a compliment.

Conversely, I don't mind criticism, nor am I unduly annoyed by bad reviews of books or insulting mail. I am basically a lazy man, but am only really happy when I'm working much too hard, just to see if I can.

Once, on the word of my agent, Harold Matson, I tore up a whole book and burned it. Matson, no man to Bowdlerize an honest opinion, had remarked of this enormous volume (of which I was quite proud) as follows: *"It seems to me you may have written an elaborate treatment of a book you may have had in mind to write some day."* It was like getting kicked in the stomach by a particularly well-coordinated mule, but I was actually relieved. I had felt a little peculiar about the book myself and didn't know why. The British publisher, who had already accepted the copy, had jumped the gun and set it in type. He cabled, wailing: "But what will we do with all this type?" and we cabled back, succinctly: "Melt it."

I actually felt a great relief when I heaved 400,000 clean words into the fireplace, and set out to rewrite the whole opus awful. I found the hair-shirt bearable, the masochism comforting, and the work went well. When I had the next 400,000 words, and my boy took a slow read and said: "Now that's more like it." I felt as if I'd just been knighted.

If you want a real nest of worms for the psychiatrists to untwist, I am as gregarious a recluse as you're ever likely to meet.

With people of my own seeking, I don't mind a mob, and in Spain we not infrequently have twenty-five people for lunch. But I hate to *do* anything with anybody in a mass movement, even something so simple as deciding who will share a cab in order to get from a restaurant to a theater. Cocktail parties drive me to real drink, after I pry myself loose from them. I wouldn't take a vacation trip with my best friends, if it involved more than two people – and I have had my last safari of more than one gun.

I revel. I literally wallow, in loneliness, which is pretty Irish of me. Give me a fire, the prospect of walls lined with books, some recordings on the machine, a sufficiency of whisky in the bar, perhaps a moon outside and nobody at all to talk to, and I could weep with sad happiness. This possibly explains an overdeveloped love of bush and sea. Space without people is my idea of the ultimate in luxury. I can sit for hours alone in a leopard blind, or ride a Somali pony for thirty miles in rocky elephant country, and be completely diverted by my own thoughts and the small sights and sounds around me. Somewhere here, there is again the conscious reversion to early poverty – whether surrounded by a multitude of books or a profusion of wild animals, there crops up the idea that *I'm doing it and the other people aren't.*

The jump from reporter to columnist is not a long one; from the very earliest days I had heeded an old-fashioned tenet, as advanced by Somerset Maugham, to write my pieces with a beginning, a middle and an end. As a matter of fact, Phillips Russell, the biographer who taught creative writing at the University of North Carolina for a great many years, once saved for me a sophomore theme I wrote at the milky age of 17, which in word-count and balance was a perfect foreshadowing of my future column form. A columnist is not much more than a reporter with a point of view, and to the attitude one adds a touch of special flavor – if possibly, one's own flavor, even if it's a touch garlicky.

And you get started with a gimmick. Mine was a simple gimmick. I came out of the war looking for an easy way to make a living, and maybe some largish money as well. I already had a fair pre-war record of magazine sales. During the war, as a journeyman Naval officer on sea-and-island duty, I had more or less provided my poker money by writing pieces for *Collier's, The Post, and Liberty.* I had no agent, but I had plenty of material, and a kind friend had once drawn me a picture of what a magazine piece looks like, skeletally, and I had no trouble selling blind.

But this was piecework, and piecework was not what I sought. The Scripps-Howard-United Feature axis had lost a whole constellation of top writers – Broun dead, Ray Clapper killed at Kwajalein, Gen. Hugh Johnson dead, Ernie Pyle killed at Ie Shima in the last days of the war. Pegler gone across the street to Hearst, Mrs. Roosevelt not so hot since the President's death – hell, there were enough vacant holes in the papers to accommodate a covey of aspiring pigeons.

At sea and on some of the dreary rocks on which I'd been stuck, while working variously for the Navy, the Marines and B-29's, I had very little to do but think, and nothing at all to drink to distract me from thinking. That kind of detached thinking was something I'd been cultivating since the early kid days in the merchant marine, when you stood a straight eight-hour night watch, with nothing to do on the focs'le head or in the wheelhouse *but* think. I thought me some fine thoughts, and finally came up with an idea: I would be out of the war, if somebody didn't kill me, at 30. World War II had come along and knocked me for a loop at the young but well-callused age of 26. Now it looked very much as if I would outlast the war and shortly be confronted with the problems of the peace. About twelve million ex-GIs would be in the same boat.

That seemed to be the germ. I would speak for this broad spread of humanity and for their wives, parents and children – not as lofty as Lippmann, not as gossipy as Winchell, not as bosom-conscious as Wilson, not as angry as Pegler. I would be a cosmic columnist – a belt-level journalist – and anything that made me mad, glad or sad was bound to react on a vast belt-level audience. That was the gimmick, and a glorious gimmick it was. It only needed a few things: a fast kickoff, and then a succession of follow-up attention-getters, and somebody would be coming around with a fat contract for syndication.

People still refer to that first piece as "The column you did on women's clothes." It was not a column on women's clothes at all, but a piece on naked sex, with a twist. Here you have twelve million Johns overseas, just waiting to get home to twelve million Marys. The script calls for Mary to meet John on the dock. They fall into each other's arms, the camera pans to the sunset, and everybody lives happily ever after.

I switched the script, Mary, bereft of Johnson, had been dressing for other women for the last four years. She had nine-inch nails, wore Dolman sleeves, flat-heeled shoes, and hauled her hair either into an Iroquois Indian topknot with a rubber band around it, or let it flop in a net like a sack of mud. She wore purple lipstick and looked like the wrath of God.

The piece I wrote was simple. I allowed John one look at Mary, in her godawful get-up, and then had him recoil in horror, and say something like: "Christ Almighty, take me back to Funafuti, because I've seen handsomer headdresses on cannibals!"

Man, it did the trick. I hit all of the front pages of our chain, and the argument was taken up on the front pages of papers not in our chain. I had insulted American womanhood most grievously. I was in business.

Then I uncovered a missing cruiser called the *Indianapolis*, which the Navy had forgotten to mention had been lost, with the ensuing deaths of 880 men, and had almost sole custody of one of the hairiest court-martials in military history. (I acquired that copyrighted story largely by accident. But it's a pretty good court-martial story when the losing Jap submarine skipper is imported to testify against the victorious cruiser skipper. It's even better when the late James Forrestal, then Secnav, has to call in a recently graduated Naval officer, now a reporter – *me* – to brief his own people on what exactly happened. The Navy should lose a cruiser on its way to Leyte from Guam, and then forget to mention it?)

Very shortly I was syndicated. Very shortly I came out against motherhood, southern cooking, and dogs. Very shortly I ran into a summit meeting of the mob in Havana, again by accident, and did bad things to Lucky Luciano's future plans for operating the narcotics business from Cuba. I also caused a considerable amount of embarrassment in Thomas E. Dewey's office, because Dewey, due to circumstances never satisfactorily explained, had sprung Charlie Lucky from a long rap up the river. That was more or less the same year that, rambling around Leghorn in Italy looking for some pieces, I ran into a series of happy accidents that resulted in the removal of Lt. Gen. John C.H. (Courthouse) Lee from his job as chief of American Armed Forces in Europe, and which stayed noisily on the front pages for weeks. That time the Army laid on aircraft so that the opposition press and news services could cover *me*.

These good stories only really happen when you're young, with strong arches, and the digestive processes of a goat. In those days I could use gin as a substitute for slumber and still write fifteen columns in a brisk afternoon at the portable. (Actually, on the second phase of the Lee story, I wrote sixteen long ones at a sitting. I had a lot I wanted to say.) The Lee story was the best I shall ever cover. I had his own staff locked up, and access to all the hot papers he tried to hide. I had more unpaid spies than the CIA, and was the complete authority on the story. It made an amusing piece for *True* called *The Bitter Tea of General Lee.*

It was a wondrous time of lucky reporting. When Farouk tumbled I spent a week with the new boy Mohammed Naguib, scared stiff that somebody was going to hand me a bomb. The same week I found a new pyramid with Dr. Ahmed Fakhry, Egypt's leading archeologist. He said I had a lucky look, and if I would come along, we would find the thing he'd been looking for for years. Jane Payne and I found it, with some assistance from Dr. Fakhry, and it just so happened I had a photographer with me.

A mere couple of weeks later I was mixed up with the first of the Mau Mau killings, in Kenya, and again I just happened to have a photographer with me. I still get a funny feeling when I flip through the scrapbooks and see a *Life* cover with "Robert Ruark Among The Mau Mau" as its only cover plug, and me wearing a great pistol in a mountain outpost called *Campi ya Simba* – "Lion's Camp."

There's no point in a detailed rundown of all the places and people, but a few years of this kind of raw meat made powerful grist for the novel mill. I had done a few books; nothing much. A funny, youngish, nose-thumbing travesty on the historical novel, called *Grenadine Etching,* and a very unfunny sequel. Then there had been a couple of collections of essays, and then quite a good non-fiction book, I thought, on my first safari to Africa and *Horn of the Hunter* is still my pet effort, for I was beginning to graduate from the fact and commencing to feel the form. This was the beginning of a long love affair with Africa. I also illustrated this one, a very slight talent I didn't know I had until a dicky liver put me on the wagon and I needed something to do with my hands.

But after two trips to Africa I was hooked on Africa, and I also had a novel on my back.

Writing it was taking a big chance. The column was still going well – although I had quit working formally for Scripps-Howard and was now doing the pieces only three times a week for United Feature Syndicate – and I could write for any good slick magazine in the country with a miniscule fear of rejection. I was settled and happy in Spain, with the new house, and taking on a fresh giant, in the novel shape, was really a fool's decision. I didn't know anything about novel writing, and there was the possibility I would live unhappily ever after if it fell on its face.

God smiled. I made no major mistakes in that one, *Something of Value,* and it certainly didn't fall on its face. It got knocked for being too bloody, but that was well before the average reader dined on a steady diet of gore from the Congo. Today it's largely regarded as authoritative history.

Then I tackled another one about the home country, *Poor No More*, and made every mistake there was, doubled and redoubled. But you learn. In the last one, again set in Africa, I didn't make many mistakes. But in *Uhuru*, this time, I didn't make the mistakes *on purpose*. You learn even more as you go – and I had to cut 165,000 words out of *Uhuru* before I discovered that I had a stupid way of saying I was going to do something, then doing it, and then telling you that I'd done it.

I'm still at loss to say what makes a book sell, any more than I know the basics behind a fact that you can make love to a woman you may have known only ten minutes on the one hand, and not reap so much as a smile after working on another one for ten years. Last year, before the newspaper strike, the *New York Times* Book Section polled a flock of best sellers from 1962, under the simple question: "What makes your book popular with the people?" And I had to confess I hadn't the faintest.

But most of the good books I ever read, from Mark Twain to Hemingway in modern times and going all the way back to *Beowulf,* told me "how it was." To tell the reader how it is, or was, with a minimum of flapdoodle, has been my principal aim, and up to now it would seem that I have been abnormally lucky.

I have been lucky, as well, in having a magnificent place to work in, and good people to help me. I work out of a big house on the beach of the Spanish Mediterranean, and the house is a 14-year-old boy's dream of what a house should be. It rambles all over the real estate, and any time I run out of book space, we just knock out another wall. The house is pocked with fireplaces – I am a steam-heat hater – and I indulge my firebug tendencies to the extreme extent of how much wood we have on hand.

This is the House that Jack Built – everything in it harks back to the personal past. There are maybe 2,000 books I treasure, including the *Encyclopedia Britannica* and my father's set of Kipling, more records than I can ever play, and about ten typewriters, in case we need spares. The phone seldom rings, because the Palamós exchange is rather torpid about calls, and for nine glorious months a year there is nobody here but me, the help, the dogs and the seagulls. The tourists are long gone, and a man can park in front of the post office once more without being mowed down by a Volkswagen.

The heads on the wall I shot. The pictures on the wall I either painted or discovered under happy circumstance. My desk is as big as an elephant's coffin, and the chairs and divans are comfortable. The ashtrays are large, and the bar convenient. I was blessed with a talented interior decorator for a wife, and she has managed to endow this robber's cave with high style, although God knows how she managed it when one tiger takes up a whole wall in the living room and two Cape buffalo glower over the fireplace in the office. A leopard is draped springing-fashion over the lady's bed, and some say that alone would induce nightmares. It could have been a zoological garden and has turned out to be the kind of joint flossy magazines take pictures of.

The whole house is geared to keeping the writer happy, because "the money tree," as the cook calls the typewriter, needs constant pruning. The house is two complete houses – one-half belonging to the guests and the other half off-limits to everybody but me and a slave named Alan Ritchie I've had chained to *his* typewriter for the last ten years. Alan, a white-haired, placid ex-sergeant of British infantry, is a rare thing. He is a secretary-major domo who actually does *not* want to be a writer himself. He also does not afflict me with unnecessary chores in order to impress me with his own importance, and he is the only person in the world who can read my handwriting.

Between us, over the years, we have cooked up quite an assembly line in the confection of books. I am convinced that, with the average writer, more time is spent doing useless chores in order to make excuses *not* to write than is ever spent in the writing. I have tried working on my own, on a big job, and it's torture.

The other great waste of a writer's time apart from conversation and drink is the necessity to cope with correspondence, go to the post office, collect the book from the store, replenish the booze, send the cable, draw money from the bank, get the spare tire vulcanized, take the dog to the vet, meet the plane, answer the phone, make the reservations, argue with the gardener, lick the stamps – an endless round of time-eating detail.

With Sergeant Ritchie I have toppled this roadblock. I merely allow *him* to do all these things, while I hit the typewriter for half-a-day and punish the pencil for the other half. I can dictate enough correspondence in two hours to keep Ritchie busy for two days. If it were left to me, it would take two weeks – or more likely, I just wouldn't answer the letters.

Between us, I would say that when we are going good on a book, Ritchie and I produce about 140 hours a week of solid toil, or ten hours a day each over a seven-day week. I have been a lusty drinker since I was 16, and I can write drunk if necessary. I have written columns and articles with a load on more than once, from accidental necessity, but on books or any big project I work dead sober. I find that complete sobriety allows you to get up reasonably early in the morning, feeling refreshed and eager to pick up the plow again, whereas if you stone yourself into slumber it takes you half-a-day and several snorts to shrug off the morning meemies. When possible I like to pull 5,000 words out of the machine before lunch, and not hitting the pre-lunch Martinis also obviates the necessity of that deadly Spanish disease, the siesta. It takes a good two hours to recover from a sodden siesta, and by that time it's the cocktail hour again and the day is shot to hell.

The snobs, the boozers, and the literary talkers rank equally among my choicest hates. I loathe the striking of off-stage attitudes in writers, to where, as in the sad late years of Hemingway, the myth obscures the man, and the writer goes away altogether. It is fatal to believe your own press clippings, especially if you are a fur-bearing author. In the case of Ernest, he finally spoke in unknown tongues and his last effort, that bullfight thing he did for *Life,* was excruciatingly embarrassing for anyone who had known the man and loved the work. It was at best, a pitiful parody of the style which had made Hemingway famous.

I was a reasonably good friend and a great admirer of Ernest Hemingway, whom I never called "Papa," "Ernie," or "Hem." We corresponded occasionally, and once got notably drunk in Pamplona ten years ago, and had a lot of mutual friends. We were both embarrassed by the title "poor man's Hemingway" that somebody once hung on me – possibly because we resembled each other physically, and certainly because my life had followed a similar pattern.

It used to bother me – at least, annoy me – until one day, well taken in wine, Hemingway said: "Look, kid. Screw 'em all. You've been a better reporter, been in better wars, seen more bullfights, shot more big game, know more about Africa, lived longer in Spain, seen more of the world, and made a hell of a lot more money, and you're twenty years younger than me. You'll probably write more books, although I doubt if any will be as good as my best or as bad as my worst. Screw this second-hand Hemingway crap. We use the same alphabet. It's a different world and it's your time at bat. I had mine. Just remember one thing: Write what you know, as true as you can, and screw the critics. If they knew anything they wouldn't be critics. If you've got balls you'll always find somebody who hasn't got balls eager to cut you loose from yours."

That was about the last time I worried about being a "poor man's Hemingway," just as I quit worrying about being a "poor man's Pegler," in the early column days. There are times when I feel like a poor man's Ruark, but that's my own fault.

It would be a lie to say that one writer is never guilty of stealing – well, absorbing – the works of another. Hemingway taught me a great many things, including his copyright trick. That trick is, roughly, that if you furbish one fingernail to a high shine, the reader will assume that you are master of hand and arm as well. The art of delicate detail, as applied to one portion of a sentence or scene, makes a detailed audit of the whole unnecessary. In short, if you write about a bullfighter wetting the edges of his muleta, and then stamping it in the sand to give it weight, you do not have to devote a chapter to how hard the wind was blowing that day.

I have always stolen as much as I could. The venerable Mr. Maugham, by his own written admission, is one of the worst writers in the world, with no feel for language and a positive devotion to the cliché. But Willie Maugham chose simplicity of style and structure, and thereby won the title of the world's champion storyteller for the past fifty years. Maugham is a self-admitted cornball in an age of impression. He always worked on stage, and in three acts, with a neat bow at the end of the package. I stole heavily from Maugham.

For sheer cream of gentle craft, with complete mastery of sympathy, humor, storytelling ability, love and understanding of mankind – and with an oddly diverging fascination for freaks and horrors – I still replenish my quiver by reading Steinbeck. It soothes me, and gives me faith in my own ability to perform some future task, even if I have to steal a little to get me over the rough spots. John's output has latterly been ragged but on the body of it all he's the most deserving Nobel-winner we've produced.

I don't think there are any exceptionally good postwar writers. If J.D. Salinger married Carson McCullers, I would not be a member of the wedding. I don't think that being either black, homosexual, or a combination of both necessarily makes a writer, nor do I think that the repeated use of four-letter words makes a war story stand up realistically. I am weary of the word "shit" being used in lieu of commas. James Jones is a one-note war writer, and Norman Mailer a clown on stage as well as off. I would rather not think of Allen Drury; it makes my ears ring.

Ultimately we will have to get around to the man I know best. What about Ruark? Is he a good writer?

I honestly don't know. He's a competent professional: we know that on the record. He's a good reporter – also a matter of record. He knows a lot of words, and he's been to a lot of places and seen a lot of things. He will not write about what he doesn't know, nor does he cloak himself in a lot of cheap mysticism. He is, certainly, not a literary poseur or a dilettante writer. He is not a philosopher, full of hidden intentions and three-dot indications of deeper meaning to saddle the reader with the burden of understanding. He suffers from being a white, non-homosexual Gentile who has been successful in other fields of writing apart from the novel form.

He does not write crap. He may write unpleasant truths, but the crap content is non-existent. He works hard, and he tries to gain on the craft, one book at a time. He would like to be a better writer, and he does not want to become the kind of myth which obscures the man, merely on account of the kind of life he's led. And, some day, he would like to see Ruark the man separated from Ruark the columnist and Ruark the magazine writer from Ruark the novelist in at least one review of a book. I am tired of having books evaluated in terms of whether or not the reviewer objects to the last column I wrote on Adlai Stevenson, or whether the reviewer disapproves of shooting for sport. That, I realize, is asking a great deal of book reviewers, a poozly lot at best.

I would have to say that the man I know best is *not* – at least not yet – a good writer. But I would also have to say that the man I know best is about as good a writer as we have around in the current flock, and a sight better, over the long pull, than a great many who think they're marvelous. We have no great writers today, but we are certainly heavy on literary lightweights with delusions of grandeur. One thing we may say in favor of the man I know best: He works hard at his trade, in research and at the machine, and one day, with luck, he may even improve himself in his chosen profession. In the meantime he vastly enjoys its fruits, and is grateful to God and man for allowing him to practice the business of writing for a living. If things had worked otherwise, The Man I Know Best might have been a pimp, a process server, or a politician, three trades to which I attach equal nobility of aim.

"The Man I Know Best," *True*, September, 1963.

People Like Us Never Grow Up

*T*his piece is being written in a bug-ridden swamp on the banks of the sluggish yellow Tana River in northeastern Kenya, where the big elephants bugle and the baboons swear at the hunting leopards, and the lean Northern Frontier lions rumble asthmatically just outside the camp. I have been watching, with mounting delight, the reactions of a couple of boys – middle-aged, white-haired boys – an editor friend from America and a reserved Londoner who never saw a hedgehog, let alone a lion, until recently. It has become almost a ritual with me in recent years to get back to Africa every couple of years with some newcomers to the scene, to watch the wonders through new eyes.

And I have been thinking, as I watched the response of my two old friends, that I have lived through the end of an era, and it's a sad thought. The pure delight of these two men in the friendliness of the lions and the surly majesty of the buffaloes and the awesome bulk of

253

the elephants was the delight of a child of my own generation, of my father's and my grandfather's generations. It was simple, unaffected glee, mingled with a disbelief that they were lucky enough to be in Africa at all. This could *not* be happening to them – one a Londoner born and bred, the other a product of the frontier state of Oklahoma when it was really woolly.

I doubt very much if the children of these men would, as the phrase has it, dig it. I am reasonably certain that many of the younger fry would scoff at us as a bunch of aging Boy Scouts for our simple pleasure in sleeping in tents, being bitten by bugs, tortured by the transport, and occasionally threatened by the wildlife. We have no TV. We have no moon shots or orbit efforts or roads for hotrods. We must be corny, because we are happy with our primitive toilet facilities and the spine-cracking progress of our vehicles. To us, in our forties and fifties, the trip to Africa – on actual safari – is the end of a boy's dream.

The dream might have begun for one when he was a King's Scout (the British equivalent of Eagle Scout) and for the other when he was shooting rabbits on his father's farm in Oklahoma. For me, certainly, it started with the Old Man and a succession of dogs and guns and boats in Carolina. People like us never grow up, even when we graduate to elephants from a timid start on rabbits. We don't grow up chiefly because we don't want to.

Unfortunately the day is past in America when you could walk five hundred yards from the town's only stoplight and put up a covey of quail, or shoot ducks so close to the trolley line that you rattled shot on the cars. The old days of drawing up beside a cornfield in a Model T and having a polite word with the farmer involving casual shooting on his place are gone, or almost gone.

We have not, in recent years – certainly not in the post-World War II years – been able to build that kind of broad outdoor background into many young lives. Perhaps today's boys will never care for the woods the way we did.

I have been tempted in the past to introduce a few younger sprouts to the fascination of safari. But having checked them out on less exotic fare, such as simple hunting and fishing expeditions, I feel disinclined to take the risk of boring them with lions or subjecting them to the torture of being bug-chewed and motionless in a leopard blind. I really would not want them to do me any favors by coming along, for safari costs a lot of money that could possibly be better spent on hotrods or ski resorts where all the girls are.

I have lately seen a couple of instances of adult heartbreak when huntin'-fishin' fathers tried to indoctrinate their juniors in rather lavish approaches to sea and field. The 9-year-old son of one would rather play canasta with adults, and the brood seemed consciously to be conferring a favor on the old man by coming on the boat for a couple of weeks' fishing. In another instance, a friend gave his son a safari as a 21st birthday present. (What I would not have given, including my soul, for an African safari in my 21st year!) The young man remained mostly in his sack, eating and reading. He sent the professional out to kill his trophies, so that Father would not be disappointed, and all he gained from the adventure was twenty pounds, which he accrued while gobbling sandwiches and drinking beer in his tent.

These may be extreme cases, but the dismaying thing I run into with the younger generation these days is their cool approach to guns and shooting. I have a houseful of trophies that some of my own age group acquaintances seem to find fascinating – a sable bull from Tabora, lions from Ikoma, big elephant teeth from the Seralippe.

But I feel apologetic when a young son turns on me and demands a justification of my right to slay God's beautiful creatures, or some younger daughter fixes me with an eye that would make Bluebeard feel sheepish about his collection of beheaded wives. I find myself mumbling, "Well, I don't actually shoot much any more – I just like to look at the animals and maybe shoot a few birds once in a while." Then the bird lovers clobber me: "And what have you got against birds?" Nothing. I just like to see them, and shoot them, and eat them. I see no difference between a fried chicken that has been butcher-killed and jointed and a breast of pheasant that has been hand-slain in the sparkling autumn woods.

I do not mean to sound bitter about this, for perhaps it is not the fault of the wet-eared young that they grew up in a world of private eyes and Jackie Gleason, or that Dagmar rather than Tarzan's Jane was their first sex symbol. I cannot help it myself if guns and dogs and plentiful free birds and rabbits are no longer available to the tads. There are times when I am sad over the retreat of American game and the sport derived from the hunting and shooting of it; there are times when I could weep over the certain knowledge that the vast game herds and exotic dangerous animals of Africa and India are rapidly dying off.

I am sad for myself and for those my age and older who love the outdoors and find its discomforts pleasant, who love its birds and fish but who do not feel guilty about shooting reasonably for sport and meat and relaxation. I am sad for the hunters and the fishermen who obey game laws and attempt to practice conservation. But I am not so sad for tomorrow's generations. Perhaps they do not care if all the elephants are poached and all the rhinos slain.

I think it is a pity that super-sophistication has combined with modern pace to cheat our younger people of the sort of fun my set enjoyed as kids. I regret a kind of thinking that regards hunting as shameful, if not sinful. I do not admire a concerted attempt to sell the idea that the killing of game is a cruel sport, because no game dies a natural death, and preys as naturally upon itself as man upon man. And above all I deplore a substitution, via movies and television, of the bloody deaths of cops and gangsters and Western bad men as high adventure, notably heroic in the mind. We may have slain innocent rabbits, but we were not taught by sponsors to applaud the wholesale slaughter of people in order to peddle merchandise.

The mosquitoes here were fearful last night, and I have just plucked a tick from a tender portion of my anatomy, and for the last day no gun has fired. Also, it has been raining. But my two middle-aged chums and I are happy here on the Tana, surrounded by wild animals and a lot of simple savages who have not yet heard of the boons of modern civilization. Perhaps my friends and I, like the elephant and the rhino, are a dying breed, but it was fun while it lasted.

"People Like Us Never Grow Up," *Field & Stream*, September, 1961.

Bibliographical Note

Somewhat surprisingly, since his death in 1965 Ruark has attracted only a moderate amount of attention in print. This is not owing to a dearth of available materials, for an extensive corpus of manuscripts bearing on his life is extant. This is where any research by a future biographer or serious student of the man's life should begin.

The single most important manuscript holding is Ruark's personal papers in the Southern Historical Collection at his alma mater, the University of North Carolina at Chapel Hill (UNC-CH). These are calendared and described in some depth in Beverly Lake Barge's "A Catalog of the Collected Papers and Manuscripts of Robert C. Ruark," a 1969 M.A. thesis prepared for the English Department at UNC-CH. This work provides not only details on the nature of the papers, but information on the somewhat controversial background underlying the deposit of Ruark's papers at the institution.

The Ruark papers are truly extensive, and to date they have been little used. Included are copies (in various forms, primarily carbon typescripts) of his columns, articles, stories, novels, plays an other items. Most but not all of these materials were ultimately published. There are scores of letters to, from, and about Ruark in correspondence files. Also included are scrapbooks, photographs, various business items and the like. These papers are available to accredited researchers.

Probably the next most important collection, and it is one I cannot describe in detail for the simple reason that I have not seen it, is material in the hands of Ruark's long-time and faithful literary agents, The Matson Agency. Harold Matson worked closely with Ruark, particularly in the writer's later years. My correspondence with Matson more than a decade ago, when I was contemplating a life story on Ruark, suggested the firm held a treasure trove of insightful material.

There are numerous items pertaining to Ruark in the Westbrook Pegler papers held at the Herbert Hoover Presidential Library in West Branch, Iowa. These include anecdotes on the man's life and work, along with correspondence he exchanged with Pegler. During the heart of Ruark's career, when he was furiously writing for fortune and hoping for a modicum of fame as well, he worked as a columnist for the Scripps-Howard Alliance. The Alliance's papers are housed in the State Historical Society archives in Madison, Wisconsin, and they are also available on eighty-five rolls of microfilm. The collection is a morgue of mimeographed feature articles and editorials (covering the period 1949-1967) along with several types of internal communications. There is Ruark material on nine of the microfilm reels.

In addition, it seems certain there is ample other manuscript material from Ruark's hand or relating to him. One of the stronger points of Hugh Foster's curiously uneven biography is that he was able to track down some of this sort of information, though his coverage of sources is sufficiently ambiguous so that we do not know the precise nature and extent of many of them (the book lacks a formal, complete bibliography). Certainly, an ambitious researcher should be able to make a listing of close acquaintances of Ruark's and then endeavor to locate material in their papers (or draw on their personal reminiscences) in helping build a fuller picture of the man. These could range from material in Southport, North Carolina, to contacts with white hunters in Africa.

Published Materials by Ruark.

Ruark was an incredibly prolific writer, as is readily revealed by any attempted analysis of the newspaper columns, magazine articles and books he published during his relatively short career. He put literally millions of words into print in less than a half-century. Whatever personal problems he had, and there were plenty of them, Ruark certainly did not lack a strong work ethic. Words came easily to him, and the literary legacy he left to posterity reveals this.

To date, there has been nothing even approaching a complete Ruark bibliography, and compiling such a listing, especially if it included all of his newspaper work, would be a daunting task. Putting together a bibliography of his magazine articles would not be quite so complex, though they number in the hundreds. He wrote regularly for